Hollywood Kids

Child Stars of the Silver Screen from 1903 to the Present

Thomas G. Aylesworth

E. P. DUTTON

New York

Page 1: Shirley Temple in an early publicity shot.
Page 2: Deanna Durbin
Page 4: Butch and Buddy with W.C. Fields in *Never Give a Sucker an Even Break* (1941).

Published in the United States by E. P. Dutton,
a division of NAL Penguin Inc.,
2 Park Avenue, New York, N.Y. 10016.

Published simultaneously in Canada by Fitzhenry and Whiteside, Limited, Toronto.

ISBN: 0-525-24562-6

W

Project Editor: Bruce S. Glassman
Associate Editor: Robin Langley Sommer
Design: Richard S. Glassman

10 9 8 7 6 5 4 3 2 1

First Edition

Hollywood
Kids

Contents

*I*n the beginning, children in movies were little more than props. Until Mary Pickford came along, they were used mainly to fill cradles or to be carried around in their mothers' arms—although sometimes they were carried off by eagles or criminals in the service of melodrama. Then came Pickford, and the new era of the child as mitigator and savior, in which the kids spread sweetness and love all over the screen, often reforming adult reprobates, tyrants, and evil-doers.

During World War I, the propaganda machines were turning out persuasive horror stories about the torture of Belgian children by the dreaded Hun, and Hollywood capitalized on the theme of the child as victim. Now the child actor was often the pitiful waif, facing unendurable mishaps, who either dies pathetically or triumphs over evil. During this same period, the child served as a symbol of unsophisticated rural America and its rapidly vanishing way of life, as simplicity and traditional values gave way to increasing complexity.

Then came the child-star craze at its height —roughly from 1925 to 1945—when an estimated 100 children every 15 minutes poured into the Hollywood marketplace. The odds against them were 15,000 to 1, but they kept trying. After all, there was gold in the Hollywood hills for youngsters, who were in demand for musicals, family dramas, cowboy pictures, and historical films. And there were hundreds of movies in which the kids were more important than the parents: now the adults were serving as props. During the 1920s the movies concentrated on the moral power of innocent children, as the nation struggled to assimilate the shifting standards

Preface

of the postwar world: the sexual revolution, unprecedented prosperity, and the lawlessness attendant upon Prohibition. With the Great Depression of the 1930s, child actors were used either in escapist (often musical) films, or as a symbol of optimism. Audiences could forget their financial woes for an hour, or transcend them in the hope that the future would be better than the present.

World War II changed the pattern again. Millions of servicemen met honest-to-goodness starving orphans scrounging for survival in the rubble-filled streets of Rome, Paris, and Berlin, and their faith in Hollywood's saccharine treatment of the orphan would never again burn bright. The bottom seemed to fall out of the child acting business. Only Margaret O'Brien, especially in *Journey for Margaret* (1942), could make the American public believe in her as the lonely waif. She was the vulnerable child personified.

Today there are several child stars making huge salaries, but things are not the same. The national disillusionment that began in the 1960s with the turbulent political and social events of that decade has been reflected on the movie screen. The actors of the "Brat Pack" play teenagers—sophisticated beyond the wildest dreams of those who loved Margaret O'Brien and Shirley Temple. Tatum O'Neal, Brooke Shields, and Jodie Foster began their careers in childhood, but they were really playing adult roles, filled with passion and conniving, in a time when innocence has lost its credibility. The days of the wholesome, scrubbed-faced, all-American child actor may be a thing of the past.

THOMAS G. AYLESWORTH

Henry Thomas and friend in *E.T. The Extraterrestrial* (1982).

1903~1909
In the Beginning

It was that appealing, swashbuckling, balcony-hopping hero of countless silent films, Douglas Fairbanks, who first observed that children and animals make the best movie actors. Except for a few cow ponies and dogs, a dolphin, and a talking mule, animals in the movies have never lived up to their potential. But from the beginning children have played a more important role in films than they ever did in the theater, and many of them became stars in their own right.

Arguably, the first child movie actress was a nameless little girl who appeared in *The Great Train Robbery* (1903), produced by the Edison Company and filmed in New Jersey. She was nameless because it wasn't until years later that motion picture producers would let audiences know just who those actors on the screen were. The movie was the first to tell a story, with a beginning, a middle, and an end, although it was a one-reeler that ran for a mere 12 minutes. *The Great Train Robbery* opens with four bandits entering a rural railroad depot and sandbagging the telegraph operator. They bind and gag him and then take over a train that has stopped for water. While the dirty deeds are being performed on the by-now moving train, the telegraph operator's little daughter discovers her father's predicament and unties him. The two of them then go for help. Since this was the first real movie as we know them today, the anonymous little girl was the first child performer.

Some child actors didn't have much to do, since they were used more as props than as performers. The child in *Rescued from an Eagle's Nest* (1907), which was also an Edison film, had only to let an eagle carry him off. The main actor in this short film was a young man named Lawrence Griffith, who played a heroic mountaineer. After working in several Edison films, the young actor adopted the professional name of D. W. Griffith and moved to Biograph Studios, where he became a director.

Although he is little remembered for his juvenile roles, the first child actor to make it from moppet to adult on the screen was the veteran actor Paul Kelly (1899–1956). He had been on the stage since he was seven years old and had child and juvenile roles in many Vitagraph pictures, beginning with *A Good Little Devil* (1908). Kelly was acting until the day he died, making many "B" movies as the hero and playing supporting roles in such "A" films as *Navy Blue and*

Mary Pickford as a boy in *Little Lord Fauntleroy* (1921).

Gold (1937), *The Roaring Twenties* (1939), *Springfield Rifle* (1952), *The High and the Mighty* (1954), and *Storm Center* (1956).

In 1909 came the debut of the most important child star of her generation or, many believe, of any generation—"America's Sweetheart," "Our Mary," Mary Pickford (1893–1979). She was born Gladys Smith in Toronto, Ontario, and when she was five years old, her father, a laborer, was killed in an accident. She found herself with the responsibility of helping her mother, Charlotte, take care of her brother Jack and her sister Lottie. At the time, Charlotte was twenty-three years old, Lottie was three, and Jack was two. Somehow, Charlotte was able to get them jobs as extras in a play put on by a Toronto stock company, at $10 a week per child.

The future Mary Pickford, then billed as "Baby Gladys," went on to play Little Eva in a stage version of Harriet Beecher Stowe's *Uncle Tom's Cabin*. In 1902 "Baby Lillian" Gish, another child actress from a fatherless family, developed anemia while touring in *The Little Red Schoolhouse*, and Gladys replaced her. The producer wanted only Gladys, but the shrewd Charlotte demanded that he hire the four of them. He caved in, and the family was earning $25 per week. By this time Gladys was nine years of age and a veteran trouper.

Life on the road was miserable. Actors were shunned by decent folk, the theaters were cesspools, and the bedbug population of the theatrical hotels was astonishing. After several years of touring, Gladys could stand it no longer, and when her current play hit New York City, she went to producer David Belasco's office and charmed him into giving her a starring role in his Broadway production of *The Warrens of Virginia*. She was 14 years old. Belasco was reluctant to bill her as Gladys Smith, a name that had no glamor. Gladys recalled that one of her grandfathers had been named John Pickford Hennessey, and her great aunt, who had been killed at a young age by a tram in London, was named Mary Pickford. Belasco had her new name. Overnight Charlotte, Lottie, and Jack became Pickfords, too.

For two years, Mary loved every minute of her life in the theater, but no play lasts for-

ever, and at sixteen she was out of work and behind in the rent again. The only option was to try to find work in the movies, so Mary went to the offices of the Biograph Studios, in a dingy old brownstone townhouse at 11 East 14th Street in New York City. What had been the ballroom of the mansion was now the Biograph set. And it was D. W. Griffith who interviewed her, asking her what she wanted. Mary replied nonchalantly, "Well, I thought I wouldn't mind working in pictures for a while, that is, if the price is right."

Griffith sized her up as being too pretty, too short, and having a reedy voice—in a word, all wrong for the stage. But on screen, since this was the silent movie era and voice didn't count, her petite beauty would be a big asset. He offered her $5 a day. Drawing herself up to her full five-foot height, she replied haughtily that she was "an actress and an artist" and must be paid "twice what ordinary performers" received. Griffith agreed.

Pickford's films revealed her inner strength —she had spent years in privation, doing hard work, and it showed. It was precisely this characteristic that made her so appealing to the moviegoing poor—and there was scarcely any other kind of moviegoer in 1909. She became best known as the plucky little orphan she portrayed in dozens of tearjerkers, but essentially she was a comedienne. Most of her films were comedies with a few episodes of pathos and excitement thrown in. She projected warmth and charm, but beneath it all was an Irish temper to be found in her characterizations.

Later, Mary would describe her technique. She never exaggerated her performances, as was common in those days of mugging, arm-waving, and chewing the scenery. When she disagreed with a director, she did her own thing. She once said, "I would *not* run around like a goose with its head cut off, crying 'Oooooh...look! A little bunny.' That's what [Griffith] taught his ingénues, and they all did the same thing. 'I'm a grown girl, I'm 16 years old. I won't do it,' I said. 'You'll do it,' he said, 'or you'll leave.' 'All right, I'll leave. I'll go. I won't do it.'" Griffith said later that there were only two people who ever outworked him—Pickford and Lillian Gish.

At the age of 24, "Little Mary" (right) could still play young girls—*The Little Princess* (1917).

Mary, late in life, expressed a rare insight into her profession: "I always tried to get laughter in my pictures. Make them laugh, make them cry, and back to laughter. What do people go to the theater for? An emotional exercise. And no preachment. I don't belive in taking advantage of someone who comes to the theater by teaching him a lesson. He can go to church, he can read the newspapers. But when people go to the theater they want to be entertained. It is not my prerogative as an actress to teach them anything. *They* will teach *me*. And that's how it should be, because I am a servant of the public. I have never forgotten that."

In her first year at Biograph, Mary was a real workhorse. In that year of 1909, she made *The Violin Maker of Cremona, The Lonely Villa, Her First Biscuits, Two Memories, The Way of Man, Sweet and Twenty, 1776* or *The Hessian Renegades, The Gibson Goddess, The Slave, Getting Even, In Old Kentucky, The Little Darling, His Wife's Visitor, The Little Teacher, The Restoration,* and *To Save Her Soul.* She even co-wrote the screenplay for *The Little Teacher.* One of her frequent co-stars was the darkly handsome Owen Moore, seven years her senior. The work was steady, and after a while Mary was also writing scripts for herself and selling them to Biograph for $25 each. She vowed that she would be making at least $500 per week by the time she was 20 years old.

Then, in 1910, came a three-month trip to California with the Griffith company; her brother Jack went along as chaperone. For those three months, Jack was an extra and Mary was a star. They lived in the cheapest lodgings they could find and were able to save $100 during the adventure. Still, something was gnawing at Mary Pickford. Like all Biograph personalities, she was not identified by name lest her publicity enable her to ask for higher wages. But the public knew her by her trademark, that head of golden curls, and she once played a character identified in the film's continuity titles as "Little Mary." Studio publicists referred to her only as "The Girl with the Golden Curls" or "Little Mary," which made it easy for Carl Laemmle to lure her from Biograph to his IMP Studios in 1910. He offered her a raise and a publicity campaign, which began with the press release, "Little Mary is an Imp now." She was given top billing, and every effort was made to establish her screen identity with the public.

In 1911 legal and business problems forced Laemmle to seek a location far from the East Coast for his next film-making venture. He chose Cuba, where the weather was favorable and labor was cheap. While Mary and Jack had been in California, Charlotte had closed the deal with Laemmle, not only for the publicity campaign and the raise in salary for Mary, but also to get her away from Owen Moore. It wasn't until they were at sea heading for Cuba that she found out Laemmle had hired Moore, too, and he and Mary were still together.

A group of some 72 people had embarked for Havana, including Mary and her family,

Owen Moore, King Baggot, and various directors and supervisors. The venture turned out to be a debacle. Charlotte was livid when she found out that Mary had been secretly married to Owen Moore earlier that year. The company found it almost impossible to get raw film stock in Cuba, and the crew disliked the climate. Unit manager Thomas Ince and Moore clashed violently. Ince's assistant insulted Mary, and Moore jumped him. The police were summoned. Charlotte arranged for Moore and the Pickford family to return to the mainland.

Once back in New York, Charlotte pretended to acquiesce to Mary and Owen's marriage, but she moved in with the newlyweds and began to dominate the household. Moore took to the bottle.

Mary Pickford returned to Biograph in 1912, joining Griffith's troupe in California right after the Christmas holidays. Griffith had promised her that he would bend the Biograph rules a little and release her name in the publicity material for her pictures, but she would not be mentioned in the film credits. This was a compromise arrangement,

The 27-year-old "America's Sweetheart" was still playing children in *Pollyanna* (1920) with Katherine Griffith and Howard Ralston.

Even in melodramas, Mary Pickford often demonstrated her talent for comedy. Here she is in one of the lighter scenes from *The Little American* (1917), a propaganda film in which she was captured by the Huns.

and Pickford didn't like it. She went back to New York to work with David Belasco again. A few months later, she was lured back to Hollywood by Harry Aitken, who had set up a company called Majestic Films.

In 1913 Mary signed with Adolph Zukor, the head of Famous Players, for that magical sum of $500 per week—just one week before her 20th birthday. Two years later she was making $4,000 a week. Mary always considered one of the films she made during this period, *Tess of the Storm Country* (1914), the real beginning of her career.

Early in her professional life, Mary was able to exercise veto power over her films and was given a choice of script, director, and co-stars. As a result of her native skills and business acumen, her movies usually boasted high production values, and most of them were immensely profitable. By mid-1916 she was signed by Zukor to an amazing contract that guaranteed a salary of $10,000 weekly with a $300,000 bonus for signing, plus $150,000 for Charlotte's assistance and good will. Mary was also given a studio devoted exclusively to the making of her films, the

Mary Pickford Company, and a share in the profits of that studio. But that was still not enough. The following year Charlotte sold out Zukor and Mary went to First National, where she was offered over $675,000 per year. Up to this time, she had been maturing on screen, but now she went back to her "Little Mary" persona of complete innocence. For the next 10 years or so, she played roles in which she was supposed to be 12 years old or younger. In *The Poor Little Rich Girl* (1917), when she was 24, she portrayed a child of 10.

Mary's innocent eyes and beautiful curls concealed one of the shrewdest minds in Hollywood history. She was always good at getting the best financial deal for herself, and she excelled in just about every area of film-making. She directed many of her biggest hits, and she had almost infallible judgment about her own material. The problem—if it was a problem—was that she could never grow up. She made *Pollyanna* (1920) when she was 27 years old. The following year, in one of those arrangements that could happen only in Hollywood, Mary played not only

Above: Pickford in a "This will hurt me more than it hurts you" scene in *Daddy Long Legs* (1919).

Above left: Charles "Buddy" Rogers and Pickford in a light moment in *My Best Girl* (1927). At the age of 34 she was finally playing adults. Pickford and Rogers became good friends while making the movie; they would marry ten years after it was completed. She was 11 years older than he.

the title role in *Little Lord Fauntleroy*, in boy's costume, but also the role of the boy's mother. Moviegoers loved it. As far as they were concerned, "Our Mary" not only could but would stay young for the rest of her life. When she was 30 years old, Pickford asked her fans to suggest some roles in which they would like to see her. Almost all the responses asked for adolescent portrayals: Heidi, Alice in Wonderland, and so on. She sighed and went along with the flow.

Mary ran a tight ship. The actors worked from 6:00 AM to 9:00 PM, and there were no coffee breaks. She was sometimes called "Retake Mary Pickford," because she was a perfectionist. She often used music on the set to put her in the proper mood. Some of her favorites were Charles Wakefield Cadman's *From the Land of the Sky Blue Water* and Jules Massenet's *Élégie*.

During World War I, Mary showed that she was fiercely patriotic by participating in numerous Liberty Bond campaigns. "I'm only five feet tall," she would say, "but every inch of me is a fighting American." Her lead role in *The Little American* (1917), which dramatized the sinking of the *Lusitania*, underlined her stance. One of the famous stars with whom she often traveled on those campaigns was everyone's favorite actor, Douglas Fairbanks, and the two fell in love,

although both were still married. Charlotte got busy, digging into her own savings to pay off Owen Moore, whose career had foundered, since it would never have done for "Little Mary" to do so herself.

Charlotte was also active for Mary on the money-making front. Adolph Zukor once complained, "Mary, sweetheart, I don't have to diet. Every time I talk over a new contract with you and your mother, I lose ten pounds." Samuel Goldwyn was later to remark that "It took longer to make Mary's contracts than it did to make her pictures."

Pickford tried again to shed her little-girl image when she made *Stella Maris* (1918), in which she played a dual role—Unity Blake, a pathetic Cockney slavey, and Stella Maris, a paralyzed rich girl. Maris is finally cured, then confronted by the world as it really is. Angered with her parents for overprotecting her, she says, "By trying to shield me you have destroyed my happiness and my faith in human nature." But the public still demanded that Mary return to her childish roles. She capitulated, but often tried to play a young girl who grew up. *Daddy Long Legs* (1919) began with its heroine as a baby rescued from a garbage can. The film went on to show her days in an orphanage and ended with a romance. She also played adult roles in *The Love Light* (1921), *Rosita* (1923), *Dorothy Vernon of Haddon Hall* (1924), and *My Best Girl* (1927).

In 1919 Pickfold entered into partnership with three other formidable luminaries of the film business — Charlie Chaplin, D. W. Griffith, and Douglas Fairbanks—to form the United Artists Corporation. That year she and Fairbanks divorced their respective mates; they were married in 1920. The marriage was not ideally happy, but it had the aura of a dream come true for the public. The couple represented Hollywood royalty at its loftiest, and their legendary home, Pickfair, was a fairy-tale castle.

Except for D. W. Griffith, Pickford and Fairbanks exerted more influence on the Hollywood movie of the time than anyone else in the history of film. They recognized talent, both in actors and in the people behind the camera. They also imported great European talent to Hollywood, most notably German director Ernst Lubitsch.

An amusing story went the rounds while Pickford was making a film called *Through the Back Door* (1921), in which one of the continuity titles was a problem. The audience was supposed to think that Mary was eloping, although she wasn't. Also, the title had to suggest that her mother was contemplating divorce. At the same time, since the audience had last seen the characters on Long Island, they had to be shown that the scene had shifted to a hotel in New York City. Finally, the title had to be funny. The furniture in the hotel room saved the title writer, who came up with "If it were not for New York hotels, where would elopers, divorcées, and red-plush furniture go?"

After Pickford married Fairbanks, they led such a social life at Pickfair that Mary had no time for the bargaining table; she left it all to Charlotte. But at the same time, family difficulties multiplied. Sister Lottie drank heavily and had several failed marriages behind her at the age of 26. Mary sued Lottie for the custody of Lottie's daughter, Gwynne, and she and Charlotte won the case, in which it was stated that Lottie was an unfit mother. Mary raised Gwynne almost as if she were her own daughter. Then Charlotte, after becoming richer than she had ever hoped, developed a drinking problem.

The signing of the incorporation papers of United Artists on April 17, 1919. Shown here are, from left, Griffith, Pickford, Chaplin, and Douglas Fairbanks, Sr. In the background are the attorneys.

The new Mary. In *Coquette* (1928), her first talkie, she dared to bob her hair and act her age.

Mary finally staged a revolt against her screen stereotype in 1928, when she had her curls cut off and adopted a contemporary shingled hair style. The following year, although she was loyal to the silent screen (she once said, "It would have been more logical if silent pictures had grown out of the talkie instead of the other way round,"), she made her first sound picture. In *Coquette*, she wore her new hair style and played the part of a swinger. Then she starred in a disastrous version of *The Taming of the Shrew* (1929) with Fairbanks.

The Pickford-Fairbanks marriage began breaking up near the end of Mary's film career. Fairbanks, in flight from the dread of aging, distracted himself with world travel and hobnobbing with the rich, famous, and titled. He was away from home most of the time. Mary sought solace with the young actor Charles "Buddy" Rogers, who had appeared with her in *My Best Girl* (1927). She divorced Fairbanks in 1936 and married Rogers in 1937.

In 1931 Mary made *Kiki*, her first and only musical, and in 1933 she made *Secrets*—her final movie. It was this last film that proved to a new generation of talking-picture audiences that she was among the greatest actresses in motion pictures. She played the wife of Leslie Howard, and they lived in a forest shack. Her outstanding performance in one scene will live forever. Gunmen begin shooting at them from outside the shack. Pickford runs to the back room to check on her baby, and finds it dead. Oblivious to the bullets flying around her, she sits, numbed by shock, in the middle of the room, cradling the dead baby in her arms. There are no histrionics—just the approaching camera mirroring the despair in her face and eyes. She later said of the scene, "That one really got me."

For 24 years Mary Pickford was the undisputed queen of the screen, and in 1975 she was awarded a Special Academy Award "in recognition of her unique contributions to the film industry and to the development of film as an artistic medium." All America loved her, but none of her fans was as loyal as the hundreds of child movie actors: as long as Mary kept playing little girls, countless kids got jobs as extras and co-stars in scenes set in orphanages, workhouses, and other heart-rending locations. □

The Rites of Puberty

Child movie actors were never given the option of running their own lives. It was as if they were a product that only adults could deal in. They were the property of their parents, merchandised by their agents and bought by the studios. Sometimes they were loaned out to other film-makers for as much as three times their salaries, and not one penny of the profit ever found its way into their pockets.

Once they were established, the child stars and their greedy producers learned to work with speed, because puberty was just around the corner and they had to earn as much as possible before the girls became busty and the boys' voices changed. The transition from cuddly infant to graceless adolescent was a serious one, to be put off at all cost. Birth dates were altered, as early biographies were burned. Childish hairdos and clothing were the rage. Childish mannerisms were encouraged. False teeth were issued when baby teeth began falling out. Painful gauze chest straps were fitted to pubescent young girls.

Still, the blossoming was inevitable. And very few young actors survived the ordeal. When adulthood came, most movie moguls dropped the former star and turned to another, younger, performer.

For all the Mickey Rooneys, Judy Garlands, and Elizabeth Taylors who remained stars after their youth had fled, there were hundreds of Edith Fellowses, Marcia Mae Joneses, Anne Shirleys, and Dickie Moores who couldn't hang on. By growing up, they had become strangers to their fans—in fact, their fans blamed them for ceasing to be the children whom they had adored. As a matronly moviegoer remarked in 1948, after lamenting the fact that Deanna Durbin had grown up, "That was a *positively wicked* thing for her to do."

Chapter Two

1910~1919

The Innocents

One of the first child stars to lead a tragic life was Jack Pickford (1896–1933). Born Jack Smith in Toronto, the brother of Mary Pickford, he changed his last name when she did and followed in his older sister's footsteps as a child actor on stage. Later, he, too, switched to the movies, where he was a juvenile actor and then a romantic lead. It was Mary who got him into the Biograph Studios in 1910, the year he made, at the age of 14, *The Kid, White Rose, A Plain Song*, and *Two Little Waifs—A Modern Fairy Tale*.

Jack Pickford went on to play in several movies about children and adolescents, including *Seventeen* (1916). When Mary signed her million-dollar deal with First National in 1917, one of her stipulations was a lucrative contract for her brother, and he went on to become a star in his own right. One of his most effective portrayals was in *The Goose Woman* (1925), with Louise Dresser, Constance Bennett, and the unforgettable Gustav von Seyffertitz. It was a Rex Beach story about a once-famous opera singer who raises geese, and the studio had to search the whole of California and part of New Mexico to get enough geese for the picture. It even went to the trouble of broadcasting appeals for the birds on the radio.

Jack Pickford's first marriage was to the beautiful actress Olive Thomas, who committed suicide by drinking a vial of liquid mercury in Paris after a night of carousing. This tragedy shattered Charlotte and Mary Pickford, who had known about Jack's fondness for the bottle, but found it difficult to cope with the rumors that spread after Thomas's death that both she and Jack had been drug users. Jack continued to drink and, many said, take drugs. He was married two more times, to actresses Marilyn Miller and Mary Mulhern; both marriages ended in divorce. In 1933, three months after his second breakup, he died in a hospital outside Paris.

Bebe Daniels (1901–71) was born Phyllis Daniels in Dallas, Texas, into a show-business family. Her Scottish-born father was the manager of a touring theatrical company whose star was her mother, a Spaniard by birth. By the time she was four years old, Daniels was appearing on stage in plays. She made her screen debut at the age of nine, in the Selig Company two-reeler *The Common Enemy* (1910), and went on to play in numerous other shorts, mostly Westerns and adventure pictures. By the time she was 14, she was starring in adult roles, notably opposite Harold Lloyd in his "Lonesome Luke" comedies.

The beautiful Lillian Gish in *Orphans of the Storm* (1922).

Jack Pickford, Mary's brother, in a tender scene with Katherine MacDonald in *The Spirit of '17* (1918).

One night, Daniels and Lloyd went to a theater to watch one of the "Lonesome Luke" pictures, and Lloyd heard a small boy say, "Oh, here's that fellow who tries to look like Chaplin." Lloyd didn't want to be known as an imitator of anyone.

He created immediately his new persona—the shy young man with the horn-rimmed glasses and straw hat—and Daniels was without her Luke. *Captain Kidd's Kids* (1919) was Daniels's last picture for Hal Roach. She and Lloyd had been at a dancing contest in 1917 where Cecil B. De Mille was among those present. He told her, "I'd like to have you in my company." Daniels pointed out that she was still under contract to Roach, and De Mille said, "Well, when you aren't, let me know." Daniels, who wanted to switch from comedy to drama, did just that, signing a long-term contract with Paramount.

She starred in many important films over the next 10 years, including *Why Change Your Wife?* (1920), *Monsieur Beaucaire* (1924), and *Miss Brewster's Millions* (1926); among her leading men were Rudolph Valentino and Wallace Reid. But she was dropped by Paramount when sound films came in. Then RKO picked her up and cast her in the title role of the musical *Rio Rita* (1929), in which she proved that she could sing.

In 1930 Daniels married Ben Lyon, an actor with whom she had starred in several pictures. By the mid-1930s, their careers were on the wane. Indeed, Daniels had not had a really good part since her role as Dorothy Brock, the star whose place is taken by Ruby Keeler, in *42nd Street* (1933). The couple accepted an offer to appear at the London Palladium in 1936, and they stayed on in London through World War II, appearing in music halls and on stage, broadcasting with the BBC, and entertaining the troops. They returned to Hollywood, where Lyon worked as a studio executive, in 1946, but went back to London three years later to start a radio show, "Life with the Lyons."

Even the First Lady of the American Theater, Helen Hayes, spent some time as a child movie star. Born Helen Hayes Brown in 1900 in Washington, D.C., she made her first picture, a two-reeler called *Jean and the Calico Doll* (1910), when she was 10 years old. After making a few more pictures, including *The Weavers of Life* (1917) and *Babs* (1920), she decided to devote her attention to the stage. But when her husband, the playwright Charles MacArthur, signed a Hollywood contract, she went to California with him and appeared in several MGM films, winning the Academy Award for Best Actress for her very first speaking role in *The Sin of Madelon Claudet* (1931). She later won the Oscar for Best Supporting Actress for her portrayal of a dotty lady passenger in *Airport* (1970).

Another child star who made her film debut in 1910 was Norma Talmadge (1897–1957), the first of the three Talmadge sisters to appear in movies. She was only 13 in 1910, when she played in five films: *Love of Chrysanthemum*, *In Neighboring Kingdoms*, *A Broken Spell*, *Uncle Tom's Cabin*, and *A Dixie Mother*. At the age of 14, she played the lead in her first important movie, *A Tale of Two Cities* (1911). She was to become one of the most idolized stars of the 1920s and specialized in playing the long-suffering heroine of many a tear-jerker.

The daughters of the celebrated actor Maurice Costello, Dolores (1905–79) and Helene (1903–57) Costello, began appearing in Vitagraph films with their father at the ages of six and eight, respectively. Two of

Helen Hayes (seated left) in *The Weavers of Life* (1917). She was 17 years old at the time.

their earliest were *The Geranium* and *The Child Crusoes* (both 1911). Dolores left show business for a time to attend school and to model for such illustrators as James Montgomery Flagg; then the sisters were reunited —dancing in the *George White's Scandals* of 1924. Both Helene and Dolores returned to the screen and became extremely successful. Helene, however, could not survive the transition to sound films.

Dolores gained sudden stardom when she was picked by John Barrymore as his leading lady in *The Sea Beast* (1926). The two were married in 1928 and divorced in 1935, after Dolores had given birth to a daughter, Dolores Ethel Mae, and a son, the future actor John Barrymore, Jr. She went on to character roles, scoring triumphs as Freddie Bartholomew's mother in *Little Lord Fauntleroy* (1936) and as Isobel Anderson in Orson Welles's *The Magnificent Ambersons* (1942).

The Australian-born actress Mae Busch (1897–1946) made her screen debut at the age of 15 in *The Agitator/The Cowboy Socialist* (1912). She had been brought to the United States at an early age and educated in a New Jersey convent. Mae Busch grew up to become a real Hollywood star, making it big in Erich von Stroheim's *Foolish Wives* (1922), in which the most famous scene had von Stroheim biting her hand. After sound came to the movies, she began appearing regularly with Laurel and Hardy.

Born Juliet Reilly in Shreveport, Louisiana in 1902, Mary Miles Minter began her stage career at the age of six, billed as "Little Juliet Shelby." She was soon to become one of the most popular child stars in American movies. She started making films in 1912, when she was a mere 10 years old, beginning with *The Nurse*. After changing her name to Mary Miles Minter, she became Mary Pickford's closest rival, although she was not nearly as good an actress. One of her directors, Edward Sloman, said after directing her in *The Ghost of Rosie Taylor* (1917), "Mary Miles Minter was quite young then—sixteen—and very beautiful. Without doubt, she was the best-looking youngster I ever saw, and the lousiest actress."

Minter was one of Hollywood's darlings, but her career suffered a fatal blow with the unsolved murder of director Desmond Taylor in 1922. Several things were discovered after the murder. Taylor was suspected of being a dealer in morphine and cocaine. And it came out that Minter had been his more-than-occasional lover, when her indiscreet letters to him shattered her public image as a girl of spotless purity. The press had a field day, and it was said that the Taylor murder sold more newspapers in the United States than any other previous event. Minter and comedienne Mabel Normand, who was also implicated in the Taylor affair, were suspected of being drug users as well, and both of them became box-office poison.

The Gish sisters, Dorothy (1898–1968) and Lillian (1896–), began their screen careers in 1912. Dorothy was 14 and Lillian 16 when they appeared in *An Unseen Enemy*, directed at Biograph by D. W. Griffith. After one of the frequent disappearances of her drifter husband, the girls' mother had taken to acting when they were very young, and realized that she could earn more money if her daughters became actors, too. They traveled with touring companies, but little money came in. Then one day they saw the film *Lena and the Geese* (1912), starring Mary Pickford, in a Baltimore theater. The Gishes had known Mary and had even shared an apartment with her and her mother when Pickford was still Gladys Smith and both mothers had sought careers for the children in vaudeville. So the Gish sisters went to Biograph's 14th Street studio to visit their old friend. While they were there, D. W. Griffith gave them a screen test—which included chasing them around the set with a pistol to test their reactions. They were hired, and from that followed *An Unseen Enemy*, which also featured a young newcomer named Harry Carey.

Early in their screen careers, the Gish sisters appeared side by side frequently, but later their paths crossed only periodically. Although Dorothy's importance as a silent-screen star has been overshadowed by her sister's fame, she was an excellent actress, and appeared in many more films than Lillian during those early days.

Griffith worked his actors hard. Lillian Gish once wrote, "It was a dedicated life then. You had no social life. You had to have lunch or dinner, but it was always spent talk-

Above: At the age of 15, Mary Miles Minter was already a strikingly beautiful woman.

Right: Minter played an innocent country girl in *The Trail of the Lonesome Pine* (1923). This image was shattered just before the picture was released, when Minter's name made headlines and the world learned that she had been the mistress of the murdered screen director Desmond Taylor, who was implicated in drug abuse and other scandals. Needless to say, this was Minter's last film.

ing over work if you were with anyone—talking over stories or cutting or subtitles or whatever."

Lillian Gish's first real triumph was as Elsie Stoneman in D. W. Griffith's monumental *The Birth of a Nation* (1915). This melodrama about the American Civil War and its aftermath became an embarrassment to the film industry for its racist theme. It was, however, exciting to watch, especially the battle scenes, and it abounded in technical innovations. If only the members of the Ku Klux Klan had not been portrayed as the heroes.

Griffith ran out of money on *The Birth of a Nation*. He had only $50,000 to work with and the picture cost $61,000. For a time, the actors worked without pay. Still, in proportion to its cost, the movie may well be the greatest money-maker of all time. In *The New York Times* review of the picture, published on March 3, 1915, no mention was made of Gish or any other actor in the film. The critic was overwhelmed by the panoramic nature of the movie, and, indeed, did not even mention its racism. Others, even at the time, objected.

Griffith came out with his answer to the critics of *The Birth of a Nation* in 1916. It was *Intolerance*, an epic film subtitled "Love's Struggle Through the Ages." It was a sentimentally conceived examination of intolerance in four periods of history, its narrative moving constantly from one story to another, with frenzied cross-cutting at the climax. Lillian Gish helped with the cross-cutting, since she played a woman who rocked a cradle, appearing between each segment—the personification of sainted motherhood, beaming seraphically down at her baby. The continuity title read: "Out of the cradle, endlessly rocking, uniter of here and hereafter."

The Gish sisters were back together in *Hearts of the World* (1918). The film was made when movies were doing all they could to further the American war effort during World War I through propaganda that depicted the dreaded Huns killing babies in Europe. Griffith decided to shoot this epic overseas, while the war was going full force. He took the Gish family with him on the same ship that carried General John J. Pershing to his command of the American Expeditionary Force in 1917.

That Gish Magic

Above: Lillian Gish (right) is dismayed at the sight of her wounded lover (Henry B. Walthall) in *The Birth of a Nation* (1915).

Above right: Lillian Gish and Ronald Colman in *The White Sister* (1923). This was Colman's first big break in films; Gish had chosen him herself after seeing him in a play.

Left: Lillian Gish in *Hearts of the World* (1918), part of which was filmed in England. The young man was the 19-year-old Noel Coward in a bit part.

Below : Lillian Gish is ordered to leave the house in *Way Down East* (1920).

The crew spent some time in London, where Griffith gave an acting lesson to Dorothy Gish. She and the director were walking in the Strand when they spotted a prostitute in front of them. Griffith told Dorothy to copy her walk and used it in the film.

Then it was off to France, and the Gish girls begged their mother not to make the dangerous crossing of the English Channel with them. She overruled them with the melodramatic line, "There are only three of our family left. If one of us is going to die, *all* of us are going to die together."

After *Hearts of the World*, Griffith came up with a most unusual film idea—a story about a rare-in-Hollywood Chinese hero who befriends a white child who had been beaten by a cruel father. It was an insensitive time, and certainly Griffith was far from being the most sensitive of men. He decided to call the picture *The Chink and the Child*. Fortunately, wiser heads prevailed, Griffith changed his mind, and the film became *Broken Blossoms* (1919). It wasn't that anyone was worried about offending Orientals in the audience: they were afraid that moviegoers wouldn't patronize a film with a Chinese as its star, even though Richard Barthelmess was playing the role, and there was no more Caucasian-looking Hollywood hero than Barthelmess.

Lillian Gish, age 23, played the part of the child, and she was expert at reaching an emotional high. When the *Broken Blossoms* closet scene—the screen's ultimate in hysteria—was shot, the screams of Gish and the cries of Griffith urging her on could be heard on the street outside the studio.

Lillian parted from Griffith amicably in the early 1920s after a salary dispute. Along the way she had directed her sister in *Remodeling Her Husband* (1920), and she went on to star at MGM under a contract that gave her control over scripts and the choice of directors. One of her triumphs there was in *The Scarlet Letter* (1926), as Hester Prynne. Modern-day critic Pauline Kael commented: "Her Hester Prynne is one of the most beautiful sustained performances in screen history." But after a few less successful movies, MGM, which now had Greta Garbo, let Lillian Gish go in 1928.

Lillian returned to the stage and appeared in plays during the 1930s, including *Uncle Vanya*, *Camille*, and *Hamlet* (as Ophelia, opposite John Gielgud). Since that time she has made several appearances in supporting roles in movies. When she made *Duel in the Sun* (1947), she and Lionel Barrymore were reunited for the first time since they had worked together with Griffith in the teens, and Griffith himself met Lillian's train when she arrived in Hollywood to make the film.

Lillian Gish was given a Special Academy Award in 1970 "for superlative artistry and for distinguished contribution to the progress of motion pictures." As recently as 1986, she appeared in her 104th film, *Sweet Liberty*.

Milton Berle (1908–), the celebrated comedian, was another child movie star. At the age of five he won a contest in which he imitated Charlie Chaplin and started playing kids' parts for Biograph and other studios, most notably in the serial *The Perils of Pauline* (1914, with Pearl White) and *Tillie's Punctured Romance* (1914, with Charlie Chaplin and Marie Dressler). By the time he reached puberty, Berle had appeared in *Easy Street* (1916), *Little Brother* (1917), *Humoresque* (1920), and *The Mark of Zorro* (1920). Berle went on to bigger things on stage and on television, returning to the screen only occasionally, often in oddities. In *Radio City Revels* (1938), he and Jack Oakie played a couple of talentless song writers who stole melodies from another tunesmith (Bob Burns) who could compose only while he was asleep. The rest of the plot was even sillier. Although Berle has demonstrated, especially on television, that he is a good actor, he continues to pop up in such forgettable films as *Can Hieronymous Merkin Ever Forget Mercy Humppe and Find True Happiness?* (1969) and *Won Ton Ton—The Dog Who Saved Hollywood* (1976).

One of the most prolific child stars of the mid-decade was Mildred Harris (1901–44). She had started in films at the age of nine, and by the time she was thirteen, she was a celebrity as Dorothy in the popular *Wizard of Oz* series (1914–15). When she became Charlie Chaplin's first wife at the age of 16, she had played prominent roles in *Enoch Arden* (1915), *The Warrens of Virginia* (1915), *Intolerance* (1916), *Hoodoo Ann*

Young Ben Alexander was one of the most talented of the kiddie crop of the 1920s, and his film career lasted for 14 years. Here he is being confronted by Henry B. Walthall in a tense scene from *Boy of Mine* (1923), when he was 12 years old.

(1916), *Old Folks at Home* (1916), *The Price of a Good Time* (1917), *Bad Boy* (1917), and *An Old-Fashioned Young Man* (1917). She and Chaplin were divorced in 1920, and she went on to play leading ladies in many silents and several early talkies.

Constance Talmadge (1900–73) was the sister of actresses Natalie and Norma Talmadge. Beginning at the age of 14, she spent two years appearing in many comedy film shorts opposite Billy Quirk. Her first big break came at the age of 16, when she played the spirited, tom-boyish Mountain Girl in the Babylonian episode of *Intolerance* (1916). She was a leading star in the comedies of the 1920s.

When she broke into films at the age of 13 as a protégée of the classical singer Geraldine Farrar, Marjorie Daw (1902–   ) had already been trained as an opera singer. As a juvenile she appeared in *The Warrens of Virginia* (1915), *The Unafraid* (1915), *The Captive* (1915), *The Chorus Lady* (1915), *Carmen* (1915), *Joan and the Woman* (1917), and *Rebecca of Sunnybrook Farm* (1917). From 1918 to 1919, she was the frequent screen partner and love interest of Douglas Fairbanks. When sound came in, she retired from the movies.

Madge Evans (1909–81) was a child star from the age of five, beginning her career in 1915 with *Alias Jimmy Valentine*, *The Seven Sisters*, and *Zaza*. She was one of the first, if not the first, child actor to grow older in the movies, making a successful transition from child to ingénue to leading-lady roles. As an adult, she appeared in such outstanding films as *Dinner at Eight* (1933), *Stand Up and Cheer* (1934), *David Copperfield* (1935), and *Pennies from Heaven* (1936). Evans retired from the screen in 1938 and from the stage in 1943, after marrying playwright Sidney Kingsley.

Born Nicholas Benton Alexander, Ben Alexander (1911–69) became a popular child actor in Hollywood at the age of four; his first directors were Cecil B. De Mille and D. W. Griffith. He made his screen debut in *Each Pearl a Tear* (1916), and it was found that he could cry on cue. It was said that his performances made even Chaplin cry, which was a high compliment at the time. He wept even more in Cecil B. De Mille's *The Little American* (1917, with Mary Pickford) and D. W. Griffith's *Hearts of the World* (1918, with the Gish sisters)—both films made to capitalize on the propaganda stories of German cruelty to children during World War I. Alexander went from tiny-tot roles to pre-pubescent parts, as in *Penrod and Sam* (1923). He graduated to post-adolescent roles in *All Quiet on the Western Front* (1930), in which he turned in a monumental performance as a young German soldier who covets his friend's new boots. In the 1930s he became a radio announcer, and in the 1950s he emerged from obscurity to play Jack Webb's partner in television's "Dragnet" series.

One of the most famous child stars of all time, Jackie Coogan (1914–84), was born in Los Angeles and made his screen debut in *Skinner's Baby* (1917) when he was 18 months old. His parents, Lillian and Jack Coogan, were stage people. She had toured in vaudeville with her family, and he had been a dancer-comedian. After they married, they worked up a stage act for themselves—she was a singer and straight man for her husband's jokes. They named their first child Jack Leslie Coogan and promptly left him with relatives while they went back on the road. But they thought better of it when little Jackie was three years old, and took him with them. So began his apprenticeship in the family trade.

In 1919 the elder Coogans signed with Annette Kellerman, a former star swimmer turned actress, in a vaudeville act. After one of Jack's turns in San Francisco, which had brought down the house, he came out from the wings to take a bow with young Jackie in his arms, setting him down in front of the footlights. The five-year-old stared out into the audience and immediately went into one of his impersonations. It stopped the show, and Kellerman offered the parents an extra $25 per week to keep Jackie in the act.

The next stop on the tour was Los Angeles. They opened at the Orpheum Theater, and it was there that little Jackie was discovered by Charlie Chaplin. Chaplin was overwhelmed when the little boy was brought onstage and did the shimmy in a bathing suit, earning an encore from the audience. Chaplin went back to his studio and thought about the boy, but it took a week for him to make up his mind, and that only after he had heard that the silent film comedian

"I'm gonna have a good feed for once."

Opposite: Charlie Chaplin and his young companion, Jackie Coogan, in *The Kid* (1921). This was the first real feature film for both stars.

Above: Once again Jackie Coogan played a homeless, hungry waif in *Daddy* (1923). It would be three more years before he had his hair cut.

Roscoe "Fatty" Arbuckle had signed little Jackie for his studio. Chaplin was relieved to find out that Jack Coogan, the father, was the one who had been signed. Chaplin immediately had the elder Coogan brought to his studio. At first he had a bit of trouble making him understand that all he wanted was to hire Jackie for one picture. But when Jack Sr. finally realized what the film-maker was asking for, he replied, "Why of course you can have the little punk. Is *that* all you wanted?" Chaplin offered $75 a week, and Jack struck a deal whereby he would be written into the script. Many years later, Jackie Coogan said that by the time the film, *The Kid* (1921), was completed, his father had played six parts in the picture. ("He played a lounge lizard in one scene and a drunk in a flophouse in another.") He had also become Chaplin's assistant and was making $150 a week to his son's $75. Even so, years later Jackie said, "It's a great life for a kid. It's wonderful to be someone before you're old."

Underneath it all, little Jackie was timid and shy. He had become dependent upon the reactions of a live audience, and he found movies very different—the only audience was the director and his minions. To prep him for the big picture, *The Kid*, Chaplin put him into a lightweight two-reel potboiler, *A Day's Pleasure* (1919), in which Jackie had a small role in the story of a family outing and its pitfalls. It was fortunate for Jackie that he was working with Chaplin. He was honing his movie skills under a perfectionist who didn't mind shooting a scene over and over until it was right. Other child stars were not so lucky. Many of them had to suffer the angry outbursts of low-budget directors when they blew a scene.

The Kid is about a tramp who picks up an abandoned child, learns to love him, and then gives him up for the child's own good; the climactic scene occurs when the workhouse officials come to drag Jackie away. Jackie had come to the set in a happy frame of mind, and no amount of description by Chaplin of the horrors of life in a London workhouse would get him out of it. After a while, Jack Coogan came to Chaplin and said that he could make his son cry. Chaplin warned him not to hurt the boy and retired to his dressing room.

Coogan had the title role in *Oliver Twist* (1922), with Gertrude Claire (left) and Esther Ralston.

A few minutes later he heard Jackie crying—just what he wanted. He left his dressing room and was met by Coogan, Sr. who said, "He's all ready." The scene went off without a hitch—the officials dragged the crying boy away, and the Little Tramp rescued him. It took Chaplin quite a while to calm Jackie down and make him stop crying. Later Chaplin asked the father what he had done to the boy. Jack bragged, "Nothing to it. I just told him that if he didn't cry, we'd take him away from the studio and really send him to the workhouse."

Thanks to *The Kid*, Jackie Coogan's name became a household word. Both critics and audiences acclaimed not only Chaplin, but also Coogan, the wistful waif who almost stole the film. Almost overnight, Jackie was famous. Irvin S. Cobb, the newspaper columnist, wrote of him: "Perhaps the kindly angels are responsible for Jackie Coogan. If so, they did a good job...if the world

Above: Another scene from *Oliver Twist* (1922). One of Coogan's co-stars was Lon Chaney (left), who played Fagin. Also in the movie were (left to right) Taylor Graves, George Siegmann, and Gladys Brockwell.

Below: Coogan played a Belgian farm boy in *A Boy of Flanders* (1924).

doesn't spoil him and God lets him live with us, he will, in maturity, be the blithest spirit that ever gave unending joy to countless millions—indeed, he is that now." And prophetically enough, a fan magazine writer summed it up: "Dear child, we have only one prayer to offer...*don't* grow up."

Jack and Lillian Coogan had been in show business for years, so it was obvious to both of them that their little son was worth a lot of money. Accordingly, they began a campaign to market the boy that would make the most avaricious film mogul blush. After *The Kid*, Jack began to merchandise his son by setting up Jackie Coogan Productions, where his next film, *Peck's Bad Boy* (1921), was made. This movie established Jackie as a star in his own right—one who didn't need to depend on a luminary such as Charlie Chaplin. In 1922 came *Oliver Twist*, *My Boy* and *Trouble*, the latter written by Jack, Sr.

By 1923 Jackie was the number-one box-office star in America, followed by Rudolph Valentino and Douglas Fairbanks. He had received a bonus of $500,000 that year to leave First National Pictures for MGM. For making only four movies in the next two years, he was to receive $1 million. By then he had investments in oil wells and real estate that totaled $1,200,000—according to his father. The child star got fifty cents for each Jackie Coogan coaster wagon sold and seven cents on every Jackie Coogan cap. He received $50,000 per year for the use of his picture on Erector Set boxes. The line of Jackie Coogan boys' clothes paid him $2,000 a week. He was supposed to get 50 cents for each Jackie Coogan doll sold: some 200,000 were purchased. There was a Jackie Coogan chocolate bar (made in the shape of his head), which gave him one cent for every five-cent bar sold.

The year after they were married, Jackie Coogan and Betty Grable danced together in *College Swing* (1938).

But little Jackie saw none of the money: his parents exercised complete control over his earnings. When he was asked, after he had signed his first million-dollar contract, what he would take for it, the boy answered, "Will you give me a dollar and a quarter in cash? I need that to get a new pair of roller skates."

Nineteen twenty-three brought two more lachrymose pictures, *Daddy* and *Circus Days*, but these saccharine sagas began to undermine Jackie's popularity. Even Chaplin expressed a negative opinion of them: "I don't like to see a child in scenes of emotion, weeping over deathbeds and such. A child should by joyous...joyous, sunny, and natural."

In the summer of 1924, Jackie led his cross-country and trans-Atlantic Children's Crusade, and he personally raised over a million dollars in funds, food, and clothing for 70,000 Greek and Armenian war orphans. For this, in addition to the adulation of his American and European fans, he received the Golden Cross of the Order of Jerusalem from Pope Pius XI.

Jackie reached a turning point in his career at the age of 12, when his famous rumpled bob was shorn to the clicking of cameras, and MGM released *Johnny Get Your Hair Cut* (1927), which showed him before and after the big event. That year he played his last role as a child star, and his contract with MGM ran out in 1928. One comic observed that "Senility finally got him at 13." After touring with his father on stage and appearing at the London Palladium, Jackie made a brief comeback in *Tom Sawyer* (1930) and *Huckleberry Finn* (1931). The two Mark Twain adaptations showed the public not only that Jackie was cute, but also that he was a real actor. But in maturity he could find no place on the screen. This early burnout was not unheard of in Hollywood, and many more child stars were to take the same road to oblivion.

Just before his 21st birthday, in 1935, Jackie was injured in an automobile crash that killed his father, who was driving, child actor Junior Durkin, and another man. Jackie, in the rumble seat, was the only survivor. In order to go to his father's funeral three days later, he had to leave the hospital against his doctor's orders.

When Jackie turned 21, he went to his mother to ask for the reputed $4 million that

The Coogan Act

There was no question that Jackie Coogan had earned at least $4 million from acting—never mind the merchandising money. But when he reached 21—old enough, he thought to ask for the money—it turned out that his mother was in no hurry to part with it. Indeed, she and her second husband had discovered that there was an old California law which would serve their purposes. It said that the parents of a minor were entitled to all of the child's earnings. Lillian refused to share any part of Jackie's fortune with the boy, and he was forced to leave the house that his money had bought.

He filed suit against his family in 1938 for the assets of Jackie Coogan Productions, Inc., but the case dragged on for months before it was finally settled. By that time the assets of the company had dwindled to a mere $252,000, of which Coogan received half. That $126,000 didn't last long, of course.

If the suit didn't do Jackie much good, it did benefit many other child actors and actresses. Impressed by Coogan's sad experience, the California State Legislature passed what is formally titled the Child Actor's Bill, but which everyone calls the Coogan Act; it was designed to prevent the repetition of such abuses. It provides that at least 50 percent of a child actor's earnings be set aside in a trust fund or some other form of savings against the time when that actor comes of age. It protected untold numbers of child performers, but Judy Garland, Edith Fellows, and Freddie Bartholomew were still to suffer at the hands of greedy relatives.

he had earned as a child star. But he was unable to collect. In 1938 he filed suit for his earnings, but was awarded only a tiny fraction of the money owed. By this time he was married to the young actress Betty Grable. As she told the press, "The 'Millionaire Kid' didn't have enough to take me out dancing, let alone get married." The trial took months, and it broke up his marriage. Still, Coogan was able to say years later, "Public adoration is the greatest thing in the world."

Jackie Coogan enlisted in the medics before World War II began, then transferred to the Army Air Corps because he was already a licensed pilot. He ended up in Burma, landing gliders and building airstrips behind Japanese lines.

Coogan never regained his former stardom, but as the years went on he managed to make a more than comfortable living out of

A theater lobby poster for *The Kid* (1921).

acting—not only in occasional film roles, but also in television appearances, most notably as the grotesque Uncle Fester in the series *The Addams Family*. In 1972, when Charlie Chaplin returned from a self-imposed exile in Switzerland (he had been driven out of the United States by political controversy in the 1950s), there was a last emotional reunion.

Sally Blane (1910–   ), born Elizabeth Jane Young, came from a show-business family. She and her three sisters, Polly Ann, Georgianna, and (the most famous) Loretta Young, went to work as movie extras at early ages to support one another and their recently divorced mother. Sally started her film work at the age of five, and by the time she was seven was playing featured roles in such films as *Sirens of the Sea* (1917). As an adult, she played feminine leads in many "B" films like *The Very Idea* (1929), in which she was a married woman hired (with her husband) to produce a baby for a childless couple. When the baby is born, they don't want to give it up. The happy ending came when it was found that the childless couple was expecting a baby of their own. Believe it or not, this was a movie farce. Blane retired shortly after her 1937 marriage to actor-director Norman Foster, who was previously married to Claudette Colbert and was probably best known for directing a number of detective movies in the "Mr. Moto" and "Charlie Chan" series.

Blane's younger sister, Loretta (born Gretchen) Young (1913–   ), was only four years old when she appeared as an extra in *The Primrose Ring* (1917). After taking time off to attend a convent school, she returned to films at the age of 14, playing a supporting role in a Colleen Moore picture, *Naughty But Nice* (1927). Actually, she got the part by default. Director Mervyn LeRoy telephoned the Young home to ask for her older sister, Polly Ann. Loretta said that her sister wasn't available, but would she do? The role set in motion a fabulous career.

Loretta Young was one of the few who progressed from child actor to adult star without a hitch, and then made a smooth transition to the talkies. For most of her roles she relied on her elegant beauty—rosy complexion, full lips, and prominent cheekbones —but occasionally she was called upon to

act. She did so convincingly as an adult in such films as *The Farmer's Daughter* (1947), for which she won the Academy Award as Best Actress, *Rachel and the Stranger* (1948), *Come to the Stable* (Oscar nomination, 1949) and *Cause for Alarm* (1951).

Young retired from the screen in 1953 to begin a long run as the hostess of television's "The Loretta Young Show," which lasted from 1953 to 1963 and won her three Emmys. When that program had run its course, she spent most of her time working for Catholic charities, but in 1986, on December 22, after a 23-year vacation from the television screen, she starred in a play called *Christmas Eve*. It was seen by more people than any of the competitors in its time slot.

The son of a circus acrobat and an actress, Arthur Lake (1905–87) was born Arthur Silverlake. He joined the family vaudeville act at the age of three and was playing child roles in films when he twelve years old, beginning with *Jack and the Beanstalk* (1917). Then he went on to juvenile leads long after he reached maturity, as in *Harold Teen* (1928), a film based on the comic strip character drawn by Carl Ed about a high school student and his friends—Lake was 23 years old at the time. In 1938 he was cast as Dagwood Bum-

Above: Loretta Young at the age of 15 in *The Magnificent Flirt* (1928). She was already a beauty.

Below: When she was only 18, Loretta Young (left) was playing mature women—*The Ruling Voice* (1931).

stead in the long-running series of "Blondie" pictures opposite Penny Singleton.

Lillian Roth (1910–80) began life as Lillian Rutstein—her parents named her for Lillian Russell. At the age of six she was taken by her mother to Educational Pictures, where she became their trademark—a living statue holding the lamp of knowledge. She was a hit on Broadway in *The Inner Man,* and debuted in movies at the age of of eight in *Pershing's Crusaders* (1918). Roth went on to be billed as "Broadway's Youngest Star" when she was in *Shavings* that same year.

By the time she was 17, Roth was an established Broadway musical-comedy star, having appeared in an Earl Carroll *Vanities* and a Ziegfeld *Midnight Frolics.* Then she signed a seven-year contract with Paramount and appeared in such pictures as *The Love Parade* (1929) with Maurice Chevalier and the 1930 films *Honey,* in which she introduced "Sing You Sinners," *Paramount on Parade, Madam Satan,* and *Animal Crackers,* with the Marx Brothers.

Roth went back to Broadway and appeared in the Earl Carroll *Vanities* of 1931 and 1932. But by this time alcohol had begun to control her life. By the late 1930s she had disappeared from sight. Her career had been wrecked by alcoholism and a procession of eight husbands. She was all but forgotten until 1953, when she told her tragic story to millions of Americans on Ralph Edwards' "This Is Your Life" television program. Over 40,000 letters poured in, and the following year her autobiography, *I'll Cry Tomorrow,* was published. It was a huge success, and once again Roth was playing night clubs and appearing on television singing the songs that she had made famous, including "When the Red, Red, Robin Comes Bob, Bob, Bobbin' Along" and "I'd Climb the Highest Mountain." The film version of her book, which had sold over 7 million copies in 20 languages, was made in 1955 and starred Susan Hayward. □

Opposite above: Arthur Lake greets Penny Singleton in *Blondie Goes To College.* The dutiful friends are Larry Parks and Janet Blair.

Opposite below: Lillian Roth (left), Helen Mann (center), and Barbara Stanwyck—*Ladies They Talk About* (1933).

Hollywood Mothers

Freddie Bartholomew and Aunt Cissie, who was appointed his legal guardian after a bitter custody battle.

As anyone who has seen the stage or screen version of *Gypsy* knows, Rose Hovick, the mother of June Havoc and Gypsy Rose Lee, was the quintessential stage mother. But many Hollywood mothers were every bit as domineering, greedy, and intimidating as she was. Some child stars had to go to court to rid themselves of parental pressure, and they were often unsuccessful. Peggy Ann Garner made headlines when her guardianship was transferred from her mother to her father in a divorce action. Jackie Coogan sued his mother and stepfather for the earnings that had accrued to him during his years as a child star—and lost. Freddie Bartholomew was almost rendered bankrupt by a series of family lawsuits over his earnings. In fact, the stage-mother syndrome can affect fathers, grandparents, and anyone else who stands *in loco parentis* to the child performer.

Darryl Hickman was six years old when he asked his mother why he was an actor. She answered, "It's something you've always wanted to do." He believed her at the time, as most children would. The child wants to get the part to please the mother. Then the mother becomes more excited than the child. When the child doesn't get the job, he or she becomes nervous, and so does the mother. Their mutual hope and anxiety feed off one another, and eventually this exchange of emotions snowballs out of control.

1920~1929

The Twenties Begin to Roar

One of the most enduring Hollywood actors started his film career at the age of five. Noah Beery, Jr. (1915–   ) the son of Noah Beery and the nephew of Wallace Beery, made his debut with his father and Douglas Fairbanks in *The Mark of Zorro* (1920). By the time he was 20, he had appeared in such movies as *Penrod* (1922), *Father and Son* (1929), *Heroes of the West* (1932), *Rustler's Roundup* (1933), and *The Call of the Savage* (1935). Beery was educated at military academies between pictures and stock-company appearances with his father.

During the mid-1930s he seemed to specialize in making serials. *The Call of the Savage*, for example, was a serial set in the jungle and concerned the search for a cure for infantile paralysis (polio). Beery played ape-man Jan·of the Jungle, but ended up discovering the lost city of Mu, populated by ruthless people who try to torture him with time-honored devices like spiked walls that close in on the victim. Beery also appeared as Skeeter Mulligan, the mechanic for flyer Tommy Tompkins, in *Tailspin Tommy* (1936 serial), then played Tompkins himself in *Tailspin Tommy in the Great Air Mystery* later that year. Then he was Jerry Meredith, the friend

Opposite: Mickey Rooney as a mischievous Puck in *A Midsummer Night's Dream.*

Above: Noah Beery, Jr., and Anne Baxter in her first film—*20 Mule Team.*

of *Ace Drummond* (1936 serial), played by John King, who later went on to Western films as "Dusty" King.

Beery generally played supporting roles, appearing as second hero to such cowboy stars as Tom Mix, Johnny Mack Brown, and Buck Jones. He married Jones's daughter, Maxine, in 1940. He has also played character parts in dramas and comedies and lead roles in some low-budget pictures. Beery's father was the only personality of star quality to play the villain in countless Westerns of the sound era. His uncle Wallace was often the good-bad man, not the outright crook with few redeeming features that Noah, Sr. portrayed. Noah, Jr. reverted to his uncle's type, and, in fact, was usually on the side of the just. In addition to making films, Beery has been seen on many television series, such as "Circus Boy," "Riverboat," "Hondo," "Doc Elliot," "The Rockford Files," "The Quest," and "The Yellow Rose."

Mary Astor (1906–) was born Lucille Vasconcellos Langhanke. Driven by her career-minded father, she entered a beauty contest at the age of 14 and was in films the following year, making her first appearance in *The Beggar Maid* (1921). She played a series of small roles and became a star in *Beau Brummel* (1924), in which her leading man was John Barrymore. Astor went on to become an important screen personality for almost 30 years, starring in such pictures as *Don Juan* (1926) *Red Dust* (1932), *Dodsworth* (1936), *The Maltese Falcon* (1941), *Thousands Cheer* (1943), *Meet Me in St. Louis* (1944), and *Little Women* (1949).

Much of Astor's fame came from her off-screen adventures. She had a love affair with John Barrymore, four marriages, a period of alcoholism, and an attempted suicide. Her first husband, director Kenneth Hawks, was killed in a plane crash. She later suffered a custody fight over her daughter with her second husband, a physician. During the trial, Astor's personal diary was introduced as evidence, and many embarrassments were brought to light, including an affair with playwright George S. Kaufman. The diary revelations almost ruined her career, but she went on to greater screen triumphs, winning the Academy Award for Best Supporting Actress for her work in *The Great Lie* (1941).

Frank Coghlan, Jr. (1917–), billed as Junior Coghlan, was a popular freckle-faced child star of the 1920s and 1930s. He made his film debut at the age of four playing Leatrice Joy's son in *The Poverty of Riches* (1921). He had problems, however, when he became an adolescent: jobs were hard to find. After he returned from naval duty at the end of World War II, he was seen in only one bit part, in *The Sand Pebbles* (1966). He also served as coordinator of special events for the Los Angeles Harbor Department.

Possibly Jackie Coogan's chief rival for public affection during the 1920s was the tremendously talented Baby Peggy. She was born Peggy Montgomery in 1917, the daughter of an extra and stuntman in Western movies, and she entered the movie industry at the age of 20 months, making 150 two-reel comedies in the next 18 months. Her first picture was *Playmates* (1921), in which she co-starred with Brownie, the Wonder Dog, for which she earned $5 a day for five days. The picture was a success, and her salary went to $75 per week at the old Century Studios on Hollywood's "Poverty Row." Each of her pictures was made in from three to five days.

After six months, Brownie, that short-haired mongrel, died, and Baby Peggy continued on her own.

The tiny brown-eyed brunette with the adorable bangs began a series of parodies of such fairy tales as "Little Red Riding Hood" and "Jack and the Beanstalk." Then she began to parody other stars of the time, including Rudolph Valentino, Harold Lloyd, Theda Bara, and Mae Murray. Then came parodies of movie spectaculars like *Carmen*, *The Girl of the Golden West*, and *The Squaw Man*. The other cast members in those films were adults. One of her favorite roles was in *Peggy of the Mounties* (1921), in which she rode Tim, a horse that stood only 36 inches tall— she had been riding since she was three months old.

In 1922 the success of Jackie Coogan inspired the five-year-old Peggy's father to sign her with Universal Studios, where Carl Laemmle put her into feature films as a child star who could compete with Coogan. Her salary soared to $10,000 a week, and she was given a studio dressing room with a window

Above: With her ebony bangs, chubby cheeks, and radiant smile, Baby Peggy stole *Captain January* (1923) from the veteran screen actor Hobart Bosworth.

Right: Baby Peggy (left) asks Edward Everett Horton for a glass of water.

and scaled-down furniture, plus a small bed for her naps. Her first feature film was *The Darling of New York* (1923), about the trials and triumphs of a five-year-old Italian orphan who, en route to America to live with her grandfather, is separated from her nurse and is cared for by a gangster called Giovanni. Stolen jewels are hidden in her rag doll, she leaves to stay with the Levinsky family, and is finally found by her grandfather. Baby Peggy was in almost every scene in the film, whether she furthered the plot line or not. She was the star.

By the time she was five years old, Baby Peggy's biography had been written and Baby Peggy products were being merchandised nationally. There were Baby Peggy dolls with real hair and eyes that opened and closed. She endorsed American Caramels, Orange Crush, and other products that her parents wouldn't even let her taste. Films like *Captain January* (1923) increased her popularity. She went on tour with *Captain January,* and there was a new Baby Peggy doll, plus Baby Peggy dresses, sweaters, handbags, toys, fairy-tale books, and a reprint of the novel *Captain January* illustrated with scenes from the movie. *The New York Globe* reported: "Baby Peggy has reached the mature age of five, but her mother holds a contract by which the baby makes as much in the next five years as all the presidents since Lincoln have drawn from the Treasury of the United States."

Baby Peggy even made an appearance at the Democratic National Convention in Madison Square Garden in 1924. She was the convention mascot, and she led the parade onto the floor of the Garden. After Franklin D. Roosevelt had nominated "The Happy Warrior," reformer Al Smith, as the Democratic candidate for President of the United States, Baby Peggy stood on the dais, waving a flag and shouting through a megaphone.

After the scandals of Desmond Taylor, Fatty Arbuckle, Thomas Ince, Jack Pickford, and others, Hollywood was anxious to upgrade its image, and Baby Peggy appeared on a float in the annual Rose Bowl Parade in Pasadena. It was cowboy star Tim McCoy who found something funny about all this display of innocence. He said: "Originally the Chamber of Commerce had planned to

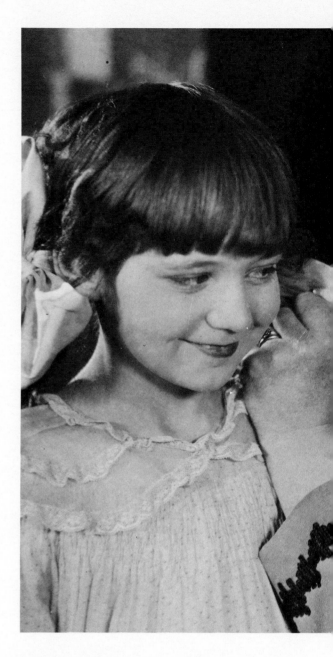

stage an impressive parade of virgins down Hollywood Boulevard, as a show of moral strength, but it had to be called off at the last moment because May McAvoy came down with the flu and Baby Peggy refused to march alone."

In a way, Baby Peggy became a has-been at the stage of seven. One of her biggest problems was that her two front teeth came out. Her father bought her false teeth, but they didn't help much. So Peggy went on the vaudeville circuit with a comedy act, retiring then from the stage in 1929. She worked

Above: Anne Shirley was 18 years old when she played a lovesick young girl in *Chatterbox* (1936).

Left: Dawn O'Day (before she became Anne Shirley) being spruced up by Louise Dresser in *Mother Knows Best* (1928).

again in films under the name Peggy Montgomery, appearing in low-budget Westerns until well into her late teens. Since then she has become a respected free-lance journalist and the author of two excellent nonfiction books about the movie industry, *The Hollywood Posse* (1975) and *Hollywood Children* (1979) under the name of Diana Carey Serra.

Born Dawn Evelyeen Paris, Anne Shirley (1918–   ) began her movie career at the age of five, billed as Dawn O'Day. She always had work in films, and appeared in such movies as *Moonshine Valley* (1922), *Riders of the Purple Sage* (1925), *Sins of the Fathers* (1928), *Liliom* (1930), *So Big* (1932), *Rasputin and the Empress* (1932), and many more. Still billed as Dawn O'Day, she made *Finishing School* (1934), in which she was a fellow student of Ginger Rogers and Frances Dee.

Then came her big break—the title role in a remake of Mary Miles Minter's 1919 film *Anne of Green Gables* (1934). For this movie she changed her name to Anne Shirley, which was the name of the picture's heroine—probably because Dawn O'Day sounded too contrived. Forever after she was identified with that character whom she played so fetchingly and warmly. The movie had all the charm of *Little Women*, and Anne Shirley became a star. She continued playing ingenues and was nominated for an Academy Award for Best Supporting Actress for her work in *Stella Dallas* (1937). She was in *Mother Carey's Chickens* (1938), which was remade as *Summer Magic* (1963) starring Hayley Mills.

Shirley maintained her virginal persona as a small-town grocer's daughter who goes to college in *Sorority House* (1939). She thinks that her life will be ruined if she is not pledged to the Gamma sorority, but when she is finally invited to join it, she realizes the hypocrisy of the sorority system and tears up her bid.

Anne Shirley played again the character whose name she'd adopted in *Anne of Windy Poplars* (1940). This time she was a school teacher who, because of her dedication and goodness, wins the hearts of her adversaries. Unfortunately, the movie didn't win the hearts of theater audiences.

Shirley retired from the screen in 1945, after the breakup of her marriage to actor John Payne and her remarriage to producer Adrian Scott, who became one of the "Hollywood Ten"—those who were cited for contempt of Congress during the Red Scare of the late 1940s and later blacklisted by the movie industry. She divorced Scott in 1949 and married screenwriter Charles Lederer.

Child star Wesley Barry was Warner Bros.' first box-office attraction. This appealing freckle-faced boy made his screen debut in *Rags to Riches* (1922), in which he was Marmaduke Clark, a rich kid. A kidnap attempt is made on him, which is foiled, and he joins a gang of regular fellows. This was an early example of the crime films and social dramas for which Warner Bros. would become famous.

Then came *School Days* (1922), a movie based on the well-known song by Gus Edwards. This time Barry was a small-town kid who couldn't cope with life in the big city. He became a criminal, but was redeemed, and returned to the country. In *The Country Kid* (1923), he played the eldest of three orphaned brothers whose two siblings kept getting into trouble, calling on him to get

them out of it. Then Barry starred in *The Printer's Devil* (1923), a comedy in which two kids start their own newspaper. Barry's partner is wrongly accused of a robbery, and Barry must track down the thief. One of his best roles was in *Heroes of the Street* (1923), in which he solved the mystery of the murder of his policeman father.

As was the case with many sons and daughters of famous actors, Douglas Fairbanks, Jr. (1909–   ) made his screen debut early, as the boy star of *Stephen Steps Out* (1923). Not surprisingly, producer Jesse L. Lasky was trying to exploit the magic of the Fairbanks name, and the picture wasn't very successful. Indeed, young Fairbanks had been raised by his mother, Fairbanks' first wife, Anna Beth Sully, from the age of nine. Also, his father took little interest in the boy's career, saying that he had "no more paternal feelings than a tiger in the jungle for his cub." Not until the early 1930s did the father and son become friends. This meant that the younger Fairbanks had to fend for himself in the Hollywood jungle, and he did it by accepting every role he was offered, including bits and extra work. He even wrote continuity titles for silent films and acted on the Los Angeles stage. Fairbanks did make one outstanding movie as a juvenile when he was 16 —*Stella Dallas* (1925), with Belle Bennett and Ronald Colman. But it was not until his marriage to Joan Crawford in 1928 that he emerged as a star. He appeared with Crawford in her first starring movie, *Our Modern Maidens* (1929). A publicity still accompanying the press release pictured Fairbanks at the wheel of a roadster in which Crawford was a passenger: the caption provided by studio flacks read "Reckless youth runs a race with death on their way to a party."

Although he was always working, Douglas Jr., despite his good looks and agreeable screen personality (nowhere more brilliantly showcased than in *Gunga Din* in 1939), never approached superstardom. But he did thrive on his political and social connections. As a lieutenant commander in the Navy during World War II, he participated in Anglo-American operations and was presented by the British with several medals and decorations. He was knighted in 1949 for "furthering Anglo-American amity." Fairbanks retired from the screen in 1950 and moved to London. Years later he and his second wife, Mary Lee Hartford, relocated to Palm Beach, Florida.

Probably most famous for her role as Peg Riley, the wife of William Bendix in the long-running television series The Life of Riley, Marjorie Reynolds (1921–), born Marjorie Goodspeed, started her film career at the age of two in *Scaramouche* (1923), followed by *Revelation* (1924). Almost ten years later, she reappeared as Marjorie Moore in *Wine, Women and Song* (1933). By 1937 she had become Marjorie Reynolds and was playing leads in minor action films. Success finally came in the 1940s, when she went from brunette to blonde and starred opposite such heavy hitters as Bing Crosby (in *Holiday Inn*, 1942) and Ray Milland (*Ministry of Fear,* 1944).

Tom Brown (1923–) was born into a show-business family, the son of vaudevillian Harry Brown and musical-comedy star Marie (Francis) Brown. He performed on radio and on the stage from infancy. At nine years old he reached Broadway, and he was ten when he first appeared on the screen in *The Hoosier Schoolmaster* (1924). Brown went on to establish himself as the clean-cut, naive, boy-next-door type in 1930s films like *Tom Brown of Culver* (1932) *Anne of Green Gables* (1934), *Freckles* (1935), *Rose Bowl (1936), Navy Blue and Gold* (1937), and *The Duke of West Point* (1938). After returning from World War II combat service as a paratrooper, he tried to shake his wholesome image by playing character parts, including villains. Called back to service during the Korean War, Brown was promoted to lieutenant colonel. After his second discharge, he appeared in a few films, but was most visible on television, in the "Gunsmoke" and "General Hospital" series.

Anita Louise (1915-70) was born Anita Louise Fremault, and began appearing on the stage in early childhood. She made her first movie, *The Sixth Commandment* (1924), when she was eight years old. She continued to make movies as a child star, then progressed to juvenile and adult roles. After shortening her name to Anita Louise in 1929, when she was 14, she emerged as one of the prettiest stars in pictures; one poll voted her Holly-

Above: Douglas Fairbanks, Jr. (right), in his first movie, *Stephen Steps Out* (1923).

Top: Douglas Fairbanks, Jr., in *Padlocked* (1926).

Below: Anita Louise and Charles Starrett, *Our Betters* (1933).

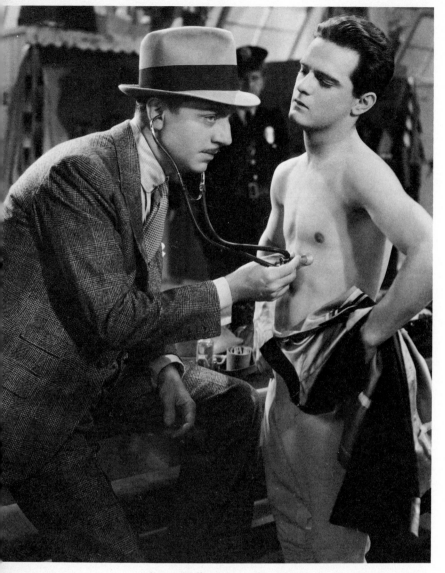

Top: Frankie Darro, Charlotte Henry (who had played the title role in *Alice in Wonderland* in 1933), and Billy Benedict (who would go on to play "Whitey" in countless "Bowery Boys" films from 1946 to 1957) in *Three Kids and a Queen* (1935).

Above: William Powell examines jockey Frankie Darro in *The Ex-Mrs. Bradford* (1936).

Right: Frankie Darro, May Robson, and Charlotte Henry in *Three Kids and a Queen* (1935). Robson is patching up a lover's quarrel.

wood's most beautiful actress. Besides that, she was an accomplished harpist. Anita Louise appeared in some of the biggest films of the 1930s, including *Madame Du Barry* (1934), *A Midsummer Night's Dream* (1935), *The Story of Louis Pasteur* (1936), *Anthony Adverse* (1936), *Green Light* (1937), *Tovarich* (1937), *Marie Antoinette* (1938), and *Reno* (1939). After she retired from films, she starred in the "My Friend Flicka" television series.

One of the most athletic actors of all time was Frankie Darro (1917–76), who was born Frank Johnson to a circus family. His parents made up an aerialist team called the Flying Johnsons. Frankie was born in Chicago, where the Sells-Floto Circus was appearing at the time. Typical circus folk, the Johnsons started training their son to become a part of the act when he could hardly walk. But as it turned out, he was afraid of heights. So they started with a tight wire stretched between two posts at a height of about a foot from the ground. Frankie walked the wire. The wire was then gradually raised to three feet, to six feet, to ten feet. But Frankie was still afraid of heights. Somehow he was able to brave it out, but meanwhile he was learning tumbling and acrobatics. He never did go up the tall rope ladder to the top of the tent.

When the circus arrived in Long Beach, California, in 1922, Frankie's mother was unable to go on; she had collapsed into a nervous breakdown. The circus moved on and the family was stranded. The father couldn't do a solo act, the mother was incapacitated, and Frankie, at the age of five, had to become the breadwinner. His father took him to Ralph Ince, a casual friend who had become a movie producer. Ince needed a boy to appear in *Judgment of the Storm* (1924) with Wallace Beery. Frankie Johnson got the role and became Frankie Darro.

Darro continued playing child parts throughout the silent era, including two films in which he had the title role, *Little Mickey Grogan* (1927) and *The Circus Kid* (1928). He matured into adolescent roles in the 1930s and often played tough kids of the Depression era. Because of his small frame he also played jockeys and pint-sized punks.

Darro was the star of *Wild Boys of the Road* (1933), a film about three young people who decide to take to the road in Depression-scarred America rather than burden their families. Traveling from city to city on freight trains, they are unable to find work. Along the way they have run-ins with railroad policemen and other authority figures. It was an effective picture until the requisite 1930s-style happy ending, which ruined its impact.

During the early 1930s, Darro started appearing in low-budget Monogram features and serials and became the studio's answer to Jackie Cooper. He starred in *The Wolf Dog* (1933) which introduced Rin-Tin-Tin Jr. to the screen. In this serial set in Alaska, Darro fought the man who had invented a death ray. In *Burn 'Em Up Barnes* (1934 serial) he was the young sidekick to veteran movie actor Jack Mulhall and Lola Lane (who later made a comeback as a member of the Lane Sisters). It was a tale about the problems of a race car driver, and in one episode Darro

performed an acrobatic stunt that left the audience stunned. Running toward his car (an old coupe with its windows rolled down), he grabbed the roof and the top of the open window with both hands and flipped his body up in such a contortion that he launched himself into the car feet-first, landing in the driver's seat and driving off.

Darro was lured back into serial work at Mascot Studios when he was 18 years old. By now he was smoking and driving fast cars in real life, but he became an innocent again for $5,000 and appeared in one of the strangest serials ever made—*The Phantom Empire* (1935). The star was Gene Autry, in his first screen appearance. It was a science-fiction Western, with Autry playing the owner of Radio Ranch, beneath which was the capital of a futuristic society bent on destroying civilization with its rocket ships and robots. Autry had his hands full in this saga. Every day he would race from the underground city of Murania to his ranch on the surface, where he broadcast a cowboy song to fulfill a radio contract. But never mind the plot. Darro was one of the kids on the ranch. Actually, he was a good horseman and actor, and he helped carry the totally inexperienced Autry in the serial.

In 1942 Darro co-starred with Paul Kelly in another serial, *The Secret Code*. He played police inspector Dan Barton, who, costumed in a solid black outfit with a black hood and gloves, turned into "the Black Commando" when he went out to smash an enemy spy ring.

Darro returned from World War II to find that his career was over. He was able to pick up some bit parts in films like *Across the Wide Missouri* (1955) and *Operation Petticoat* (1959), and appeared occasionally on the Red Skelton television show, but he had to rely on a bar that he owned to support himself.

Marcia Mae Jones (1924–   ) made her film debut at the age of two, playing Dolores Costello as a baby in *Mannequin* (1926). She had a typical stage mother in Frieda Jones, who managed the careers of her children, Margaret, Macon, and Marcia Mae. Their father was a telegrapher with the *Los Angeles Times*. During the 1930s Marcia Mae played child roles in many Hollywood films, including *The Champ* (1931), *Heidi* (1937), *The*

Adventures of Tom Sawyer (1938), and *The Little Princess* (1939); she once went to work with scarlet fever so that shooting time would not be lost. Jones was not the prettiest of the child stars, but she had an expressive face and often demonstrated that she could act, as in *These Three* (1936), in which she portrayed a terrorized little girl. Her career went downhill in the 1940s and she began drinking heavily and attempted suicide. However, she emerged from retirement in the 1960s to appear in occasional character roles in movies and on television, often using the name Marsha Jones.

Nancy Kelly (1921–) was a model as a baby and later played child roles on stage and in the movies. Her screen debut came when she was a five-year-old tot, in *Untamed Lady* (1926). Kelly went on to play children in *Mismates* (1926), *The Girl on the Barge* (1929), *Convention Girl* (1935), and *Submarine Patrol* (1938). She acted in many fine films, including *Jesse James* (1939), *Stanley and Livingstone* (1939), and as an adult in *The Bad Seed* (1956), the film version of the Broadway play in which she had won a Tony Award for her portrayal of the mother of an evil child.

Johnny Downs (1913–) began making films as a child and was one of the first youngsters to appear in the "Our Gang" comedies. He became a young song-and-dance performer in vaudeville and on Broadway, then returned to movies as a juvenile lead in "B" musicals and light romantic films, often with a college setting. Some of his more prominent pictures were *Babes in Toyland* (1934), *Pigskin Parade* (1936), *Turn Off the Moon* (1937), and *Rhapsody in Blue* (1945).

Virginia Grey (1917–) was the daughter of silent-comedy film director Ray Grey, who died when she was eight. She was raised by her mother, who was a cutter at Universal Studios. Her first screen role came when she was 10 years old and played Little Eva in *Uncle Tom's Cabin* (1927). She was a bit robust for the part of the dying child, and the movie wasn't helped when director Harry Pollard showed her winging her way to heaven—literally. Grey appeared in a few more movies as a child—*The Michigan Kid* (1928) and *Heart to Heart* (1928), for example, then left the studio to finish her school-

Above: The beguiling Marcia Mae Jones played Mary Sawyer in *The Adventures of Tom Sawyer* (1938).

Below: Virginia Grey, as Little Eva, comforts Uncle Tom in *Uncle Tom's Cabin* (1927).

Above: The frightened Marcia Mae Jones (left) is confronted by the evil Bonita Granville in *These Three* (1936).

Left: Eleven-year-old Virginia Grey is comforted by Mary Astor in *Heart to Heart* (1928).

ing. She came back in the early 1930s, first to play small roles in major films, then graduating to the lead or second lead in numerous MGM films.

Dickie Moore (1925-   ) was in the movies from infancy. He was born in Los Angeles, next door to a secretary at Fox Pictures who worked for studio president Joseph Schenck. She was a family friend, and was picked up at the Moore home one day by the studio's casting director, who was looking for a hand-

some baby to play John Barrymore as an infant in a forthcoming picture. So Dickie got his first job at the age of 11 months, playing Barrymore as a baby in *The Beloved Rogue* (1926). All he had to do was lie in a crib and cry for 30 seconds, but he did it so well that they raised his salary from $5.00 a day to $7.50.

Moore made several more pictures before he was seven years old, notably *Passion Flower* (1930), a remake of *The Squaw Man*

Opposite: Dickie Moore with Marlene Dietrich and Herbert Marshall in *Blonde Venus* (1932).

Right: Moore (center) was one of the younger *Little Men* in the 1935 film. Frankie Darro is holding him. To the right of Darro is Richard Quine. Dickie Jones is second from the left, and the schoolmaster is Ralph Morgan.

Below right: Moore played the title role in *Oliver Twist* (1933).

Below: Dickie Moore was Barbara Stanwyck's son in *So Big* (1932).

(1931), *So Big* (1932), and *Blonde Venus* (1932), in which he played Marlene Dietrich's young son whom she took along when she went on the prowl for customers. He made *The Expert* (1932) with Charles "Chick" Sale, playing the orphaned kid next door who strikes up a friendship with a benevolent old man. During its filming, Moore lost a front tooth and was fitted with a bridge. The relationship between Sale and Moore was the best thing in the film. *So Big* (1932) was

based on the Edna Ferber novel about Selina Peake (Barbara Stanwyck) who, after the death of her father, becomes a school teacher in the farm country of Illinois. She marries a farmer who dies shortly afterward and she must raise their son (Moore) alone. In the film, Moore grew up to be Hardie Albright.

When he was seven, Moore was signed by Hal Roach to appear in some "Our Gang" comedies, although he later claimed that he never understood the jokes that they played in the series. In these comedies, he usually played a rich kid, and his starting salary was $225 a week—much more than any other Our Gang member was earning. But Roach knew what he was doing. While Moore was under contract he was able to loan him out to other studios—usually for $1,500 a week. Some of his more notable films of that time were *Oliver Twist* (1933), *Peter Ibbetson* (1935) and *The Story of Louis Pasteur* (1936), in which he played a boy dying of rabies who was cured by Pasteur.

For all his fame, Moore led a rather prosaic private life. He went to public schools, belonged to the Boy Scouts, and even sold magazines door-to-door. Even so, he was a real star, with a line of clothing named for him and his picture inside a packaged ice cream cup—a proof of fame equal to that of a baseball card.

Unlike many other child stars, Moore made the transition to older roles easily. As a teenager he played Gary Cooper's brother in *Sergeant York* (1941) and he appeared with Don Ameche in a delightful comedy, *Heaven Can Wait* (1943). He also had the distinction of giving Shirley Temple her first screen kiss (a peck on the cheek) in *Miss Annie Rooney* (1942). Photographers from the wire services, newspapers, and magazines were there to record the historic moment. Moore later claimed that this was the first time he had kissed a girl. Another part of the movie involved Temple teaching Moore to jitterbug. She, of course, was a great dancer, but Moore said he "stumbled over curbs." Finally, the studio had to make a rubber mask of his face and put it on another actor who could dance, in order to finish the scene.

The name "Dickie" was becoming increasingly unsuitable for a strapping young man, and it was Dick Moore who went into wartime service. He was a reporter for the Army newspaper *Stars and Stripes*, in the Pacific theater. After his discharge, he worked briefly for a Los Angeles newspaper, then had a few more movie roles. Moore was dissatisfied with the latter part of his acting career, during which he appeared in such forgettables as *Bad Boy* (1949) and *Killer Shark* (1950). He even starred in a serial, *Cody of the Pony Express* (1950), which featured him as a young William F. "Buffalo

Above: Helen Parrish and Frank Morgan in *There's Always Tomorrow* (1934).

Opposite top: Jackie Searl, Helen Parrish, and Frankie Thomas in *Little Tough Guys* (1938).

Opposite below: Parrish (left) in *First Love* (1939).

Bill" Cody. Moore did go out in style, however. He was outstanding in *The Member of the Wedding* (1953), his last picture.

In 1957 Moore became the public relations director of Actor's Equity. In 1964 he went to New York, where he set up his own public relations firm, Dick Moore Associates, which specializes in producing industrial shows. Looking back on his life, Moore recently commented: "There was a time when I bridled whenever a fan bothered me for an autograph or someone started with the jokes about dimples, but now I'm rather pleased that someone remembers. Since my two boys no longer watch my 'Our Gang' pictures on television, it's nice to know that someone is impressed."

Helen Parrish (1922-59) began her film career at the age of five, playing the daughter of Babe Ruth in *Babe Comes Home* (1927). She and her sister Beverley, and two brothers, Gordon and Robert, had come to Hollywood from Columbus, Georgia, when their father, a Coca-Cola salesman, was transferred to southern California. He was on the

Sex and Child Stars

With the possible exception of Mickey Rooney, Hollywood's kids of the 1920s, '30s, and '40s were a pretty staid bunch. To begin with, their parents, agents, and studios did everything they could to keep them childlike and innocent in the hope of prolonging their careers. Many of them were deliberately kept away from other children who might well be competitors for the same roles. Finally, children who were not in the business often thought of the child stars as odd and different—people to shun. Consequently, these talented kids were pretty naive. Dickie Moore was terrified on the day he was to give Shirley Temple her first screen kiss, because he had never kissed a girl before—and he was 16 years old. Donald O'Connor later confessed that he was so nervous when called on to kiss Marilyn Monroe on screen that "My lips were shaking all over and I couldn't find Marilyn's lips and she couldn't find mine, and I had to turn my back to the camera so the audience couldn't see these four lips trying to find each other." Edith Fellows got her first screen kiss from Leo Carillo when she was 13. She had been expecting a kiss on the cheek, and when Carillo kissed her mouth, she feared she'd become pregnant. Diana Carey Serra, the former Baby Peggy, perhaps summed it up best: "Everyone thought we were swinging and wild, sexing it up at ten years of age. But nobody ever told me anything about sex, menstrual periods, anything, ever." And Cora Sue Collins remarked, "We were the squarest group of kids in the world. I was terrified of sex. So were all my girlfriends."

This is not to say that they didn't have crushes. Jane Withers and Peggy Ann Garner were mesmerized by Peter Lawford. Bonita Granville secretly worshipped Joel McCrea and Ronald Reagan. Gloria Jean was enamored of Donald O'Connor, and Edith Fellows had a yen for Bobby Jordan. Still, according to Dickie Moore, many child stars remained virgins until they married.

road most of the time, so their mother, actress Laura Parrish, decided to get her children into the movies. All four of them were listed in the 1928 *Casting Directors Album of Screen Children* and the kids were earning $5 a day working as extras. Parrish went on to appear in "Our Gang" comedies and some feature films. In *There's Always Tomorrow* (1934), she was one of the children of Frank Morgan, trying to break up his romance with Binnie Barnes. She was also featured in Deanna Durbin movies. Parrish died of cancer at the age of 37.

Mickey Rooney (1920–   ) was born into a theatrical family. His mother, the former Nell Carter, was a chorus girl in a third-rate burlesque troupe, earning $14 a week. After she married Joe Yule, a burlesque comic, she continued to sing and dance in the chorus. As soon as he was old enough, she put her son, Joe Yule, Jr., into the act, but the dressing room wasn't big enough for all three of them. Finally, she bought out her share of the act from her husband for $29 and went off with her son to make it on their own. (Mickey Rooney would later find his father and bring him to Hollywood once his own career was

well under way. Yule, Sr., got work as an extra and also appeared as the star comic in a second-rate burlesque house in Los Angeles.)

Nell first opened a restaurant in Kansas City—the kind of place that served chicken, biscuits, and coffee for 25 cents. She was skimming the newspaper one day when she saw an ad announcing that Hal Roach, the Hollywood producer, was looking for talented children for his "Our Gang" series of comedy shorts. Nell bought a second-hand car, a Montgomery Ward tent, and some groceries, and the next day she and Sonny were headed for Hollywood. But the interview with Roach was a disaster. First of all, she had to wait weeks for an appointment. And when Roach's assistant offered Joe, Jr., $5 a day, Nell argued that he was worth three times that amount; rather than have him work for peanuts, she would take him back to Kansas City. It was suggested that she do just that. So it was back to Missouri for a year. Then a local theater owner thought of taking a troupe to Hollywood himself. Eleven people in two cars, sleeping beside the road at night, made it to California in ten days flat—something of a record in

Right: A theater lobby poster for Mickey Rooney's *The Adventures of Huckleberry Finn* (1939).

Opposite: Freddie Bartholomew and Mickey Rooney in *Little Lord Fauntleroy* (1936).

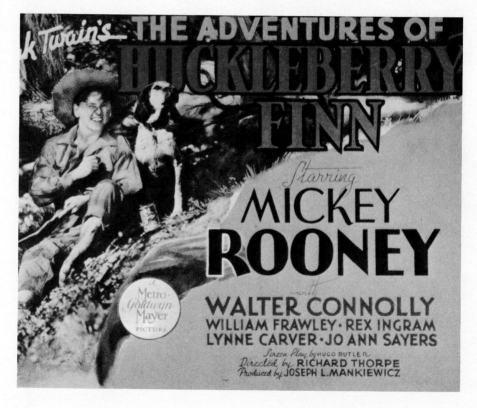

those days of rutted highways. When they hit Hollywood, Nell got a job as a telephone operator in a studio—through which she learned of roles for young actors by tuning into the telephone grapevine.

Joe, Jr., the six-year-old master singer, dancer, mimic, and comedian, made his screen debut playing a midget in a short called *Not to be Trusted* (1926). The next year he appeared in his first feature, *Orchids and Ermine* (1927), with Colleen Moore. He was a midget again, but the part wasn't completely successful. He bit off the end of a cigar and spit it toward a spittoon, and along with it went one of his baby teeth. Nell retrieved the tooth and replaced it in his mouth with the aid of some chewing gum.

Larry Darmour's studio on Poverty Row in Hollywood was about to launch a series of kids' comedies. These moppet laughers were all the rage then, especially the "Our Gang" and the "Us Bunch" series, and Darmour was set to produce his own, based on the character Mickey McGuire, in the popular syndicated "Toonerville Folks" comic strip drawn by Fontaine Fox. But the kid had to be a small pugnacious brunette. Joe, Jr. was small and pugnacious-looking enough, but he had blond hair. All it took, however, was an application of shoe polish by Nell, and the boy was ready for the screen test.

After five days of nail-biting, Nell decided to call the studio to find out when they were going to decide among the screen-tested candidates. She also decided to lie a little, saying "After all, the kid's had five other offers since it was made." The bluff worked, and Joe Yule, Jr., was called back to the studio for more tests. All he had to do was look and act a bit tougher than he already was, wear big shoes, torn pants, and a derby two sizes too large, and chomp on a big brown rubber cigar. He got the part at $75 a week, and Nell quit the phone business.

After the Mickey McGuire series became a complete success, the studio got an idea. They had been paying cartoonist Fontaine Fox a royalty for the use of his character's name—$1,000 a picture. They figured that they could save that money if Joe Yule, Jr., were to change his name to Mickey McGuire. After all, the kid's name would be the same as that of the series, and Fox would have no

claim. It didn't work: Fox was too smart. He sued, he won, and the series fell on hard times. All in all, Joe, Jr., had appeared in some 50 Mickey McGuire two-reelers between 1927 and 1933. He had also played in several feature movies, including the Western *My Pal, the King* (1932), in which he played the boy monarch of Ruritania who was educated into the ways of a true Westerner by Tom Mix and his horse, Tony. Waiting in the wings after the demise of the Mickey McGuire series was Universal Studios, who wanted the boy. But because of the lawsuit publicity, they insisted that he change his name again. Joe Yule, Jr., alias Sonny, aka Mickey McGuire, became Mickey Rooney.

Rooney made a few forgettable films for Universal and then signed with MGM in 1934. His first big break came in *Manhattan Melodrama* (1934), a crime picture in which he played Clark Gable's character as a young boy. It is probably remembered mostly by trivia buffs, as the film that John Dillinger watched in Chicago's Biograph Theater before being gunned down by the FBI.

In 1935, Rooney, on loan from MGM to Warner Bros., accomplished one of the most remarkable acting feats ever by an adolescent on screen, playing a memorable Puck in Max Reinhardt and William Dieterle's production of Shakespeare's *A Midsummer Night's Dream*. It was all the more remarkable since he had broken his leg halfway through the production and had to be wheeled around on a bicycle, which was cleverly hidden behind the bushes.

One of the three people who died in the car crash that also killed Jack Coogan was Junior Durkin, a talented young actor of the time. He had been signed to do *Ah, Wilderness!*, based on Eugene O'Neill's only comedy, about a boy breaking through the shackles of adolescence. The part went to Rooney by default and he made it an acting triumph.

Rooney played the son of a disgraced jockey who inherits his father's bad reputation in *Down the Stretch* (1936). In it, he gets a chance to prove himself as a jockey, but is framed by a syndicate. He made another racetrack film in 1937—*Thoroughbreds Don't Cry*—the first of many movies that he would make with Judy Garland.

In 1937 MGM had the idea of using Rooney in a film version of a Broadway play called *Skidding*. That domestic comedy was retitled *A Family Affair*—the first Hardy Family picture. It was a hit, and over the next 6 years MGM made about $20 million on the first 14 Hardy films—which it spent only $4 million to produce. Rooney played Andy Hardy, an almost painfully typical teenager, in *A Family Affair*. His father, Judge Hardy, was played by Lionel Barrymore; Spring Byington was his mother. For the rest of the Hardy series the parents were played by two reliable members of the MGM stock company—Fay Holden and Lewis Stone. Judge Hardy was always good for a stern but kind lecture when Andy went wrong out of sheer youthful spirits.

MGM won a Special Academy Award in 1942 "for its achievement in representing the American way of life in the production of the 'Andy Hardy' series of films." The series consisted of 15 films, beginning with *A Family Affair*, and many of them also gave some important starlets their start in MGM movies. The second picture was *You're Only Young Once* (1938, with Ann Rutherford). Then came *Judge Hardy's Children* (1938, with Ann Rutherford), in which Rooney officially became the star of the series. *Love Finds Andy Hardy* was released in 1938, with Judy Garland and Lana Turner—the latter was on a trial contract because the studio thought she had something, and she did; she spent 18 years at MGM. The rest of the series consisted of *Out West With the Hardys* (1938, with Ann Rutherford and Virginia Weidler), *The Hardys Ride High* (1939), *Andy Hardy Gets Spring Fever* (1939), *Judge Hardy and Son* (1939, with Martha O'Driscoll), *Andy Hardy Meets a Debutante* (1940, with Judy Garland), *Andy Hardy's Private Secretary* (1941, with Kathryn Grayson), *Life Begins for Andy Hardy* (1941, with Judy Garland), *The Courtship of Andy Hardy* (1942, with Donna Reed), *Andy Hardy's Double Life* (1942, with Esther Williams), *Andy Hardy's Blonde Trouble* (1944, with Bonita Granville and the Wilde Twins, Lyn and Lee), and *Love Laughs at Andy Hardy* (1947, with Bonita Granville). The last Andy Hardy film was made in 1958. It was *Andy*

A theater lobby poster for *Judge Hardy and Son* (1939)—the eighth Hardy family film.

The great team of Judy Garland and Mickey Rooney.

Hardy Comes Home, in which Rooney was a grown-up Andy. It just didn't work.

But Andy Hardy wasn't the only role that Rooney played during those years. He starred with Freddie Bartholemew and Jackie Cooper in *The Devil Is a Sissy* (1936) as a slum kid. Bartholomew was the rich kid and Cooper was the middle-class kid: they all went to the same school. He was outstanding in *Boys Town* (1938), the picture about Father Flanagan's orphanage in Nebraska, in which he played a roughneck who refuses to reform. That same year he received a Special Academy Award for his "significant contribution in bringing to the screen the spirit and personification of youth." He had the title role in *Young Tom Edison* (1940); he was impressive in the film version of William Saroyan's novel *The Human Comedy* (1943); he did all those hectic musicals with Judy Garland. By 1939 he had taken over the title of America's most popular star from Shirley Temple.

After his service in World War II, Rooney's career went into a decline. In 1948 he left MGM and formed his own production company, which went broke. He fought back by taking roles in quickie films, but proved that he was a fine adult actor in such films as *The Bold and the Brave* (1956) and *Baby Face Nelson* (1957).

Rooney's private life has been far from serene—he is a short man (five feet, two inches) who seems to have a penchant for marrying tall women (eight wives, including actresses Ava Gardner and Martha Vickers). But he has bounded through life with the endless energy that he showed from the start. Appearing in everything from tired comedies (*Francis in the Haunted House*, a 1956 film featuring a talking mule) to serious dramas (he was nominated for an Academy Award for *The Bold and the Brave*), Rooney has always given his audiences a good performance.

Early in 1978 Rooney told reporters that he was going to retire after he finished his current film. His agent told the press, in effect, not to pay any attention. He said that Rooney always talked about retiring when he was in the middle of a film, and always changed his mind when the next part came along. Sure enough, after that came his long

Above: Mickey Rooney and Judy Garland had chemistry. Here they are in *Love Finds Andy Hardy* (1938).

Below: Rooney and Garland were great in *Strike Up the Band* (1940). Also in the film were future stars William Tracy (far left), who would go on to do a series of comedy films about a hapless army private, and Sidney Miller (over Garland's head), who would become a regular in Rooney's films.

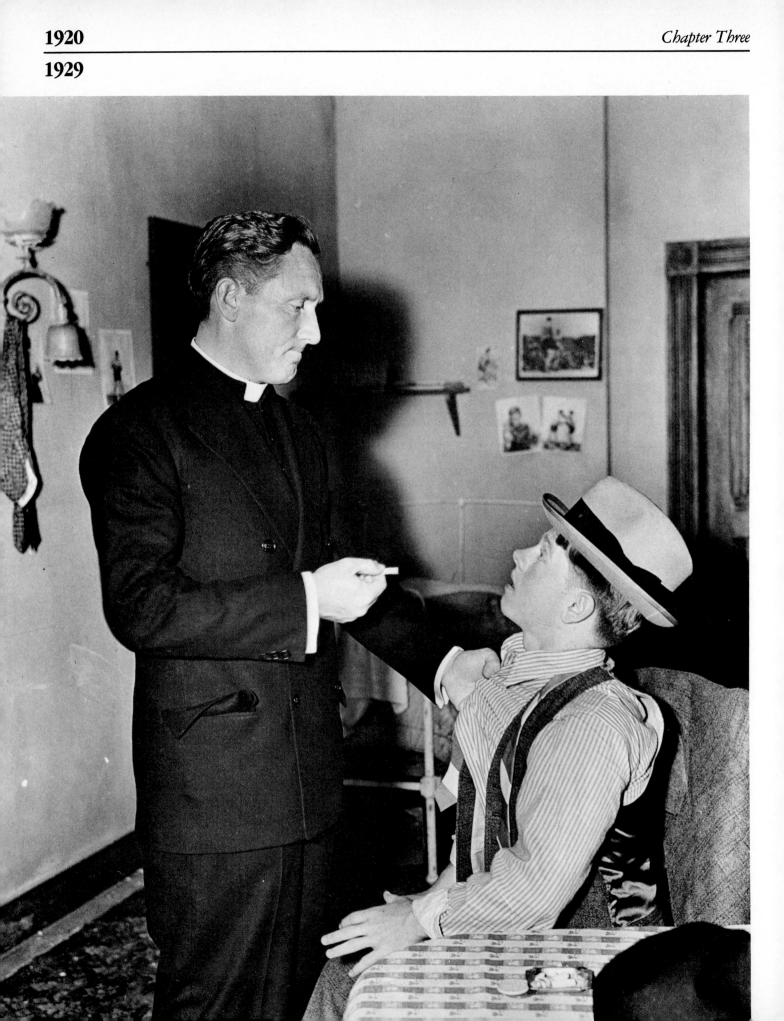

run on Broadway in *Sugar Babies* and his Emmy Award-winning television performance as "Bill."

Rooney once reflected on that terrible period from 1946 to 1956 when he was virtually without a job: "Everything moved in funny ways. I was a child actor making money before I went to school.... Then I was in my teens. That's supposed to finish a child actor. Temple, Jackie Coogan and the rest went downhill after puberty. But not me. I became bigger than I'd ever been and the money came faster than any ten children could spend it. Finally I was a man.... I could vote. I could marry. But in my manhood, in my immature manhood, I made my childish mistakes. It was almost as if, never a child, I turned childish as a man."

In 1982 Rooney received another Special Academy Award "in recognition of his 60 years of versatility in a variety of memorable film performances." The life-long actor has been philosophical about his ups and downs, citing the familiar show-business adage on the cyclic process of fame: "First a guy says, 'Who is Mickey Rooney?' The next stage in the career is 'Get me Mickey Rooney.' The next phase is 'Get me a fella *like* Mickey Rooney.' Then, 'Who is Mickey Rooney?' That's just the way it goes."

He was born John Charles Holt, Jr., but the son of screen actor Jack Holt and Margaret Holt was always called Tim (1918–73). He entered Culver Military Academy at Culver, Indiana, in 1933, where he excelled at sports and was also active in dramatics. Holt graduated *cum laude* in 1936 and won the Golden Spurs, Culver's highest award in horsemanship. Since he had been a child actor in some of his father's silent pictures, most notably in *The Vanishing Pioneer* (1928), he determined to pursue acting. Walter Wanger, the producer, saw him in a play, *Papa Is All*, and cast him in a series of pictures he was producing for United Artists, beginning with *History Is Made at Night* (1937), with Charles Boyer and Jean Arthur, and *Stella Dallas* (1937), with Barbara Stanwyck.

Holt then went into Westerns, playing juveniles and boyish cowboys in numerous "B" pictures and occasionally getting a break in a high-quality film like *The Magnificent*

Ambersons (1942), Orson Welles's filming of the Booth Tarkington classic, in which he gave a splendid performance as the spoiled scion of the Amberson dynasty.

Holt enlisted in the service early in 1942. He served with distinction in the Air Corps and was decorated for valor. After his discharge he returned to the screen in several excellent films such as *My Darling Clementine* (1946). Probably the best role of his career was that of Curtin, Humphrey Bogart's conscientious partner, in *The Treasure of the Sierra Madre* (1948).

At the end of his career Holt remarked, "I never did feel there was anything mystic about Hollywood. I never did really like it." Holt went on to own a traveling rodeo company (he was cheated by his partner), manage a ranch, build suburban houses, and serve as advertising manager of KEBC-FM in Oklahoma City. He died of brain cancer at the age of 55.

Above: Tim Holt, left, in *Swiss Family Robinson* (1940) with, clockwise, Baby Bobby Quillan, Edna Best, Terry Kilburn, Thomas Mitchell and Freddie Bartholomew.

Opposite: Tracy and Rooney in *Boys Town* (1938).

Jackie Searl and John Barrymore in *Topaze* (1933).

Jackie Searl (1920–   ) was one of the kids audiences loved to hate. He made his debut in *Daughters of Desire* (1929) and went on to play brats, sissies, and meanies. He was memorable as the whiney Sid Sawyer in *Tom Sawyer* (1930), in which Jackie Coogan had the title role, and played Sid Sawyer again in the Coogan vehicle *Huckleberry Finn* (1931). He was sniveling opposite Cooper in *Skippy* (1931) and turned timid and shy as the dormouse in *Alice in Wonderland* (1933). Searl played the cowardly rich kid in two movies with the Dead End Kids—*Little Tough Guys* (1938) and *Angels Wash Their Faces* (1939). In the 1940s he played adult supporting roles in occasional films and later appeared in character parts on television.

Mitzi Green (1920–69) began performing on stage at the age of three in her parents' vaudeville act. By the time she was nine she was in the movies, debuting in *The Marriage Playground* (1929). Soon she was the child star of Paramount's early talkies. Publicized as Little Miss Mitzi, she remained popular on the screen for several years through such parts as Becky Thatcher in *Tom Sawyer* (1930, with Jackie Coogan) and in the title role in *Little Orphan Annie* (1932, with Edgar Kennedy), which was based on the popular comic strip. After retiring at the age of 14, she returned to films to do two minor movies in 1952.

Edith Fellows (1923–   ) was a spirited child and teenage performer in many Hollywood films. She once said that she enjoyed playing a brat "because I was doing things I couldn't do at home!" She felt that when she threw something at Claudette Colbert, she was really "throwing it at Grandma."

Fellows was deserted by her mother when she was only two years old, and was taken to the Atlanta home of her paternal grandmother. Because she tended to be pigeon-toed, a doctor recommended dancing lessons, and by the time she was four, Edith was so good that she was appearing in a one-woman, or rather one-child show. She could dance both ballet and tap and sang with a voice that showed great promise. It was in that show that she was discovered by a talent scout.

The talent scout almost guaranteed Edith a screen test if her grandmother would bring her to Hollywood, and asked only a $50 fee for himself, which was paid. But Edith's grandmother couldn't afford the trip to Hollywood, so the dancing school staff took up a collection that paid the train fare for both of them. The day after they arrived in Hollywood, they set out to find the agent. It turned out that the address on the talent scout's business card was a vacant lot.

Grandmother Elizabeth Fellows was made of stern stuff. Rather than return to Atlanta, she found a job as a housekeeper in Beverly Hills. After work, she would rehearse Edith. She also paid for some singing lessons for the child. During the day, Edith played with a boy in the neighborhood who worked occasionally in films. One day he was called by the Hal Roach studio for an interview, and his mother, unable to leave Edith at home alone, took her with them. Edith was chosen over the boy for the part. That taught her grandmother something about the terrible competition between child actors, and she resolved to make sure that Edith did not socialize with other young actors lest they steal some important professional information from her. When Edith tried to strike up a friendship with Jane Withers, her grandmother told her, "Don't you let me catch you so much as *speaking* to that girl."

Edith made her screen debut in *Madame X* (1929) and appeared in the 1930 *Children's Casting Directory* as: "Edythe Marilyn Fellows—Long Golden Brown Curls, Deep Blue Eyes, Age 5 years, Height 42 inches, Weight 36 pounds, Dramatic Readings, Comedies, Singing, Playing Uke, Dancing, Imitator, Impersonator of Characters, Different Types." Fellows went on to appear in such films as *Huckleberry Finn* (1931, with Jackie Coogan), *Emma* (1932), *Mrs. Wiggs of the Cabbage Patch* (1934), and *The Keeper of the Bees* (1935).

Above: Edith Fellows in *Tugboat Princess* (1936).

Below: Fellows with Michael Bartlett and Claudette Colbert in *She Married Her Boss* (1935).

Bottom: Fellows with Bing Crosby (center) and Tom Dugan in *Pennies from Heaven* (1936).

Then Edith became the center of a family squabble over her earnings. She had been working since the age of five, mostly as an extra. She was soon making $1,000 a week, but her grandmother was reluctant to buy her even a decent wardrobe, so poor had they been before. Then her mother and her maternal grandmother suddenly appeared on the scene. They wanted custody of the child, who was becoming wealthy, and they charged Elizabeth Fellows with kidnapping. For the next few weeks Edith was spending the morning on the set and the afternoon in court. Finally, the judge ruled in favor of Elizabeth Fellows, to whom Edith was really attached, and the two remained together. The trial had cost several thousand hard-earned dollars, but Edith went on to score in *Pennies From Heaven* (1936, with Bing Crosby), *Little Miss Roughneck* (1938), *The Five Little Peppers* (1938), and *Her First Romance* (1940).

Fellows was dropped by the studio when she was 17 years old and went to New York to do stage work. In 1944, when she reached the age of 21, she returned to Hollywood to collect the earnings from her trust fund. Because of the heavy court costs, the total was a meager $900.60, and she went back to New York.

Jackie Cooper (1921–   ) was another child star whose parents were vaudevillians. His father was a performer, and his mother played the piano for a singer of off-color songs. The father deserted the family when Jackie was a baby. Cooper recalled later that his father "had walked out for a pack of cigarettes when I was two and didn't come back until I was 13." His mother still had to go on the road, so he was left with a grandmother. At the age of three, he was making the rounds of the studios and taking on some extra jobs in Bobby Clark and Lloyd Hamilton two-reel comedies.

Cooper made his first feature film, *Sunny Side Up* (1929), when he was seven, and was spotted by a Hal Roach scout and hired for "Our Gang" comedies. He appeared in eight episodes in 1929 and 1930. His big break came when he was selected to play the title role in *Skippy* (1931), a film based on the enormously popular comic strip of that era, drawn by Percy Crosby. It was, in part, a

"Our Gang" in the late 1920s. At the far right is the young Jackie Cooper, who signed up when he was eight.

Best of Friends

Left: Wallace Beery and Jackie Cooper in *The Bowery,* in which they were enemies.

Below left: Cooper as Jim Hawkins and Beery as Long John Silver in *Treasure Island* (1934), in which they were friendly enemies.

Below: Cooper as Dink and Beery as an aging boxer in *The Champ* (1931), in which they were father and son.

tear-jerker, and Cooper was magnificent. *Skippy* made him the first child ever nominated for an Academy Award for Best Actor, and he became a star overnight. His next triumph was with Wallace Beery in *The Champ* (1931), the sentimental story of a washed-up boxer (Beery) and his son, Dink (Cooper), who worships the ground he walks on. It was another five-handkerchief production.

By this time, MGM had bought Cooper's contract from Hal Roach. Almost immediately, Jackie's salary went from $50 a week to $1,100. Then there was *Young Donovan's Kid* (1931), in which he played the title role. It was the story of a six-year-old orphan (Hollywood was still filled with orphan stories) who was adopted by a gunman (Richard Dix). Naturally, this dirty-faced urchin reforms him. Pathos reigned again in *When a Feller Needs a Friend* (1932), in which Cooper played a crippled boy who overcomes all adversities. (The word *Feller* was changed to *Fellow* in the British release, in case audiences might think it was a film about a lumberjack.) Then there was *Divorce in the Family* (1932), in which Cooper's stepfather (Conrad Nagel) must, and does, win Cooper's love.

Treasure Island (1934) was a wonderful rendition of the Robert Louis Stevenson thriller, and Cooper (as Jim Hawkins) and Wallace Beery (as Long John Silver) were captivating, as usual. Also in 1934 came *Peck's Bad Boy*, which Jackie Coogan had made as a silent. During its filming, young Cooper was having a hard time producing tears on cue. He was too smart to fall for the usual shabby tricks, like being told that his dog had died, but when the producer blamed the director for the child's failure to cooperate and fired him on the set, Cooper burst into tears. Of course, this was just another trick—the producer was playing on the close relationship between the boy and the director.

About this time, Cooper's father turned up again, handicapped by paralysis. Cooper's mother had had him declared legally dead after a seven-year absence, but she wanted to avoid scandal and had him sign an agreement that he would never enter the state of California or approach either her or Jackie again. For this, he was to receive $100 a week for

life. Years later, after World War II, Cooper found out that his father was playing piano in a bar from a wheelchair, and that he had married his nurse.

Cooper and Beery were reunited in *O'Shaughnessy's Boy* (1935), in which Cooper played the son of a circus wild-animal trainer (Beery), who gave his father encouragement a la *The Champ*. But the magic had gone out of their partnership, possibly because Cooper was aging so fast that "Our Gang's" Spanky McFarland had to be hauled in to play him as a child. By the time Cooper appeared in *Tough Guy* (1936), he was an adolescent, but he still knew how to cry in a movie. He played a runaway with an intelligent dog—unblushingly billed as Rin-Tin-Tin, Jr.

Although Cooper was a successful co-star with Mickey Rooney and Freddie Bartholomew in *The Devil Is a Sissy* (1936), it was decided to pair Bartholomew and Rooney in subsequent films like *Little Lord Fauntleroy*

Jackie Cooper, Alice Brady, and Frank Morgan in *Broadway to Hollywood* (1933).

(1936), *Captains Courageous* (1937), *Lord Jeff* (1938), and *A Yank at Eton* (1942). The two became so popular at MGM that Louis B Mayer lost interest in young Jackie Cooper and offered him a new contract at a reduced salary. Cooper refused and was dropped by the studio. He began freelancing in 1937, after earning $600,000 in six years at MGM.

Oddly enough, Cooper went on to team up with Freddie Bartholomew again. In *Spirit of Culver* (1939), he played a cadet who discovers that his heroic father, believed dead, is both alive and unheroic. Bartholomew (why this English boy found himself at a military school in Indiana was not explained) and Tim Holt (who actually had gone to Culver Military Academy) played Cooper's fellow cadets in this remake of *Tom Brown of Culver* (1932), which had starred Tom Brown. Cooper and Bartholomew were reunited in *Two Bright Boys* (1939), in which Cooper inherits a ranch in Texas which he needs help to run. In come Bartholomew and his father (Melville Cooper), to help Jackie save the farm from unscrupulous oil men.

Cooper's career began a temporary skid in the late 1930s, especially when he made a serial called *Scouts to the Rescue* (1939), in which he led his scout troop in capturing a bunch of counterfeiters. The device by which an Indian tribe spoke a strange language in this low-budget adventure was nothing more than a reversed sound track. Other clunkers included *Gallant Sons* (1940), which featured some grown-up juveniles like Cooper (with a moustache), Tommy Kelly, Leo Gorcey, Gene Reynolds, and Bonita Granville playing a gang of kids who solve a murder mystery. However, Cooper had a good co-starring role in *The Return of Frank James* (1940), opposite Henry Fonda.

Cooper joined the Navy early in World War II and was greeted, like many celebrities, with the suspicion that he would expect special treatment. "So you're Jackie Cooper, eh? Well, if you think you're going to get away with anything here, you're in for a big surprise," said one of his officers in boot camp. While he was in the service, he taught himself to play the drums and became so good that he played with Claude Thornhill's Navy Band (Thornhill went on to lead one of the top-ranked big bands of the 1940s).

Little Sibling Actors

The Gish Sisters.

Hollywood has always been a place where relatives mean a lot. And often siblings are popular simultaneously. On the adult side, there were such sets as Olivia De Havilland and Joan Fontaine; Frank and Ralph Morgan; Barry Fitzgerald and Arthur Shields; Shemp, Moe and Curley Howard of *The Three Stooges*; the Ritz Brothers; and the Lane Sisters.

On the juvenile side, sibling stars have been much more numerous: Mary and Jack Pickford; Sally Blane and Loretta Young; Lillian and Dorothy Gish; Constance and Norma Talmadge; Darryl and Dwayne Hickman; Dean and Guy Stockwell; Gordon, Robert, Beverly, and Helen Parrish; Leo and David Gorcey; Moochie and Donna Corcoran; and Hayley and Juliet Mills. Probably the champion family, however, was the Watsons. Bobs Watson, the charming actor who cried so convincingly in *Boys Town* and 124 other films, was the best known and youngest of Coy Watson's nine children. They lived near the old Mack Sennett studio, so when a child was needed for a film, the producer would say to the casting director, "What size do you want? Go down to the Watsons'."

This predilection for using two or more children from a single family was logical in that a child whose brother or sister was already in the acting game would know some of the Hollywood ropes before he or she first faced the cameras. And if the siblings were in the same picture, the more experienced child could help the other get on with the job.

But deep down, there was probably a more compelling reason. If four youngsters were needed and they all came from the same family, that meant that there was but one stage mother on the set rather than four.

Above: Jackie Cooper and Bonita Granville in *White Banners* (1938)—smitten with the fudge-maker.

Below: Cooper and Betty Field are in trouble with a teacher in *What a Life* (1939)—the first in a series of Henry Aldridge pictures.

After his discharge as an ensign, Cooper went back to Hollywood and made a couple of bad movies. His mother had set aside most of her son's earnings, so money was no problem—but his Hollywood career was apparently over. He was twice married and divorced before 1949, had started to drink heavily, and was tearing himself apart. But he came to grips with himself and rebuilt his career. He started touring in the National Company of *Mister Roberts*, playing Ensign Pulver. Then he launched a highly successful career on television, first with the situation-comedy series called "The People's Choice," in which he played along with a talking basset hound named Cleo, then in the wonderfully funny series "Hennessey," in which he was a Navy doctor. It ran for three seasons. Since "Hennessey" went off the air, Cooper has been a television executive producer and director. One sign of his new-found talent was the Emmy he won for directing an episode of "M*A*S*H" called "Carry On, Hawkeye" in 1973. In 1978 he received another directing Emmy for an episode called "Pilot" on "The White Shadow." He still appears in small parts in movies, most notably as newspaper editor Perry White in the *Superman* films. Cooper started as a winner and has kept it up ever since.

But Cooper the director doesn't like to work with children. He feels that "They ought to be out roughhousing; they should not be made to drain themselves." ☐

Chapter Four

1930~1939

Mom, Dad, and the Kids

*P*robably the first child star of stature to emerge in the 1930s was a young English lad, Freddie Bartholomew (1924–), who was born Frederick Llewellyn in London. This curly-haired, dimpled, angelic-looking boy was raised by his aunt, Millicent "Cissie" Bartholomew, whom his parents had selected as his tutor. He first appeared on the London stage at the age of three, and apparently Cissie knew a good thing when she saw it. Figuratively, Bartholomew was divided into three parts by his aunt. She would get the first $2,500 of his annual earnings, plus one-third of the remaining income. His grand-parents would get another third, and the rest was to be set aside in a trust. Bartholomew's parents were completely shut out.

Bartholomew appeared in a couple of British films: *Fascination* (1930, when he was six years old) and *Lily Christine* (1932). Then, in 1934, Cissie learned that MGM was looking for a boy to play the title role in the film *David Copperfield* (1935), and she took him to Hollywood. In fact, producer David O. Selznick and director George Cukor were familiar with the boy's work. They had seen him act while they were in England looking for locations for the picture. Although these locations were never used, and the entire

Above right: Freddie Bartholomew in *David Cooperfield* (1935), with W. C. Fields as Micawber.

Opposite: Bartholomew played Greta Garbo's son in *Anna Karenina* (1935).

73

film was shot in Hollywood, Bartholomew got the role as the young Copperfield (Frank Lawton played David as an adult), beating out Jackie Cooper, who really wanted the part. Bartholomew was captivating, and he was signed to a seven-year contract at $175 a week. The movie turned out to be possibly the richest and most satisfying of all Dickens films, and soon Bartholomew was earning $1,000 per week at MGM.

Cissie went to court and had herself appointed Freddie's guardian. When this news reached London, Bartholomew's parents and grandparents headed for California. That was the start of the litigation that kept the family in court at least twice a month for three years. By the time that Bartholomew was 15 years old, there had been some 27 different lawsuits filed by members of his family against each other—and he had to pay for all of them, thus losing most of the million dollars he had earned in the previous six years.

Bartholomew went on to play the son of Basil Rathbone and Greta Garbo in *Anna Karenina* (1935) and to appear with rough, tough Victor McLaglen in *Professional Soldier* (1936). He was acclaimed in the title role of *Little Lord Fauntleroy* (1936), which was taken seriously then, but would be laughed off the screen today. C. Aubrey Smith appeared as his grandfather. Many think that Bartholomew's finest role was in *Captains Courageous* (1937), that adaptation of the Rudyard Kipling novel in which he played a spoiled rich brat who had fallen off a luxury liner and been rescued from the ocean by the crew of a fishing boat. Forced to work to earn his passage, he becomes a man for the experience. Also in the cast were Spencer Tracy, Mickey Rooney, and Lionel Barrymore.

After *Captains Courageous*, Bartholomew began to show telltale signs of advancing age: after all, he was a ripe old 13. The 1938 movie *Kidnapped*, an excellent film version of the Robert Louis Stevenson romance, saw him still at his peak, but parts became sparser after that. In 1942 he made his last memorable film, co-starring with Rooney in *A Yank at Eton*, in which Rooney played havoc with the traditions of the venerable English public school.

Mickey Rooney, Freddie Bartholomew, Melvyn Douglas and Lionel Barrymore in *Captains Courageous* (1937).

During World War II, Bartholomew enlisted in the Air Corps; when he came back, his career was at a standstill. All he could come up with were parts in such long-forgotten movies as *The Town Went Wild* (1944), *Sepia Cinderella* (1947), and *St. Benny the Dip* (1951). Subsequently, Bartholomew went into television, hosted a daytime show, became an associate director of a New York television station, and carved out a successful career in advertising.

The future Hollywood sex goddess Betty Grable (1916–73) was a mere 14 years old when she appeared in the chorus lines of four 1930 musical films: *Let's Go Places, New Movietone Follies of 1930, Happy Days,* and *Whoopee!* In 1931 she was signed by Samuel Goldwyn, who changed her name to Frances Dean and gave her bit parts. In 1932 her contract was picked up by RKO, and her name was changed back to Grable. By now

the attractive young blonde was playing leads in "B" movies. In 1937 she switched to Paramount and began her short-lived marriage to Jackie Coogan. They were divorced in 1940, the year that Fox signed her as a threat to Alice Faye, who was being difficult about financial arrangements with the studio.

Suddenly, Grable became a top box-office attraction. Her vibrant personality, fresh complexion, and great legs made her the star of countless musicals for the studio. She was the number one pin-up girl of the troops during World War II. From 1943 to 1965, Grable was married to trumpeter/band leader Harry James. After her film career deteriorated, she made night-club appearances and

Opposite: Bartholomew with his Aunt Cissie (Millicent Bartholomew) on the set of *Little Lord Fauntleroy* (1936).

Below: Bartholomew, Warner Baxter, and Arleen Whelan in a tense scene in *Kidnapped* (1938).

was one of the many stars who played Dolly Levi in the stage production of *Hello Dolly*!

By far the longest-running series of comedy shorts in film history was the one that featured children in a variety of escapades. Of course, it was "Our Gang," which was in production from 1922 to 1944 and reached its peak in the 1930s. "Our Gang" was born in the fertile imagination of Hal Roach, an American original who got into the movie business in the early years of the century after drifting around the world. By 1920 he had his own studio in Culver City, near Hollywood, and was making comedy films. Roach launched the careers of such comedians as Harold Lloyd, Snub Pollard, Charlie Chase, and Laurel and Hardy. He got the idea for "Our Gang" from the success of the "Sunshine Sammy" comedies (1921–22), which starred Ernie Morrison, an appealing black child. Roach decided to make a series featuring plain kids who were up to ordinary mischief rather than a bunch of artificial child stars. He was right.

The cast was assembled in a talent search that emphasized physical types rather than acting experience. The original "Our Gang" was recruited partly from the ranks of child actors and actresses and partly from families and friends of people around the studio. For the record, the cast of the first film in the series, titled *Our Gang* and made in 1922, consisted of Peggy Cartwright, Jackie Condon, Winston Doty, and Ernie Morrison. They were soon joined by Allen "Farina" Hoskins, Joe Cobb, Jackie Davis, Mary Kornman (the daughter of Harold Lloyd's still photographer), and Mickey Daniels (Kornman's next-door neighbor in real life). Ernie Morrison and Allen Hoskins were black children, who, fortunately, were not subjected to the worst of the crude racial humor of that time. Joe Cobb became famous as the fat boy of the series. Mickey Daniels was tough but cute. The girls were real beauties with whom any parent (and any kid) could identify. The series was off and running.

Above: Ann Dvorak clutches Buster Phelps in *Three on a Match* (1932).

Below: Henry Travers, Buster Phelps, and Frances Farmer in *Too Many Parents* (1936).

From the start, the key to "Our Gang's" success was realism. Hal Roach had wanted believable kids, and the studio had the sense to put those kids into lifelike situations. The many imitators who tried to follow the path of "Our Gang" almost always went wrong in the same way—they had exceedingly clever child stars doing exceedingly clever things: singing and dancing with great aplomb, putting on thoroughly professional performances. But Roach had discovered the secret that has ensured the success of "Our Gang" to this day—there is nothing quite as engaging as perfectly ordinary kids getting into perfectly ordinary trouble. Roach and his directors had only to carry everyday mischief one step too far, and they had a great product.

Along the way, some of the "Our Gang" kids became so popular that Roach was able to loan them out to other studios for feature films. Mickey Daniels, for example, appeared with Sally O'Neal in *Frisco Sally Levy* (1927), in which they played the children of a Jewish father and an Irish mother—a reprise of *Abie's Irish Rose*. Then Jean Darling of near-

"Our Gang" in the 1920s. Farina Hoskins is at the top in the center and Joe Cobb kneels at the right.

by Glendale and Mary Ann Jackson of Santa Monica were added to the cast.

When the "Our Gang" series became a success, applications from would-be cast members came in from every state in the Union. In the first 17 years, Roach and his staff interviewed some 140,000 children. The result? Only 176 of these kids ever appeared in an "Our Gang" comedy, and only 41 were given contracts. At the time, the wages ranged from $37.50 to $75.00 a week. Among those turned away were Mickey Rooney and Shirley Temple. But such child stars as Edith Fellows, Marcia Mae Jones, Helen Parrish, Darryl Hickman, Scotty Beckett, Robert Blake, and Jackie Cooper cut their professional teeth in the series.

Roach also made money on the "Our Gang" kids' endorsements, although the children did not share in the profits. There were lunch boxes, coloring books, clothing, balloons, roller skates, chewing gum, and many other products. Roach also signed with the Kellogg Company, and Gang members' faces appeared on giveaways and ads—"Our Gang peps up with Pep, the peppy cereal food." Some of the kids toured in vaudeville. Peggy Eames, Mickey Daniels, and Johnny Downs made personal appearances in theaters located where the Kellogg ads had been especially successful.

The only non-human member of the "Our Gang" cast was Pete the Pup, that phlegmatic canine with the unlikely circle around his eye. Hardly anyone ever noticed that sometimes the circle was around the right eye and sometimes around the left.

When Joe Cobb grew too old for his role, Roach held a nationwide contest to find a fat boy to replace him. The winner was Norman "Chubby" Chaney, who took over the part in 1928. Ernie Morrison bowed out after a couple of years. Allen Hoskins grew up and was replaced by Matthew Beard, Jr., whom everybody called "Stymie," and who was famous for his derby hat. The cast kept changing, but the series remained the same.

Beard had started acting when he was 17 months old, and his mother was a movie extra. In *Hallelujah!* (1929) she carried him in her arms. Later he adopted the derby because Stan Laurel was his favorite actor; sometimes he would visit Laurel's set and put the comedian's derby on his own head. One day Laurel said, "Get the kid a derby. Make him happy."

Beard was dropped from "Our Gang" in 1935, and he recalled later that it had been a terrible shock: "It was a heck of a transition. I felt very bad because nobody explained to me what had happened. They'd brought "Buckwheat" in when I started getting too large, just as they had brought me in when Farina started getting too large; and I knew that Farina had the same feeling when I took his place." Beard couldn't find another job, and eventually he drifted into drug use. He was arrested and sentenced to nine years in prison for possession and sale of heroin. After his release, he entered Synanon, a drug rehabilitation center, and recovered from his addiction, but he died later of a stroke. A sad footnote to his life is the fact that he always thought of Dickie Moore as his best friend because Moore never called him "Nigger."

Matthew Beard, Jr. (left) played "Stymie" of Our Gang.

Spanky McFarland (left) with William Henry "Buckwheat" Thomas in an Our Gang episode titled *Little Sinner.*

Our Gang throws a party. Buckwheat is at left and Spanky is second from left. Third from left is the very young Robert "Bobby" Blake.

Generally, the "Our Gang" kids spent a few years with the group before they gave up their film careers and went back to normal life. Most of the kids tried for other roles, and a few had some success, but "Our Gang" was the whole story for most of them. Mary Kornman, for example, did tour in vaudeville after her original four-year stint with "Our Gang," and she got some parts in "B" films when she grew up. Eventually, she left show business for marriage. Mickey Daniels also did some film work after he left "Our Gang"—among other things, he appeared in another Hal Roach series, this one about teenagers, called "The Boy Friends"—but he never hit the heights again. He ended up going into the construction business.

Perhaps the most popular of all the "Our Gang" kids was George Emmett "Spanky" McFarland (1928–   ), who lasted an incredible 11 years in the series because he stayed short. As a baby, McFarland was a chubby little model in Dallas, Texas, plugging baby clothes and bakery products. An aunt sent Hal Roach his photo, and the McFarlands drove to Hollywood for a screen test. Spanky was signed to a four-year contract in 1931, shortly after his third birthday. He would eventually make 95 "Our Gang" comedies.

Spanky took over the part of the chubby leader of the gang in 1932. He was at the peak of his fame by the mid-1930s, and he made a lot of money for Hal Roach, not only in the series, but when he was loaned out to other studios like RKO, Paramount, and Warner Bros. for major films. Roach was pocketing fat fees (loaners never got a piece of the action), and he showed his gratitude by using Spanky in only half a dozen "Our Gang" comedies one year instead of the usual 12.

Spanky was in the 1934 version of Robert Louis Stevenson's *Kidnapped* and appeared with Fred MacMurray, Henry Fonda, and Sylvia Sidney in *The Trail of the Lonesome Pine* (1936), the first Technicolor outdoor film. In *Kentucky Kernels* (1934), with comedians Bert Wheeler and Robert Woolsey, he played a precocious child who is adopted by the two men, who take him to Kentucky to claim his inheritance. The boy starts a feud between two families, and Wheeler and Woolsey have to use their wits to keep him out of trouble. McFarland was also in *Peck's Bad Boy with the Circus* (1938). And he starred not only in the "Our Gang" episode that won an Academy Award for One-Reel Short Subjects (*Bored of Education*, 1936), but also in the only full-length feature that the gang ever made: *General Spanky* (1936), a Civil War melodrama.

After appearing in the war-time movie *Johnny Doughboy* (1943), at the age of 16, McFarland was out of a job and back in Texas. He served in the Air Corps and, after his discharge, worked as a chauffeur in Dallas. Later he worked for Coca Cola, sold insurance for a while, and took a job with an aircraft company. Fourteen years after the end of his "Our Gang" career, McFarland placed an ad in an actor's trade journal: "Childhood (3–16) spent as a leader of "Our Gang" comedies. Won't someone give me the opportunity to make a living in the business I love and know so well? Have beanie, will travel."

In the late 1950s, McFarland went into television, hosting a children's show in Tulsa, Oklahoma. Then he became a successful salesman and a business executive. Looking back on his career, he once said, "I had a ball."

Darla Hood (1931–79) was the "Our Gang" girl whom everyone remembered. This pretty little brunette was born in Liddy,

Oklahoma, and her talent was such that her parents provided her with dancing lessons in faraway Oklahoma City—a 300-mile round trip twice a week. Her teacher, Kathryn Duffy, took her to New York, where Darla had the luck to be discovered in classic movie style. One night in the hotel dining room, the orchestra leader let the little charmer lead the band in a number, and in the room was a Hal Roach talent scout. He gave her a screen test in a New York studio and immediately took her to Hollywood, where she was awarded a nine-year contract. Darla never saw Liddy, Oklahoma, again. Her parents joined her in California, and she began her "Our Gang" work in 1935, at the age of four. She stayed with the gang until she was 14, making 150 segments of the series and earning $750 a week for several years. Hood appeared in occasional features, including *The Bohemian Girl* (1936) and *Born to Sing* (1942), but she never made it big in full-length pictures. After her movie career ended, she did quite well in other kinds of show business— playing background music for films, making television and stage appearances, even doing voiceovers for television commercials.

Overleaf: Carl "Alfalfa" Switzer and Darla Hood.

Below: A scene from one of the MGM Our Gang shorts.

Carl "Alfalfa" Switzer (1926–59) was the freckle-faced kid whose hair was parted in the middle and whose singing voice was delightfully squeaky. Carl and his brother Harold had made a few public appearances in their home town of Paris, Illinois. When they went to visit their grandparents in California, they went to the Hal Roach Studio to see if they could crash show business in the "Our Gang" comedies. The story goes that they couldn't get past the guard at the gate, who was constantly beseiged by aspiring child actors, so they sneaked into the studio commissary and launched into their song-and-dance routine. Naturally, Hal Roach was eating in the commissary. He liked what he saw and signed the boys to contracts on the spot. (Things like that really happened in those days.)

Starting with *Beginner's Luck* (1935), Carl appeared in 61 "Our Gang" episodes over the next six years (Harold had a much shorter career; he was dropped after just a few episodes). As Alfalfa, Carl made an art of atrocious off-key singing, although he actually had a trained voice and had started out in show business as a singer. When he had outgrown "Our Gang," his earnings, which were $750 a week at the peak (an awful lot of money for those days), dropped precipitously. He got the lead in a 1940 Republic movie called *Barnyard Follies*, but a few years later he was taking bit parts. Carl supplemented his income by working as a hunting guide in the woods of Northern California. He had several brushes with the law and was once shot at and wounded by an unknown assailant. Eventually, he became a bartender and in January 1959 he got into a drunken argument over $50 with a former hunting-venture partner and a gun went off. Shot in the stomach, Switzer was dead at the age of 31. The slaying was ruled "justifiable homicide."

William Henry "Buckwheat" Thomas spent ten years with "Our Gang." One of many black children who were featured in the gang, Thomas played a role modeled on that of Farina Hoskins—even the nicknames were similar by design. Hoskins, who made more than 100 "Our Gang" shorts, had a few movie roles later on, then dropped out of sight. He spent most of his adult life helping others, working with the mentally retarded. Thomas became a film technician when his "Our Gang" career was ended and showed the same concern for public service as his former colleague. He was killed in 1968 while flying food to the starving in Biafra.

Norman "Chubby" Chaney, the fat boy who succeeded Joe Cobb, died when he was just 18, in 1936. Tommy Bond, another "Our Gang" regular, went on to a successful adult acting career in the 1940s. Darwood Kaye, the bespectacled boy who appeared in "Our Gang" episodes in the mid-1930s, became a missionary. Porky Lee, who was active at about the same time, became a teacher. Shirley Jean Rickert, a beautiful little blonde, became a beautiful big blonde who worked in burlesque for a while before becoming a business executive.

Literally dozens of kids appeared in "Our Gang" shorts over the years: some of them became regulars; many made only fleeting appearances. Few became rich, because the salaries were not high. The biggest stars in the gang earned perhaps $300–400 per week, with the lesser lights getting as little as $40 per week. And all was not sweetness and light. With big money over the horizon for those who could move on to starring roles in feature films, as Scotty Beckett, Jackie Cooper, and others did, there were inevitable rivalries and pressures. The surprising thing is how well the group held together, even as its membership shifted over the years, and how little Hollywood phoniness came across on the screen.

"Our Gang" survived for so long, and was revived in a new era for a different medium, because the people in charge let the natural high spirits of childhood shine through. Their competitors—kids' series that included such talents as Shirley Temple and Mickey Rooney—flourished occasionally, but they have almost all vanished without a trace. Talent wasn't the real secret of the "Our Gang" success. It was the skill with which Hal Roach selected the members of the group, and the ability of such directors as Robert McGowan, Anthony Mack, Gus Meins, Gordon Douglas, George Sidney, Edward Cahn, and Cy Enfield to make the chemistry work.

What killed "Our Gang" was not a shortage of ability, but a change in the economic

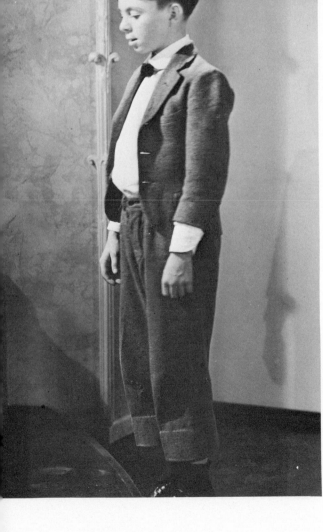

Above: A rare photograph of Carl "Alfalfa" Switzer, showing him without his cowlick.

Left: Alfalfa playing a dual role.

Our Gang at the height of its popularity. Alfalfa often appeared in a cowboy costume.

structure of the movie industry. Toward the end of the 1930s, movie distributors began to place less emphasis on short subjects like the "Our Gang" comedies. The distributors and the movie theaters they served wanted full-length features more than short subjects, at least short subjects of the length that just suited "Our Gang." The standard evening's entertainment was becoming the double feature—one "big" movie of top quality, one "B" film that served more or less as filler, and perhaps a 10-minute one-reel short to usher people into and out of the theater. The standard "Our Gang" products were two reels, or about 20 minutes long—too short to be features and too long to be fillers. Roach

tried to adjust them both ways, making longer and shorter "Our Gang" episodes, but he wasn't happy with the results, either artistically or at the box office. In 1938 he sold the whole "Our Gang" operation to MGM, the great film factory of that era. MGM kept grinding out "Our Gang" shorts into the war years, making more than 50 one-reelers in all. Fans of "Our Gang" maintain that the MGM products were decidedly inferior to the Hal Roach episodes, even though some of the old (or young) regulars lingered on to the end.

In 1944 MGM made the last "Our Gang" episode, *Dancing Romeo.* In a real sense, however, the end never came. In the early 1950s, "Our Gang" shorts from the classic period were being revived in movie theaters. And after some hassles about copyrights and contracts, "Our Gang" comedies began to appear on television, labeled "The Little Rascals." The reason that they were not billed as "Our Gang" comedies was that the rights to that title belonged to MGM. Oddly enough, "The Little Rascals" was originally supposed to be the name of the group, but the title of their first short caught on as their name. At any rate, nearly 100 of the Roach shorts began to be seen by new generations, even though occasional crude cuts were made in order to fit in commercials.

The "Our Gang" television revival was good news for some retired regulars, who were invited to make appearances on television shows. It was also good news for children, who got a chance to watch those products of Hollywood's Golden Era. However, talk of producing some contemporary "Our Gang" episodes has come to nothing. One problem seems to be a short supply of bright-eyed, innocent kids in this modern, television-wise world.

Virginia Weidler (1927–68) had good looks, played good parts, but never really achieved acting success after she grew up. The daughter of an architect and a former German opera singer known professionally as Margaret Theresa Louise, she was escorted by her stage-struck parents through the standard auditioning tour of the Hollywood studios with her six brothers and sisters. Virginia was the one who caught on. She made her film debut at the age of four in a movie called *Surrender* (1931). However, she didn't make the big breakthrough until the advanced age of seven, when she played a brat named Europena in *Mrs. Wiggs of the Cabbage Patch* (1934), which starred W. C. Fields and Zasu Pitts. In this film she was wonderful as the child who threatens to hold her breath until she turns blue. Weidler promptly became Paramount's resident child star. Although she never really scaled the heights at that studio, she had good roles in such movies as *Girl of the Ozarks* (1936) and *Souls at Sea* (1937).

Paramount cut Weidler loose after five years of her seven-year contract had elapsed, and she went to MGM at the age of 11. This marked the beginning of a new phase in her career. She appeared with Mickey Rooney in

Virginia Weidler hands Joan Crawford a sponge in *The Women* (1939).

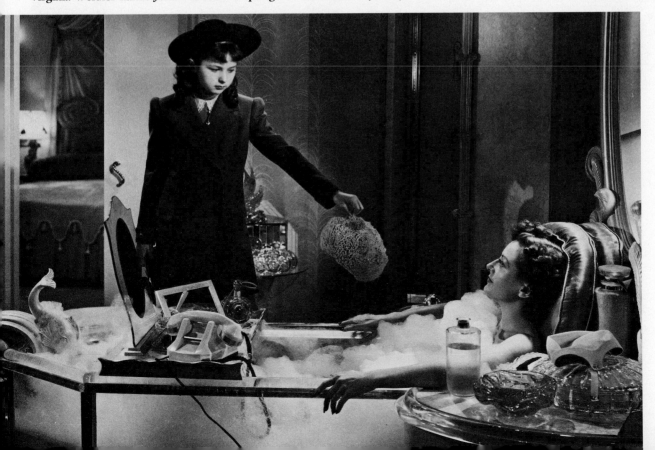

Left: Virginia Weidler (right) played the sister of Katharine Hepburn (left) in *The Philadelphia Story* (1940).

Below: Weidler (left) and Jean Porter (center) were incurable autograph hounds in *The Youngest Profession* (1943). Many MGM stars made cameo appearances in the film, including Agnes Moorehead (right).

Love Is a Headache (1937), in which the two played orphans who were adopted by a stage star (Gladys George) as a publicity stunt. The kids stole the show. She appeared with Tom Brown in the adaptation of Gene Stratton Porter's novel *Freckles* (1935). Brown played Freckles, an orphan who gets a job as a night watchman in an Indiana lumber camp at the turn of the century and rescues Weidler from a group of bandits. She portrayed Lucky, the little mascot of the roughneck mining camp, in *The Outcasts of Poker Flat* (1937), and was back with Rooney in one of the Andy Hardy movies, *Out West with the Hardys* (1938).

Weidler was one of Mother Carey's neighbors in *Mother Carey's Chickens* (1938)—a little girl whose mother made her wear her shoes on the wrong feet three times a week so that they would wear down evenly. She played opposite an aging John Barrymore in a cynical comedy, *The Great Man Votes* (1939); was back with Rooney in *Young Tom Edison* (1940); and did some of her best work in a sparkling film version of the Broadway play *The Philadelphia Story* (1940), in which she played Katharine Hepburn's wasp-tongued little sister. She teamed up with two other child stars—Scotty Beckett and Marcia Mae Jones—in *The Youngest Profession* (1943).

Those were good years for Virginia Weidler. But the movie business is tough—she learned that one day on the set of *The Great Man Votes*, when Barrymore, who thought that she was trying to steal a scene from him, literally threw her across the room. The fact that she was getting older made things tougher. When MGM picked up Shirley Temple in 1941, it was the end for Weidler, because the studio needed only one adolescent female star. For all practical purposes, her film career was over. She made her last picture, *Best Foot Forward*, in 1943, flopped in a Broadway play, tried a night-club career, and retired into marriage. Largely forgotten by the public, she died of a heart attack at the age of 40.

The story of Shirley Temple (1929–   ) has no parallel in Hollywood history. No other child star has had the impact that she had from the time she walked out of a nursery school and into stardom. Temple was born in Santa Monica, California, within hailing dis-

Shirley Temple as a beautiful baby.

tance of Hollywood, the daughter of a bank manager, George Temple, and his wife Gertrude. When she was a toddler she started dancing to music from the Victrola, and she sang almost as soon as she could talk. At the age of three, she was taking dancing lessons.

Before she was four years old, Temple was discovered at dancing school by Charles Lamont, a director and scout for a second-line studio called Educational Pictures. She was cast in a series called "Baby Burlesks" and paid $10 a day. These films were modeled on the early Baby Peggy comedies, featuring children but aiming at adults with take-offs of current movies. In these one-reelers, *The Front Page* for example, became *The Runt Page*. Shirley imitated stars like Marlene Dietrich, and all the cast members wore costumes above the waist and diapers (with huge safety pins). Good taste was not a factor in the "Baby Burlesk" shorts. In one of them, *Polly Tix in Washington* (1932), Temple appeared as a call girl in lace panties and a brassiere, acting much like Mae West. In another, *Glad Rags to Riches* (1932), she wore a flouncy hat and a festive blouse and was taken to a dance by another moppet in

top hat and tails—both of them in diapers. When Temple's parents took her to a theater to see her "Baby Burlesk" films, she often fell asleep. Later she moved into another series called *Frolics of Youth*.

Fox Studios had its eyes on the talented little girl, and decided to use her in a film that was to be called *Fox Movietone Revue*; the title was later changed to *Stand Up and Cheer* (1934). The weak plot focused on the formation of a Depression-era presidential commission set up to lighten the country's spirits, and the film starred Warner Baxter, Madge Evans, James Dunn, and John Boles. But Shirley Temple stole the show with her song-and-dance production number "Baby Take a Bow." When the number was being shot, the Hollywood comedic genius Harold Lloyd was on the set and exclaimed, "My God! Another Coogan!" Temple was an immediate hit and signed a seven-year contract with Fox at a salary that seemed immense— $150 a week.

Above: Shirley Temple in *Baby Take a Bow* (1934).

Below: Temple goes into her dance wearing a diaper in one of the "Baby Burlesks" shorts.

Temple with Claire Trevor in *Baby Take a Bow,* one of the nine movies she made in 1934.

Hollywood stars turned out movies at an assembly-line clip in those days, and Shirley Temple was no exception. She made nine films in 1934. She was loaned out to Paramount for her first starring vehicle, *Little Miss Marker* (1934), opposite Adolphe Menjou. It was based on the Damon Runyon short story about a little waif who is left in a bookie joint as security for a $20 loan made to her father by the hard-boiled Sorrowful Jones (Menjou). When the father does not return (there is a hint of suicide), Sorrowful is put into the anomalous position of having to care for "Marky" (Temple). He reads her bedtime stories from the *Daily Racing Form* and puts chairs together to make a bed for her. *The New York Times* raved: "Tiny Shirley Temple is a joy to behold and her spontaneity and cheer in speaking her lines are nothing short of amazing ... No more enchanting child has been beheld on the screen."

The studio initiated an advertising campaign: "She was an I.O.U. for 20 bucks ... Hocked to the toughest mugs on Broadway—this million-dollar baby carved romance into the hearts of Broadway chiselers. Damon Runyon's *Little Miss Marker*, with Shirley Temple, the child wonder star of *Stand Up and Cheer*." The remake, *Sorrowful Jones* (1949), with Bob Hope, Lucille Ball, and Mary Jane Saunders, never came close to the charm of this film.

Bright Eyes (1934) featured juvenile villainy on the part of Jane Withers in the tale of a custody battle over the recently orphaned Shirley. It was not much, but it gave her fans her great number "On the Good Ship Lollipop." Her other 1934 films were *Carolina, Mandalay, Now I'll Tell, Change of Heart, Baby Take a Bow,* and *Now and Forever.*

At the end of her first year in the big leagues, Shirley Temple received a Special Academy Award "in grateful recognition of her outstanding contributions to screen entertainment during the year 1934." It was also said that she had brought "more happiness to millions of children and millions of

Temple with Lynn Overman (left) and Adolphe Menjou in *Little Miss Marker* (1934)

grownups than any child of her years in the history of the world." Perhaps the greatest accolade of all came from the venerable Mae West, who called her "a 50-year-old midget." It was typical Hollywood talk, but it was probably nothing but the truth. After *Little Miss Marker*, her original contract had been torn up and she was earning $1,500 a week, although she was limited by her parents to an allowance of $4.25 a week. By 1939 her salary would be $300,000 a picture, at a time when a worker could support a family of four on about $40 a week. Even when Temple was too young to read the scripts of the movies she acted in—she learned her lines by having her mother read them to her at bedtime—she was the center of a remarkable cult.

Temple was so popular that President Franklin D. Roosevelt, in the depths of the Depression, said, "It is a splendid thing that for just 15 cents an American can go to a movie and look at the smiling face of a baby and forget his troubles." Indeed, when Mrs. Temple heard that Roosevelt would welcome a visit to the White House by Shirley, she asked, "Why can't he come here?"

Shirley's father, George, had to retire from the bank so that he could become his daughter's full-time banker. (There were rumors, of course, that he had to quit because so many mothers were bringing their daughters to the bank to dance for him, hoping he would find the kids a movie job. It must have been noisy on those marble floors.) But Shirley needed her father's expertise. She was on her way to becoming the top box-office star in America between 1935 and 1938. She would earn more than $3 million dollars before she reached puberty, and save 20th Century-Fox from bankruptcy when they started earning about $6 million a year from her films. The studio was paying Shirley's mother $150 a week to be her coach and hairdresser, so the whole family was in the movie business as a result of Shirley's success. As she recalled later, "I

Right: Temple walks up the gangplank of *The Queen of Bermuda* with her mother and father—1938.

Opposite: Shirley poses in a replica of Sir Joshua Reynolds' famous painting, *The Age of Innocence.* She was five years old.

stopped believing in Santa Claus at a very early age. Mother took me to see him in a Hollywood department store and he asked me for my autograph."

Money was pouring into the studio coffers from endorsements, too. There were Shirley Temple dolls and Shirley Temple dresses and Shirley Temple plates and dishes. In addition, there were Shirley Temple imitators galore—even a Shirley Temple cocktail, non-alcoholic, of course. Every other studio in Hollywood felt that it had to have a singing, dancing moppet to match Shirley Temple. Literally thousands of kids auditioned for the jobs, but none of them ever had the charm that Shirley Temple had.

The plots of Temple's movies were not noted for their originality. In most of them she was either an orphan who found a happy home with a new family, or the child of a single parent (widowed, of course, since Hollywood did not recognize the existence of divorce in those days) who found a new mate for her father or mother. There was

always a pause for a song like "On the Good Ship Lollipop" or "Animal Crackers in My Soup" and a dance or two with Bill "Bojangles" Robinson or Buddy Ebsen. Even non-fans (and there were precious few of them) enjoyed *The Little Colonel* (1935), in which Temple starred with Lionel Barrymore, as her grandfather. She and Bill Robinson created a movie legend by tap-dancing up and down a stairway.

In *Curly Top* (1935), Shirley starred with John Boles and Arthur Treacher and played Cupid again, matching up her sister (played by Rochelle Hudson) and Boles. No one could ever forget her "Animal Crackers in My Soup" number and her tour de force— the "When I Grow Up" sequence, in which she went from child to teenager to old woman. The title song was nice, too.

She danced again with Bill Robinson in *The Littlest Rebel* (1935), and rescued her father, a Confederate soldier (John Boles), from Civil War imprisonment by sneaking in to see President Lincoln to ask for his release.

Two Oscar winners in 1934. Shirley Temple won a Special Academy Award for "her outstanding contribution to screen entertainment" that year, and Claudette Colbert won the Best Actress award for *It Happened One Night* (1934).

Temple decorates her 1937 Christmas tree.

Captain January (1936) featured Shirley and Buddy Ebsen dancing charmingly against the backdrop of a New England fishing village. Once again, she was an orphan, who had been taken in by a kindly lighthouse keeper, Guy Kibbee. And as usual, the mean old law was trying to break up their relationship.

Poor Little Rich Girl (1936) starred Temple with Alice Faye and Jack Haley, and it was one of her best. The story had Shirley running away from home and joining the vaudeville team of Faye and Haley; eventually, she managed to get her father (Michael Whalen) married to Gloria Stuart. The film's best musical number was Shirley's "Military Man."

Dimples (1936) was set in New York's Bowery just before the Civil War and had Shirley practically selling herself to a rich lady to save her poor daddy. The best

Opposite: Shirley Temple with her screen mother, Lois Wilson, in *Bright Eyes* (1934).

Below: Shirley tackles an oversize lollipop.

A collection of Shirley Temple lobby posters.

Right: *The Littlest Rebel* featured Shirley as a cute little Confederate who saves the life of her father, John Boles. She also got a chance to dance with the late, great Bill Robinson.

Opposite top left: Temple pretends to play the clarinet with a band before she goes into her dance in *Rebecca of Sunnybrook Farm* (1938).

Opposite top right: Jean Hersholt played Shirley's gruff grandfather in the dramatization of the nineteenth-century children's story *Heidi* (1937).

Opposite below: Slim Summerville, Temple, and Guy Kibbee harmonize in the sentimental favorite *Captain January* (1936).

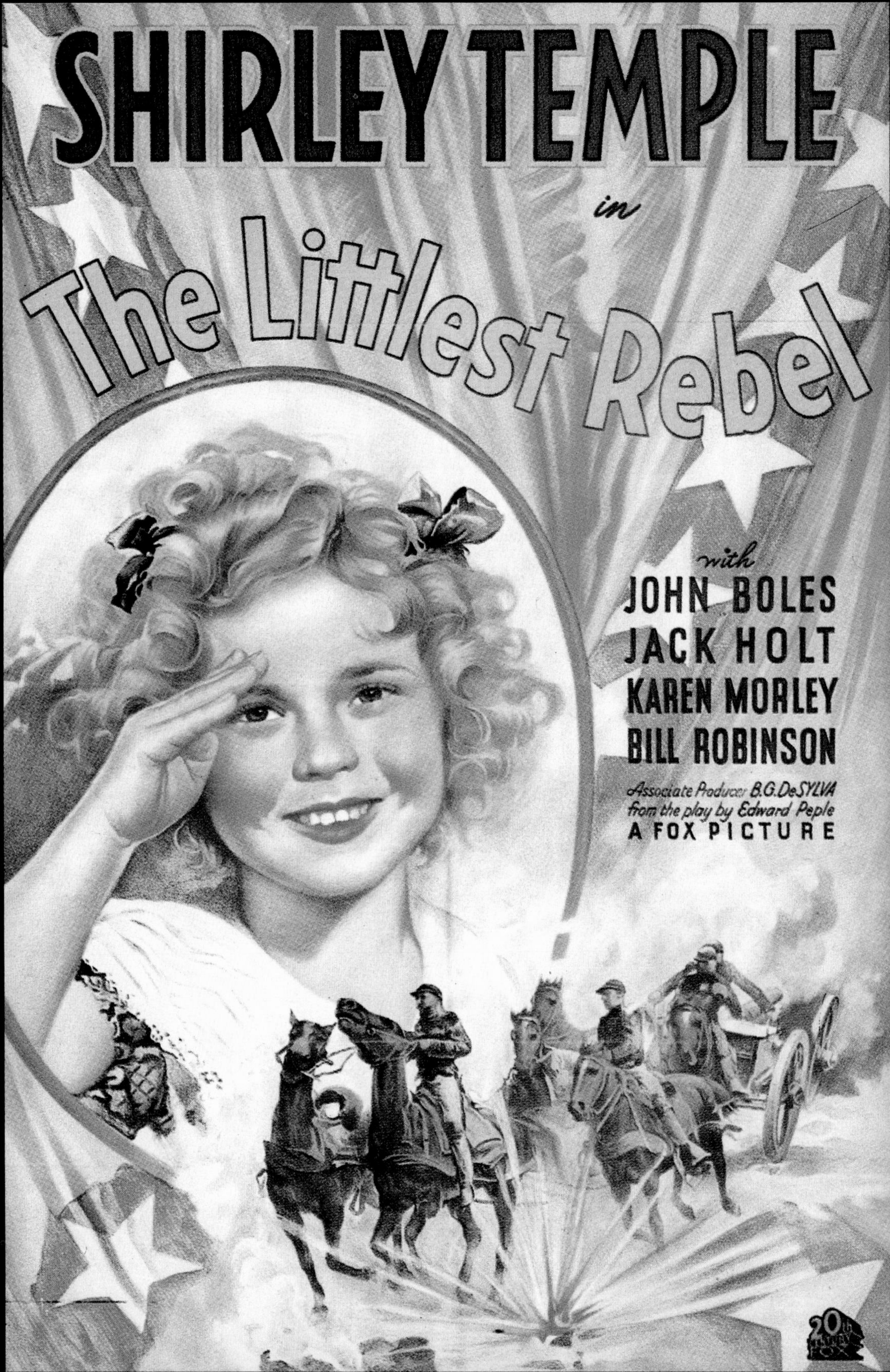

SHIRLEY TEMPLE

in

The Littlest Rebel

with

JOHN BOLES
JACK HOLT
KAREN MORLEY
BILL ROBINSON

Associate Producer B.G. De SYLVA
from the play by Edward Peple
A FOX PICTURE

20th FOX

Above: Shirley's in trouble in *Curly Top* (1935).

Below: Temple and Randolph Scott in *Susannah of the Mounties* (1939).

Bottom: Temple (right) in *The Little Princess* (1939).

moments—Temple singing "Oh Mister Man Up in the Moon" and "What Did the Bluebird Say?"

Temple demonstrated her gift for impersonation when she attached a doll to her toes for a clever Astaire-Rogers number in *Stowaway* (1936). It was a film about the orphaned daughter of a missionary to China (Temple) who stows away on a playboy's yacht and succeeds in solving everyone's problems. She also gave entertaining impressions of Al Jolson and Eddie Cantor in the film.

Through it all, Shirley remained remarkably unaffected, even though the studio made her eat lunch in her bungalow so that she wouldn't hear adult conversations at the studio commissary and lose her girlishness. When her baby teeth started to fall out, she was equipped with a set of tiny dentures. She said later, "I never knew I was famous until I went on a trip. In 1937, when I was eight, my mother and I went to Hawaii. There was a tremendous crowd that met the ship and shouted for me. There was a motorcade through Honolulu to the palace, where I had to sing "The Good Ship Lollipop" from all four sides of the palace to huge crowds. And my mother made it seem perfectly normal for thousands of people to be cheering me, as if there was nothing special going on. I thought all children must live as I did. It wasn't until a year later—in Boston—that I was aware of a crowd shouting, 'We love you, Shirley! We love you!' I wondered why. I asked my mother, and she said, 'Because your films make them happy.' I class myself with Rin-Tin-Tin. People in the Depression wanted something to cheer them up, and they fell in love with a dog and a little girl."

Rebecca of Sunnybrook Farm (1938) had nothing to do with the famous children's book. In this one, Temple became a radio star while Randolph Scott and Gloria Stuart romanced. But Shirley got to dance again with Bill Robinson. Later she said that her favorite musical number of all time was "The Toy Trumpet" dance with Robinson in that film.

Shirley starred with Jimmy Durante and George Murphy (the senator-to-be) in *Little Miss Broadway* (1938), in which she livened up a theatrical boarding house. The three

Left: Temple in one of her dances in *Captain January* (1936). Her partner is the veteran Buddy Ebsen.

Below left: Another Temple dance routine, this time with Jimmy Durante—*Little Miss Broadway* (1938).

Below: The famous stairway dance with Bill "Bojangles" Robinson in *The Little Colonel* (1935).

Above: Not only was she a beautiful baby, Temple also turned into a beautiful teenager.

Right: Shirley teaches the shy Dickie Moore to dance in *Miss Annie Rooney* (1942). In the picture Moore gave Temple her first screen kiss.

outstanding songs were "Be Optimistic," "If All the World Were Paper," and "Hop Skip and Jump."

Just Around the Corner (1938) had Shirley dancing with Bill Robinson again, but it was a maudlin offering and one of her least successful films. One of her best was *The Little Princess* (1939), about a poor Victorian waif who makes good. About this time the powers that be decided that she had had it as a tiny-tot star and began putting her into teenage roles. She was never to be the same again. By 1940 she was quickly approaching the status of a has-been. Her contract with Fox ran out in 1940, and she was cut loose by the studio without much sentimental reminiscing. In the hard world of Hollywood, the people who kept track of the money had noticed that her last few pictures had not been nearly as successful as her earlier efforts.

Temple moved over to MGM, where she made only one movie, then signed with

David O. Selznick. Her career as a teenage star was not distinguished, although she did have moderate success in such movies as *The Bachelor and the Bobby Soxer* (1947) with Cary Grant, *Fort Apache* (1948) with John Wayne, and *Mr. Belvedere Goes to College* (1949) with Clifton Webb. However, what may have been her worst picture was also made during this period. It was *That Hagen Girl* (1947), in which she had her first grown-up part. She plays an illegitimate girl who becomes the butt of malicious small-town gossip. A lawyer (Ronald Reagan) is suspected of being her father, but à la *Lolita*, they get romantically involved with each other. It was a bomb, and it was reported that Reagan had tried desperately to avoid making the film because he knew how bad it would be.

At the age of 17, Shirley married John Agar, who had appeared with her in *Fort Apache* and whose professional future

Right: Temple proved herself to be a gifted comedienne playing opposite Cary Grant in *The Bachelor and the Bobby Soxer* (1947). In the movie she had a terrible crush on the rich playboy Grant, who tried to talk her out of it.

Family Time

Undoubtedly the precursor of all the "Hey, Mom, I'm home! Can I have some milk and cookies?" type of movies was the Andy Hardy series. Between 1937 and 1947, 15 highly successful modest-budget films were made by MGM about the vicissitudes of a "typical" family in a small Midwestern town. Of course, this typical family was headed by a judge who liked to have man-to-man talks with his son, the very untypical Mickey Rooney. Everybody was insufferably nice in these films, and they made millions for MGM.

Another, less successful, family series was that of the Jones Family, which starred Jed Prouty as the father and Spring Byington as the mother, along with their assorted kids. The series started in 1936 with *Every Saturday Night*, and during the next 4 years, 16 more Jones Family pictures were made. The humor was more slapstick that that of the Hardy movies and not nearly as sentimental.

The Bumstead family appeared first in 1938, when Columbia Pictures adapted Chick Young's comic strip about a dumb but honest family man, Dagwood Bumstead, and his pretty wife, Blondie, to the screen. The series was so successful that an average of one Blondie movie came out every six months for the next ten years. Starring were Penny Singleton (Blondie), Arthur Lake (Dagwood), Larry Simms (Baby Dumpling, later Alexander), Jonathan Hale (Mr. Dithers), and a dog with star quality (Daisy).

If Andy Hardy was taken seriously by MGM, the studio obviously regarded Henry Aldrich as nothing more than an amusing way to kill some time. The 1944 Aldrich series titles told the story: *Henry Aldrich, Boy Scout; Henry Aldrich Plays Cupid, Henry Aldrich's Little Secret*. But they were entertaining little teen-age comedies that starred Jimmy Lydon as Henry and John Litel as his long-suffering father.

Arthur Lake (left) as Dagwood Bumstead, with Penny Singleton (Blondie) and Larry Simms (Alexander).

Jane Withers starred with Irvin S. Cobb in *Pepper* (1936). Withers was an accomplished mugger.

Opposite: Ever the tomboy, Withers poses for an outdoor photograph in 1936.

seemed bright. But Agar's acting career fizzled out, and the marriage ended in divorce in 1949. The following year she married Charles Black, whose father was president of the Pacific Gas and Electricity Company, and she concentrated on rearing children and working with the Republican Party until 1969. In that year, President Richard M. Nixon named her to the United States delegation to the United Nations General Assembly. Temple underwent a traumatic but successful mastectomy in 1972 and returned to political work almost immediately. She was appointed the United States Ambassador to Ghana in 1974. In 1976 President Gerald Ford appointed her Chief of Protocol—the first woman to hold that post. Today she serves on the boards of many corporations, charities, and educational institu-

tions, and trains newly appointed ambassadors at the request of the State Department.

When Shirley Temple Black received the Life Achievement Award of the American Center of Films for Children in 1977, it seemed hard to believe that this poised, beautiful woman of 49 had once been the curly-haired moppet who tap-danced her way to stardom. Those who had been involved in films at the time were very much aware of what Shirley Temple had meant to the industry, but she herself said briskly, "I'm not sentimental about the past; the most important moment is now."

Looking back on her film career, Temple once said, "I have no regrets, but I've paid my dues all the way. Anything good that happens is balanced by something else. I never get too content or too happy, because

Above: Withers poses as a Gypsy fortune teller in
Paddy O'Day (1936).

Opposite: Tom Brown shares a secret with Jane
Withers in *Gentle Julia* (1936).

I don't want to tempt fate. I've not had a
happy, happy, enchanted life. But I've
learned from tragedies that happen, and that's
good enough." This Hollywood legend who
says that she almost never sees a movie unless
she is "trapped on an airplane" retains her
sense of humor. She claims that she always
wanted to be a brain surgeon, but "I realized
that no one would come to Shirley Temple
for brain surgery."

Temple's fans have not forgotten her. In
1987 national magazines carried a two-page,
full-color ad for a porcelain Shirley Temple
doll wearing the costume she wore in *Heidi*
(1937). It was a beautiful collector's item
priced at $90.

The 1930s were the heyday of the young
actor in Hollywood. Kids had big box-office
potential, and every studio had to have its
complement of fresh-faced boys and girls
who radiated wholesomeness and who could
also cry on cue, if desired. Those were innocent times, and sweetness and light were in
style. One big exception to that rule was a
not-especially-beautiful screen child named
Jane Withers (1926–   ). She was a pudgy
little thing, but made up for her lack of Shirley Temple glamor with mischievous charm
and boundless vitality. Her mother, Lavinia
Ruth Winters, had been forbidden an acting
career of her own when she was a child.
When she married, she made her husband
promise that if they had a daughter, the child
would be encouraged to pursue a career in
the performing arts. Fortunately, her baby
had a lot of talent. When Jane was four years
old, she had her own radio show in Atlanta,
her home town, where she appeared as
"Dixie's Dainty Dewdrop," often giving impersonations of famous people. In 1932 her
mother took her to Hollywood, where she
modeled, did voices for "Loony Tunes" car-
toons, and made her screen debut in a bit
part in *Handle With Care* (1932).

After two years of small roles, Withers
struck it rich in the Shirley Temple picture
Bright Eyes (1934). Shirley played the good
little girl, of course, and Jane played a nasty,
kicking, biting tomboy. In the course of the
film Withers kicked Temple, asked Santa
Claus for a real machine gun (and fired a toy
gun at Temple when the real gun was not
under the Christmas tree), and roughed up

little Shirley mercilessly. Audiences loved it—although Jane was sometimes stopped on the street and criticized for the mean way she had acted in the movie.

Bright Eyes was the beginning of a string of 47 pictures over the next 12 years. From then on, Jane Withers was a star, and her father took pains to make sure that little Jane learned how to do bookkeeping. By 1937 she was number seven in a poll of favorite box-office attractions and was earning $2,000 a week. She alternated between tough-kid parts, as when she slugged it out with Jackie Searl in *Ginger* (1935), and sweet roles, as in *The Farmer Takes a Wife* (1935).

Every Sunday was open house at the Withers' place, with kids and their parents attending a party—sometimes the parties had 150 guests. One of the most famous bashes was

held on the occasion of Jane's 13th birthday, which was covered in the May 8, 1939, issue of *Life* magazine. The young guests were asked to come costumed as what they wanted to be when they grew up. Jane was a cowgirl, and, dancing with Foster Grundy (15), won the waltz contest. Hospitably, she relinquished her prize to Bonita Granville, who came dressed as an old maid. Tommy Kelly was a baseball player and Freddie Bartholomew was a wounded football player (winning first prize for the funniest costume). Also at the party were Gene Reynolds (a convict), Carl "Alfalfa" Switzer (a cowboy), Marcia Mae Jones (a nurse), Jackie Searl (a jockey), and five-year-old Bobs Watson (as Daniel Boone), who won first prize for the most original costume. The kids feasted on creamed chicken, peas, aspic, and ice cream.

Bonita Granville (left) with Frieda Inescort in *Call It a Day* (1937).

Withers kept working after Shirley Temple had retired, but her popularity, too, began to wane as she grew into her teen years. She gave up acting in 1947 and married a Texas oil millionaire. She returned to Hollywood nine years later, but despite good roles in such movies as *Giant* (1956), never regained her former stardom. She did make it big, in a world that television had revolutionized, in a series of commercials for the abrasive cleaner, Comet. She appeared in dozens of commercials as Josephine the Plumber, who invariably wore overalls and solved someone's dirty-sink problem in the 60-second time limit set for a commercial drama. The cheerful, slightly homely face that had made Jane Withers an appealing child star also helped to make her a convincing Josephine.

Maria Ouspenskaya, Bonita Granville, and Margaret Sullavan in *The Mortal Storm* (1940).

Another young woman who spent a lot of time before the cameras in nasty roles was Bonita Granville (1923–   ). She was the daughter of show people and made her stage debut at the age of three. She made her screen debut playing small parts in two 1932 movies—*Westward Passage* and *Silver Dollar*. Then she had a small role playing Ursula Jeans as a child in *Cavalcade* (1933). This was a most unusual film, since it had an almost all-British cast, won the Academy Award for Best Picture that year, and is almost forgotten today.

Granville's future was shaped by her role as a malicious student who ruined the lives of two teachers by speading rumors about a lesbian relationship between them. The film was *These Three* (1936), a movie version of Lil-

Nancy Drew, Girl Wonder

Left: Frankie Thomas as Ted Nickerson and Bonita Granville as Nancy Drew in *Nancy Drew and the Hidden Staircase* (1939), the last of the series.

Opposite top: *Nancy Drew—Detective* (1938), the first of the series.

Opposite below: A tense moment for Nancy and Ted in *Nancy Drew—Trouble Shooter* (1939).

Below: Ted is obviously not very skilled with a camera in *Nancy Drew—Reporter* (1939).

lian Hellman's Broadway play *The Children's Hour*, and the teachers were played by Merle Oberon and Miriam Hopkins. Young Bonita won an Academy Award nomination for Best Supporting Actress for the role, which she played at the age of 13.

Granville then played a vicious witch-baiter in *Maid of Salem* (1937). In *Beloved Brat* (1938), she was a spoiled rich girl who had problems with her parents. Her mother and father didn't know how to handle her, but everything was fixed by Dolores Costello, who played an understanding school teacher. In *My Bill* (1938), she and Bobby Jordan turned against their mother (Kay Francis) after Francis became a widow; Dickie Moore played their good brother.

Not all Granville's roles were nasty ones, however. She had a sympathetic part in *White Banners* (1938), which also starred Jackie Cooper. She also appeared as a good girl with the Dead End Kids in *Angels Wash Their Faces* (1939). And she was properly prim when she visited Andy Hardy's home town of Carvel in one of the Hardy Family movies.

One of the roles for which Granville is best remembered is that of Nancy Drew, the teenage girl detective in the series that Warner Bros. hoped would compete with the Andy Hardy films. Nancy's attorney father (John Litel) let her come and go as she pleased. Her boy friend, Ted Nickerson (he was Ned Nickerson in the books on which the films were based), was played by Frankie Thomas, who had been the star of *A Dog of Flanders* (1935) and the serial *Tim Tyler's Luck* (1937), based on the comic strip by Lyman Young.

Nancy Drew—Detective (1938) was the first of the series; it centered on the disappearance of an elderly lady who had promised her school a large endowment. In 1939 came such bits of fluff as *Nancy Drew—Reporter*, which also featured Dickie Moore; *Nancy Drew—Trouble Shooter*, and *Nancy Drew and the Hidden Staircase*, the best of the lot. The Nancy Drew series collapsed after *Hidden Staircase*. The problem was that Nancy Drew wasn't really old enough to be kissed by boys, much less, like Andy Hardy, to have innumerable romantic problems. And even her murder plots were not sufficiently

Tim Holt, Bonita Granville, and Harry McKim in *Hitler's Children* (1942).

exciting to keep a juvenile audience interested.

Then came *Hitler's Children* (1943), one of the greatest sleepers in Hollywood history, starring Granville and Tim Holt. It was produced on the proverbial shoestring, costing $178,000 and grossing $3,250,000—more than any other RKO picture up to that time, including *King Kong* (1933) and *Top Hat* (1935). *Hitler's Children* was publicized by the first all-out radio campaign for a motion picture. It purported to be a catalogue of the horrors inflicted on young girls who refused to bear children for the Third Reich—including such Nazi brutality as the flogging of well-developed (and often demurely uncovered) women for their refusal to cohabitate with Prussian supermen. The film avoided the censors because of its patriotic theme and propaganda uses.

Granville's adult roles were successful, and she made a good many television appearances in the 1950s. But it turned out that her real future was not in front of the camera. She had married John Wrather, a wealthy Texas oil man, and became an executive of his vast business empire, which included hotels and the Muzak Corporation. Wrather bought the popular television show "Lassie" in 1950, and Bonita Granville Wrather became the program's associate producer, then its producer—a position she held until "Lassie" went on to syndication in 1972. She also produced some of the "Lone Ranger" programs. When "Lassie" was revived for a 1972 movie, she co-produced it. The former brat had made good in another facet of show business.

Cora Sue Collins (1927–), a fine young actress and a great tap-dancer, made her

Opposite: Jackie Cooper
throws a party at his
house—1939. Left to right:
Bonita Granville, Cooper,
Judy Garland, Junior Coghlan, Virginia Fahy, and
Buddy Pepper.

Right: Myrna Loy, Cora Sue
Collins, and William Powell
in *Evelyn Prentice* (1934),
in which Collins played an
obnoxious brat.

Below right: Baby LeRoy
seems terrified of W. C.
Fields—with good reason.
On the right is Alison Skip-
worth. *Tillie and Gus*,
(1933).

Overleaf: Baby LeRoy,
Helen Twelvetrees, and
Maurice Chevalier in *A
Bedtime Story* (1933).

screen debut at the age of five in *The Strange
Case of Clara Deane* (1932). The following
year she played the Greta Garbo character
as a child in *Queen Christina* (1933). Collins
had roles in many great films, including
Treasure Island (1934), *Little Men* (1934),
Anna Karenina (1935), *The Adventures of
Tom Sawyer* (1938), and *Blood and Sand*
(1941). She retired from the screen at the age
of 17, in part because she grew up too soon:
by the time she was 15, she was quite busty.
She married a wealthy Virginian and became
a society leader in Nevada and Mexico.

Baby LeRoy (1932–), born LeRoy
Winebrenner, had made four movies before
he was two years old. They were all produced in 1933—*A Bedtime Story*, *Torch
Singer*, *Tillie and Gus*, and *Alice in Wonderland*. He was best known for several appearances with W. C. Fields, whom he plagued in

Above: Scotty Beckett, Errol Flynn, and J. Carrol Naish in *The Charge of the Light Brigade* (1936).

Right: Scotty Beckett (right) when he was a member of Our Gang. With him is Spanky McFarland.

four films, getting his share of abuse in return. There was a story that Fields once laced LeRoy's bottle of milk with a couple of shots of gin. When the child was unable to walk in front of the camera, Fields said to the director, "See, I told you the kid was unreliable." Baby LeRoy retired from the screen at the ripe old age of four.

One of the more prominent graduates of "Our Gang" was Scotty Beckett (1929–68). After a couple of parts in other movies, beginning when he was three, he joined the gang in 1934 at the age of five. He stayed with "Our Gang" for two years, appearing in 15 episodes. In most of them he was the kid in the baggy turtleneck sweater and cap who teamed with Spanky McFarland. Success with "Our Gang" brought Beckett offers for roles in Hollywood features, which is why his stay with Hal Roach didn't last long.

Beckett always seemed to be someone's son in his early feature films. He was Spencer Tracy's son in *Dante's Inferno* (1935), a movie about an unscrupulous adventurer who makes his money in a carnival. He was Madeline Carroll's son in *The Case Against Mrs. Ames* (1936). For a change of pace, he was slaughtered by marauding tribesmen in India in *The Charge of the Light Brigade* (1936), the Errol Flynn swashbuckler. Then he was the son of Greta Garbo in *Conquest* (1937), of Wallace Beery in *The Bad Man of Brimstone* (1938), of Norma Shearer and

Tyrone Power in *Marie Antoinette* (1938), and of Ralph Bellamy in *Blind Alley* (1939). When he wasn't playing someone's son, he was the younger incarnation of an adult star. In *King's Row* (1941) he grew up to be Robert Cummings.

Even when he reached adolescence, an age that was disastrous for many young Hollywood stars, Scotty Beckett continued almost without a break. He was the teenaged Al Jolson in the musical biography *The Jolson Story* (1946). Without skipping a beat, he played William Bendix's son in a radio serial that was to become a television series, "The Life of Riley." Everything seemed to be going well for him. He had an adult role as a young soldier in a fine film story of World War II, *Battleground* (1949). But then began a long series of arrests for drunken driving, and his career began to tail off. Beckett was

Above left: Beckett with Claude Rains in *King's Row* (1941). Rains was the town physician, and Beckett was the young Robert Cummings, who also became a doctor.

Above: Charles Boyer (as Napoleon), Scotty Beckett, and Greta Garbo (as Countess Walewska) in *Conquest* (1937). Alan Marshal is in the background.

Left: Beckett (right) played Barbara Stanwyck's son in *My Reputation* (1946).

Opposite: Conway Tearle, Natalie Moorehead, Dickie Jones, and Alameda Fowler in *Fifteen Wives* (1934).

on television in a series called "Rocky Jones, Space Ranger" for a while in the mid-1950s, but the story was coming to an end. Beckett was found dead, a probable suicide, in his Hollywood home in 1968, at the age of 38. It was a tragic ending to a life that had begun so brightly.

Richard Quine (1920–) was an actor's son who began performing in vaudeville and on the radio as a child singer, dancer, and actor, then made his screen debut at the age of 12 in *The World Changes* (1933). He made several more films as a juvenile, including *Counselor-at-Law* (1933), *Jane Eyre* (1934), *Dames* (1934), *Little Men* (1934), *A Dog of Flanders* (1935), and *Dinky* (1935). In the 1940s he played adult supporting roles, was married to the actress Susan Peters for six years, and turned to directing, beginning with *Leather Gloves* (1948). Some of his best directorial work can be seen in *So This Is Paris* (1955), *My Sister Eileen* (1955), *The Solid Gold Cadillac* (1956), *Bell, Book and Candle* (1958), *The Notorious Landlady* (1962), and *The Prisoner of Zenda* (1978).

The amazing Dickie Jones (1927–) became a rodeo and circus stunt performer at the age of six, and by the time he was eight he had made his screen debut in *Little Men* (1935). Jones went on to specialize in child and juvenile roles in Westerns such as *West-*

ward Ho! (1935), *Daniel Boone* (1936), *Wild Bill Hickock* (1938, a serial), *Destry Rides Again* (1939), *Virginia City* (1940), and *Brigham Young* (1940). In 1940 he provided the voice of the title character in Walt Disney's *Pinocchio*. After service in World War II, he came back to Hollywood to appear as an adult supporting actor, but was more noted for his work on television, especially in the lead role of the series "Buffalo Bill, Jr." in the mid-1950s.

Above: Jack Haley, Patsy Kelly, Stuart Erwin, Judy Garland, Johnny Downs, and Betty Grable in *Pigskin Parade* (1936). This was Judy's first feature film.

Opposite: Judy Garland, the fresh-faced kid. This was taken when she was 16 years old.

Judy Garland (1922–69), "the Little Girl with the Great Big Voice," was born Frances Gumm in Grand Rapids, Minnesota, the daughter of vaudevillians Frank and Ethel Gumm. Her parents billed themselves as "Jack and Virginia Lee, Sweet Southern Singers." The two had met in the Princess Theater in Superior, Wisconsin, where Frank, a handsome Irish tenor, had led the community singing, and Ethel had played the piano accompaniments to silent movies. They went on to manage the New Grand Theater in Grand Rapids, where they played and sang old favorites during the intermissions.

The Gumms had three daughters—Jane, Virginia, and the baby, Frances. All of them were taught to sing and dance, and they appeared at the New Grand as The Gumm Sisters when Frances was three years old. In 1926, when Frances was four, her mother, an ambitious woman whom her youngest daughter would later describe as "the real-life Wicked Witch of the West," persuaded her husband to take them all on a vacation—to Hollywood. The idea was to buy a new theater in California. When they arrived in Hollywood, Ethel Gumm gave her three children dancing lessons at the same studio where

Right: Judy Garland appeared in one of the few films that the great Sophie Tucker, "The Last of the Red-Hot Mammas," ever made—*Thoroughbreds Don't Cry* (1937).

Below: Judy had a musical turn in *Thoroughbreds Don't Cry.*

Shirley Temple was to be discovered in 1931, often paying for the lessons by playing the piano at the studio. Nothing much came of the trip, and the girls went back to being the "Gumm Sisters Kiddie Act."

In 1931 the girls changed their stage name, on the advice of the show-business legend George Jessel, to Garland; a year later Frances changed her first name to Judy. The trio wasn't very successful under any name, and it finally broke up when one of the sis-

ters married. Judy continued to sing on her own, ending up in the mid-1930s back in Hollywood, where, at the age of 13, she was interviewed by MGM's production boss, Louis B. Mayer. He was so impressed by her stirring, soulful voice that he signed her to a contract immediately. Garland was the first person in the history of MGM to be signed without a screen or a sound test.

There were plenty of other child actresses on the MGM lot in those days, and Garland did not jump ahead of the pack instantly. She was put on a strict diet to slim her down (the studio commissary was told to feed her nothing but chicken soup, no matter how much she pleaded for banana splits). Her first film was a short subject, *Every Sunday* (1936), with another young MGM contract singer, Deanna Durbin. Both of them looked good, and things began to happen. Universal Studios had a script called *Three Smart Girls*, which called for a popular style singer, and the studio asked MGM to loan out Garland for the role. MGM said no. The script was rewritten to fit a classical-style singer, and Durbin got the part. Garland, instead, was loaned out to 20th Century-Fox for a routine musical called *Pigskin Parade* (1936), in which she appeared with Stuart Erwin, Jack Haley, and a young Betty Grable. This football musical was Judy's first feature film, and included such songs as "It's Love I'm After" and "You Say the Darndest Things." The picture got good, but not sensational, reviews for her.

Right: Freddie Bartholomew and Judy Garland in *Listen, Darling* (1938). They played brother and sister.

Below: Frank McHugh, Fanny Brice, and Garland in *Everybody Sing* (1938).

Garland returned to MGM and triumphed in *Broadway Melody of 1938* (1937). She stole the show from such veteran stars as Robert Taylor, Eleanor Powell, George Murphy, Sophie Tucker, Binnie Barnes, and Buddy Ebsen—all of whom were billed above her—by singing "You Made Me Love You" to a photograph of Clark Gable. Then came four more films. *Thoroughbreds Don't Cry* (1937) cast her opposite Mickey Rooney for the first time—they would go on to make a total of nine films together. *Everybody Sing* (1938) was a musical in which Garland shared the spotlight with Allan Jones. *Listen Darling* (1938) featured Garland and Freddie Bartholomew as teenagers trying to get their widowed mother, Mary Astor, to marry Walter Pidgeon. In this film, which also featured Scotty Beckett, she sang "Zing! Went the Strings of My Heart," a song that would become one of her trademarks. Finally, there was *Love Finds Andy Hardy* (1938), which featured the classic scene with Mickey Rooney in the malt shop where they are sharing the same libation—using two straws.

Above: Garland singing "Over the Rainbow" in *The Wizard of Oz* (1939).

Left: Ray Bolger, as the scarecrow, makes himself known to Dorothy and Toto in *The Wizard of Oz*.

Opposite: Garland as Dorothy Gale and Billie Burke as Glinda, the Good Witch of the East, in *The Wizard of Oz*.

In the foreground are
Donald Meek, Virginia
Weidler, Mickey Rooney,
and Judy Garland—*Babes
On Broadway* (1941).

Then came *The Wizard of Oz* (1939), in which Garland became a star at the age of 17. Actually, she got the lead by a fluke. MGM had wanted Shirley Temple to play Dorothy, and they were willing to work a trade-off with 20th Century-Fox by borrowing Shirley in exchange for Jean Harlow and Clark Gable, who were working on the film *Saratoga* (1937) at the time. When Harlow died during the filming of that picture, the deal fell through and MGM decided to risk everything on Garland (who was making a piddling $330 a week at the time). She was, however, a blossoming 16-year-old when she was assigned the part, so the studio made special caps for her teeth, strapped her into a corset that hid her maturing figure, bound her breasts with gauze bandages, and made her diet even stricter—thereby turning her into 11-year-old Dorothy Gale of Kansas.

The movie was a triumph for Garland as the innocent Dorothy, singing such songs as "Somewhere Over the Rainbow." *The Wizard of Oz* is one of those films on which people are brought up and which they never forget. Children and parents who see it year after year on television never seem to tire of it. After the picture was released, Garland received a Special Academy Award in 1939 "for her outstanding performance as a screen juvenile during the past year." She went on to star with Mickey Rooney in a string of musicals showing the rosy side of teenage life, such as *Babes in Arms* (1939), *Strike Up the Band* (1940), *Babes on Broadway* (1941), and *Girl Crazy* (1943). During this time, perhaps her biggest disappointment had been in the MGM commissary. It was common then to name dishes after stars—the Joan Crawford Casserole, for example. At Universal, Deanna Durbin was a salad, but at MGM, Judy Garland was a sandwich.

Although Garland's career was blooming, her personal life began to go downhill. She was still plagued by her weight problem, and, in an effort to contain her tendency to overeat, the studio put her on a stricter diet and a doctor recommended pills; among them were amphetamines. At the same time, the strain of constant work began taking its toll on her nervous system, and soon she was living on pills to put her to sleep, to keep her awake, and to suppress her appetite. By the time she

was 21 she was seeing a psychiatrist regularly. She was to have a drug problem for the rest of her life, later complicated by alcohol.

During the 1940s Garland made some of MGM's greatest musicals, including *For Me and My Gal* (1942), in which she co-starred with Gene Kelly in his first movie. It was a film about pre-World War I Broadway life. Directed by Busby Berkeley, it featured wonderful duets for the two stars.

Rooney, Garland, and Tommy Dorsey and his orchestra in *Girl Crazy* (1943).

Then came *Meet Me in St. Louis* (1944), an enjoyable period musical that had charm at a time when it was most needed. It told of the ups and downs of a middle-class family in St. Louis at the turn of the century during the 1904 St. Louis World's Fair. Many think that this was Garland's best film, and it showcased some of the finest acting talent of the 1940s. Directed by Vincente Minnelli, the picture had wonderful songs—among them "The Trolley Song," "Have Yourself a Merry Little Christmas," "The Boy Next Door," and "Meet Me in St. Louis."

Garland also starred with Ray Bolger, Angela Lansbury, and John Hodiak in *The Harvey Girls* (1946), the tale of a group of young women who go to the Wild West to become waitresses in a Fred Harvey restaurant and succeed in taming the town. It was a big, bustling musical and featured such

Judy has a tryout in *Ziegfeld Girl* (1941). At piano is Charles Winninger. At the right are Paul Kelly, Edward Everett Horton, and Jackie Cooper.

hit songs as "On the Atchison, Topeka and Santa Fe." Then there was *Easter Parade* (1948), in which she starred with Fred Astaire, Peter Lawford, and Ann Miller. It was a delightful Irving Berlin musical, and the critics went wild over Judy and Fred's clowning in "We're a Couple of Swells."

Garland co-starred with Van Johnson in an odd little musical entitled *In the Good Old Summertime* (1949). It was based on the Nikolaus Laszlo play *The Shop Around the Corner*, which had been made into a film of the same name in 1940, directed by Ernst Lubitsch and starring James Stewart and Margaret Sullavan. It told the story of two pen pals working in a turn-of-the-century notions shop, unaware that they are carrying on a post-office romance with each other—at the shop, they can't get along at all. For the musical, starring a chubby Judy Garland, the setting was switched to a music store in Chicago, with S. Z. Sakall as the owner. Judy sang "I Don't Care" and other delightful songs. (Later, the same theme was switched to a Budapest perfume shop in the Broadway musical *She Loves Me*.)

Domestically, things were increasingly difficult for Garland. In 1941 she had married orchestra leader and composer David Rose, Martha Raye's ex-husband. They were divorced in 1945, and she married her director from *Meet Me In St. Louis*, Vincente Minnelli. Their daughter, Liza Minnelli, was born the following year, but Garland and Minnelli divorced in 1951. Because of her personal problems, she began showing up late for work or not at all. She was suspended a few times and finally fired by MGM, in 1950, whereupon she made her first suicide attempt. Then she married Sid Luft, who became her manager and engineered a triumphant engagement at the London Palladium, followed by a 19-week appearance at New York's Palace Theater. Garland was ready to return to Hollywood.

The picture that many Judy Garland fans think of as her best was *A Star Is Born* (1954). It was also her last musical. Janet Gaynor and Fredric March had made the original, non-musical *A Star Is Born* in 1937. It was the story of a girl's overnight success in Hollywood and the corresponding decline of her alcoholic husband's film career. By the time Judy made the musical, the story had often been told, but it didn't matter because of her musical genius and a fine supporting cast, especially James Mason as her husband. Garland was at her pinnacle singing "The Man That Got Away" and "Born in a Trunk." And she was at her most winning in "Here's What I'm Here For," where she sang, danced, and pantomimed the woman in pursuit of the man. The advertising for *A Star Is Born* read, "$6,000,000 and 2½ years to make it!" But it was worth the money and the wait. After a four-year hiatus from film-making, two divorces, and an attempted suicide, Judy Garland had staged a spectacular comeback. The premiere, on September 19, 1954, outglittered anything that Hollywood could have invented about itself. The film met with rave reviews.

Although Garland continued to make fine films and give great concerts, her private troubles proved overwhelming. There were lawsuits, countersuits, nervous breakdowns, suicide attempts, and numerous breakups with Luft. Their marriage finally ended in 1965 with an ugly custody battle over their two children, one of whom became the singer Lorna Luft. In spite of all this, Garland gave a magnificent concert in New York's Carnegie Hall, played a great dramatic vignette in *Judgment at Nuremberg* (1960), and scored another dramatic triumph in *A Child Is Waiting* (1962).

After her divorce from Luft, Garland married Mark Herron, an actor who was seven years her junior. This marriage lasted for six months, when they separated, with a divorce

Below: Judy Garland attends the opening of *The Grapes of Wrath* (1940) with Helen Parrish and Forrest Tucker.

Opposite: Deanna Durbin with some of the hundred men in *One Hundred Men and a Girl* (1937).

following in 1967. Her fifth husband was Mickey Deans, whom she married in 1968 in London. He was a 35-year-old discothéque manager, and she was now 46. Garland began an engagement in a London cabaret, but she was constantly late, had trouble remembering her lines, and her voice frequently cracked. It was a disaster. She was booed, jeered, and pelted with debris by the audience. But she was still planning another comeback when she died on the night of June 22, 1969, in her London apartment. The coroner's verdict was death by an accidental overdose of sleeping pills. Ray Bolger, her friend and co-star in *The Wizard of Oz* and *The Harvey Girls*, said, "She just plain wore out."

Despite her demons, if not because of them, Garland was still a draw even in death. Her funeral in New York brought out 22,000 fans to pay their last respects, the greatest tribute to a deceased film star since the funeral rites for Rudolph Valentino in 1926.

The most important musical star at Universal in the late 1930s and early 1940s was Deanna Durbin (1921–   ). She was doubly important since her films had saved the studio from bankruptcy. Hers was another of those improbable Hollywood success stories. Durbin was born in Winnipeg, Canada, but the family moved to California when she was 11 years old. She began taking singing lessons and, in her early teens, was seen by a talent scout and signed to a six-month MGM contract. At the age of 14, she was in the previously mentioned musical short *Every Sunday* (1936) with Judy Garland.

MGM seemed to favor Garland, and did not renew Durbin's option. She had tried out for the voice of *Snow White*, the Disney film of 1938, but was rejected because she sounded "too old" for the part—she was 15. She got some attention making her radio debut on "The Eddie Cantor Show," and was signed by Universal to do *Three Smart Girls* (1936). It was alleged that MGM's Louis B. Mayer hit the ceiling when he found that Durbin's option with his studio had lapsed and she had been signed by Universal for starring roles. "We'll make Judy Garland an even bigger star," was his response.

In *Three Smart Girls*, Durbin enjoyed immediate success in her first feature film. She had an appealing wholesome quality and a

Above: Deanna Durbin (left) with Judy Garland in their 1936 short *Every Sunday*.

Opposite: Durbin and Melvyn Douglas in *That Certain Age* (1938). She had a crush on this older man.

bubbling personality, and her excellent soprano singing voice enthralled the nation and helped bring "serious" music closer to public acceptance. Nan Grey and Barbara Read were the other two principals in this film about three sisters trying to reunite their estranged parents. It was a simple tale that served merely to frame the remarkable performance of Durbin, who would become the financial salvation of Universal Studios. She sang two songs that became hits—"My Heart Is Singing" and "Someone to Care for Me"—plus some operatic arias.

Durbin made *One Hundred Men and a Girl* (1937) with conductor Leopold Stokowski and a symphony orchestra (the 100 men), in which she urged Stokowski to give work to unemployed musicians, including her widowed father, played by Adolphe Menjou. Finally, she had to march all the men to Stokowski's house, where he re-

lented and conducted Lizst's *Hungarian Rhapsody Number Two* from the top of his staircase. Again, Deanna got a chance to sing both popular and classical music. After the picture was released, her contract was revised, doubling her salary to $3,000 a week with a $10,000 bonus for each subsequent movie.

Mad About Music (1938) was Durbin's third straight box-office hit. It was set in a Swiss boarding school, where Durbin starts telling stories about a non-existent explorer father. When the other students become suspicious, she drafts a stand-in father, Herbert Marshall. Helen Parrish and Marcia Mae Jones were also in the film. The picture was lavishly produced; Durbin sang Schubert's *Ave Maria* with the Vienna Boys Choir, plus some pleasant popular tunes. She was now identified with the wholesome teenager, and that same year she won a Special Academy Award for her "significant contribution in bringing to the screen the spirit and personification of youth."

In *That Certain Age*, (1938) Durbin was cast as a late-teens character who has a crush on an older man (Melvyn Douglas), but ends up with Jackie Cooper. As before, she sang both operatic arias and popular songs in the film.

Durbin got her first screen kiss in *First Love* (1939) from Robert Stack (who would later play Eliot Ness in the television series "The Untouchables"), and the event made headlines. She played an orphan living with nasty relatives who was rescued by the handsome Stack. Helen Parrish was the hateful cousin—a glamorous sourpuss. Deanna got in a few popular songs as well as the demanding "Un Bel Di Verdremo" from Puccini's *Madama Butterfly*.

Nan Grey (again) and Helen Parrish were the other two sisters in *Three Smart Girls Grow Up* (1939), and Durbin tried to marry them off. She sang "Because," which turned out to be one of her biggest recording hits. By this time 18-year-old Deanna was rich and living in a pink-stucco Italianate villa done in rococo style, with fountains, arches, ornate grillework, tropical gardens, and a swimming pool bejeweled with lights, all with a panoramic view of Los Angeles.

In *It's a Date* (1940) it was obvious that Durbin was maturing. Her voice was getting better, as was her acting. She might have gone on playing teenagers forever, but she decided that it was time to grow up on the screen.

She married assistant director Vaughn Paul in 1941, and that same year starred opposite Charles Laughton in *It Started with Eve*, in which she had a more mature part than those she had been playing. Laughton is a cantankerous billionaire who wants to meet his son's bride before he dies. The son (Robert Cummings), who has no fiancée, picks up Durbin, a hat check girl, and the first girl he can find, and introduces her when Laughton seems to be on his death bed. Of course, Laughton finds her irresistible and decides not to die after all. This complicates Cummings' life, but all turns out well.

Can't Help Singing (1944) was possibly the Durbin film with the best music—by Jerome Kern and E. Y. "Yip" Harburg. There was the title song, plus "More and More," "Cal-i-for-ni-ay," and "Any Moment Now." Deanna played a nineteenth-century woman who headed West to marry her sweetheart, an army lieutenant, against her father's wishes. But she met Robert Paige along the way and the rest is history.

Durbin finally shed her ingenue personality for good to play a disillusioned singer in a sleazy night club in *Christmas Holiday* (1944). And in *Lady on a Train* (1945), she appeared in a murder mystery-comedy. Durbin was back with Laughton in *Because of Him* (1946). He played a famous stage actor, and she was a waitress who tried to get him to further her singing career. He wouldn't have anything to do with her until she sang "Danny Boy" to him; then, of course, he got her a starring role. In *For the Love of Mary* (1948), Durbin played a White House telephone operator.

Up In Central Park (1948) was an old-fashioned musical even when it premiered on Broadway in 1945. It told the story of an Irish colleen (Durbin) and a reporter (Dick Haymes) in turn-of-the-century New York City and their efforts to expose "Boss" Tweed—the head of Tammany Hall. The plot was corny, but the songs were good, including "The Small Carousel in the Park," "When You Walk in the Room," and "We'll Be Close As Pages in a Book."

But audiences did not seem to want a grown-up Deanna Durbin, and her box-office draw declined. In her 12-year career at Universal Studios, she had made 21 films, and in 1948, at the age of 27, she turned her back on her movie career. Quite well off financially, she divorced her second husband and left for Paris. She later married a French film director, Charles David, and settled down to life as Madame David in the small town of Neauphle–le-Château.

Robert Cummings and Deanna Durbin in *Three Smart Girls Grow Up* (1939).

Kid Stars and the Three Rs

Hollywood's idea of what life in a secondary school is all about—Jane Withers (center) in *High School* (1940).

When the 1930s arrived, every studio was compelled by law to maintain special schools where child actors could continue their studies while appearing in pictures. School was generally in session from nine to noon if the children weren't needed on the set, but they had to have three hours of instruction a day. And sometimes the teacher would close down the set at four in the afternoon if the three hours hadn't been completed. When MGM shot *Boys' Town* (1938), with its cast of hundreds of young-

sters, this presented a problem, so the picture was made during the summer vacation. For many child stars, the studio school was a refuge, since they were often shunned in the public schools. Judy Garland, for example, tried to enroll at Hollywood High School and was told by a vice-principal, "Children like you should not be allowed to go to school with *normal* children."

Mrs. Fern Carter was the regular teacher of the "Our Gang" kids at the Hal Roach studio for years. She even went along with

Darla Hood, Spanky McFarland, and William Henry "Buckwheat" Thomas when they were on tour. She was the one who had the unpleasant task of explaining to Darla why Buckwheat and his mother often had to ride in separate railroad cars and stay in different hotels in some parts of the country. Sometimes she had to teach the white children separately and go back to the "Jim Crow" car to instruct Buckwheat, who was isolated from his lifelong friends.

Mary McDonald ran the "Little Red Schoolhouse" (which wasn't red) at MGM, where Darryl Hickman and Elizabeth Taylor used to play tackle football during recess. She also taught Roddy McDowall, Margaret O'Brien, Mickey Rooney, Judy Garland, and Freddie Bartholomew. But she lost Bartholomew when the studio bigwigs noticed he was losing his British accent because of association with the American kids; he was handed over to a private tutor, a Mrs. Murphy from Ireland. Murphy also taught Bartholomew's stand-in, Ray Sperry, who ended up speaking like an English lord. Another Hollywood teacher was Paramount's Mrs. West, who faced down the great Cecil B. De Mille. De Mille criticized Dickie Moore one day, saying, "I didn't like the way you played that scene." Tired and irritable, Moore answered, "Who cares?" De Mille was about to slap the boy when Mrs. West stepped between them, shouting, "You lay one hand on that child and *this picture doesn't move!*"

There was also Lawlor's Professional School on Hollywood Boulevard, where as many as 150 young performers might be enrolled at a given time. It was a haven for the kids, who preferred studying with others of their own kind where they were not regarded as freaks. The head was Viola F. "Mom" Lawlor, who loved movie children. Her favorites were Mickey Rooney and Frankie Darro, probably because they both came from broken homes. She put up with a lot from these kids, including Darro dancing on a library table and Rooney giving imitations of Lionel Barrymore or Clark Gable during class time.

In addition to Deanna Durbin (and much later, Eddie Fisher), one of Eddie Cantor's important discoveries was a child actor and singer named Bobby Breen (1927–   ). This curly-haired little boy made his stage and night-club debut at the age of seven; by the time he was nine, he had made his first film, *Let's Sing Again* (1936), and become RKO's leading child star. The film was about a boy who runs away from an orphanage to join a traveling show. When he gets to New York, he is reunited with his father through the miracle of music. The boy soprano sang a lot. Soon the public could hear Breen on all the big radio shows and see him in movie after movie. His young soprano voice, invariably described as "sweet," was the key to his success.

In *Rainbow on the River* (1936), Breen is sent from the South to New York City, where he is ignored by his grandmother (May Robson) and made miserable by his nasty cousin. Singing all the way, he finally wins his grandmother's heart and brings his old black nurse to New York. This was one of the few features in which "Our Gang's" Stymie Beard appeared.

In *Make a Wish* (1937), Breen plays a singing prodigy and Basil Rathbone is a Broadway composer. Some villains try to steal Rathbone's operetta, but Breen saves the day. (One of the screenwriters was Gertrude Berg—the writer and star of the radio, and later television, series, "The Goldbergs.") A reviewer noted sourly that Breen "exudes sweetness all over the screen to an annoying degree" and that "He sings like an angel but he acts like the devil." Despite the complaints, the money rolled in (and was thoughtfully put away in a trust fund by Breen's sister Sally).

In *Breaking the Ice* (1938), Breen leaves the Pennsylvania Dutch country for Philadelphia, where he becomes a singer in an ice-skating rink. The movie was almost stolen from him by Irene Dare, a six-year-old figure skater who went on to star in *Everything's on Ice* (1938), in which she plays a child skating star whose uncle wants to use her to make money.

In *Hawaii Calls* (1938), Breen was a shoeshine boy who stows away on a boat bound for Hawaii, gets caught, but finds a

Bobby Breen and May Robson (center) in *Rainbow on the River* (1936).

home in that tropical paradise. He was in pre-Civil War Louisiana in *Way Down South* (1939), fighting a cruel lawyer who was after his inheritance. The film was a fantasy that depicted slavery as a desirable way to spend one's life. It also starred Stymie Beard, who, as usual, was required to smile a lot.

Escape to Paradise (1939) was a mess. Breen was a South American kid who played Cupid for Kent Taylor and Marla Skelton. This was Breen's last picture. He had turned 12, and his voice changed. After his retirement from the screen he went on to study at UCLA and The American Academy of Dramatic Art, and appeared occasionally in night clubs and on stage as a tenor.

Ann Gillis (1927–) was born Alma Mabel O'Connor; by the time she was nine,

she had appeared in her first movie, *The Garden of Allah* (1936), with Marlene Dietrich. She went on to become the definitive Becky Thatcher in the best film treatment of the Twain classic, *The Adventures of Tom Sawyer* (1938). Gillis played the title role in the original *Little Orphan Annie* (1938), and appeared in *Peck's Bad Boy* (1938), *Beau Geste* (1939), *Edison the Man* (1940), *Little Men* (1941), and *Since You Went Away* (1944). As a child, she was extremely popular with audiences, but she never made it as an adult actress. She retired and moved to England, and was last seen in a bit part in *2001: A Space Odyssey* (1968).

Perhaps the most outstanding case of arrested teenage development in Hollywood history is that of the group which most people remember as the Dead End Kids, although they appeared under many different names. For close to a quarter of a century, this group of actors stayed frozen in time, somehow convincing their producers (if not their audiences) that they were reasonable imitations of teenagers.

The group got its start in 1936, when Sidney Kingsley's play *Dead End* was produced on Broadway. A stark drama about the bitterness of poverty in a New York slum during the years of the Great Depression, it was filled with raw talk (at least for that era) and concluded with a shootout in which a gangster hero of the neighborhood boys was killed. Among the boys in the original cast were Huntz Hall and Charles Duncan. Later, Duncan was replaced by a young actor named Leo Gorcey. Gorcey and Hall, with other members of the Broadway cast, appeared in the film version of the play, which was released by Samuel Goldwyn in 1937. The adult stars of the picture were Humphrey Bogart as the gangster, Allan

Myrna Loy, Ann Gillis, and William Powell (who played the title role) in *The Great Ziegfeld* (1936).

Jenkins as his stooge, and Joel McCrea and Sylvia Sidney as the love interest.

If there was a leader of the gang of young toughs in *Dead End*, it was Billy Halop (1920–76). The son of a lawyer and a professional dancer, and the brother of Florence Halop—an actress best remembered for her role as the short brunette court clerk on the television series "Night Court"—Halop was raised on Long Island. At the age of six, he began working professionally. He played the title role on radio's early serial "Bobby Benson at the B-Bar-B." He also starred in the title role of the radio serial "Skippy," and at 12 played Romeo in a radio production of *Romeo and Juliet*. By then he was appearing on radio's "The March of Time" and on Nila Mack's all-kiddie radio show "Let's Pretend," for which he was paid $3.50 per performance.

By the time he was 17, Halop was making $750 weekly on radio, although his parents restricted him to an allowance of $10 per week. He appeared with the Ringling Brothers Circus and in a rodeo. Then came *Dead End* on Broadway in 1936, in which he played the leader of the gang—the one with a rudimentary conscience. Then he played the same role in the film version, in which his sister was played by Sylvia Sidney. Halop and the other kids made several more pictures together, despite the real-life antagonism between Halop and Leo Gorcey, the other popular member of the gang. (Indeed, Halop didn't get along well with any of the others except for Gabriel Dell.) In the 1940s he broke away from the gang, but could land only secondary film roles, although he was quite good in *Tom Brown's School Days* (1940), with Freddie Bartholomew, and *Mob Town* (1941), with Anne Gwynne and Dick Foran. After service with the Coast Guard during World War II, he returned to Hollywood to discover that he was still thought of as one of the Dead End Kids.

Halop was arrested on a charge of drunkenness in 1954, threatened to commit suicide, and had a nervous breakdown. Then his wife contracted multiple sclerosis, and Halop gave up drinking to take care of her,

The Dead End Kids—Leo Gorcey, Gabriel Dell, Bobby Jordan, Bernard Punsley, Billy Halop, Huntz Hall.

Halop, Gorcey, Dell, and Punsley (above), and Jordan and Hall in *Dead End* (1937).

Streetwise

It would seem that Hollywood always had its share of screen brats—the type played by Jane Withers, Jackie Searl, and Bonita Granville. But these kids were rather innocent—obstreperous, but not really bad. Then, in 1937, a new type of child actor came to the screen—the streetwise tough. *Dead End* served up a gang of street kids who were the precursors of those featured in *The Blackboard Jungle* (1955) and *A Clockwork Orange* (1971). These kids were not only tough, but also vengeful, cunning, and often downright mean.

The film *Dead End* was a powerful melodrama based on Sidney Kingsley's play about a New York slum and the kids who lived there. It was an indictment of juvenile delinquency and the adult failure of responsibility. Shot on a single huge set, it seemed to draw the audience into the story, and made stars of the Dead End Kids. They were victims of society, true, but they were also amoral punks, for the most part. It was this picture's success that led Hollywood to produce more social dramas.

The Dead End Kids went on to make more hard-hitting movies about delinquency, such as *Angels With Dirty Faces* (1938), *Little Tough Guys* (1938), *Hell's Kitchen* (1939), and *Angels Wash Their Faces* (1939). They even made prison pictures, such as *You Can't Get Away with Murder* (1939) and *Off the Record* (1939). Although they later turned to low comedy and cheap serials, these young stars served to initiate national concern about the issue of juvenile crime. Not all the answers have been found, but the problem is no longer swept under the rug.

becoming a registered nurse. Toward the end of his life, apart from the occasional bit role in films, the best he could find was the small part of Mr. Munson, the owner of the cab that Archie Bunker drove sometimes on the television series "All in the Family."

Leo Gorcey (1915–69) was the son of the veteran stage and screen actor Bernard Gorcey, who apprenticed him out to his brother, who ran a plumbing shop. The father relented, and urged his son to try out for the stage production of *Dead End.* Despite his lack of acting experience, he looked convincing as the hard-boiled, tough-talking, larcenous slum boy, Spit. Gorcey went with the rest of the boys to make the movie version and, with them, was signed by Warner Bros. to make additional crime melodramas. Unfortunately, Gorcey carried his tough little punk image into his off-screen life. He had several brushes with the law and was married five times.

The lovable oaf in the Dead End Kids gang was Huntz Hall (1920–), one of 14 chil-

dren in the family of an Irish-born engineer. He attended New York's Professional Children's School and got work on radio when he was quite young. After appearing in *Dead End* on Broadway, he went to Hollywood to do the film and never looked back. Rubber-faced and mashed-nosed, he played Dippy, the dumbbell, who was Spit's sidekick.

After the group broke up, he appeared in some films, on television, and in night clubs. He also directed a television movie, *Lost Island.*

If there was an innocent among the Dead End Kids, it was Bobby Jordan (1923–65). He was always the lookout, because he was so young, and his long, floppy hair and innocent face won the hearts of audiences. Probably the most intelligent of the Dead End characters was Gabriel Dell (1920–), who went on to become an important television and Broadway actor in the 1960s.

The Dead End Kids made *Angels with Dirty Faces* (1938), with Halop as Soapy, Gorcey as Bim, Hall as Crab, Jordan as Swing, Dell

Billy Halop learns boxing from John Garfield in *They Made Me a Criminal* (1939).

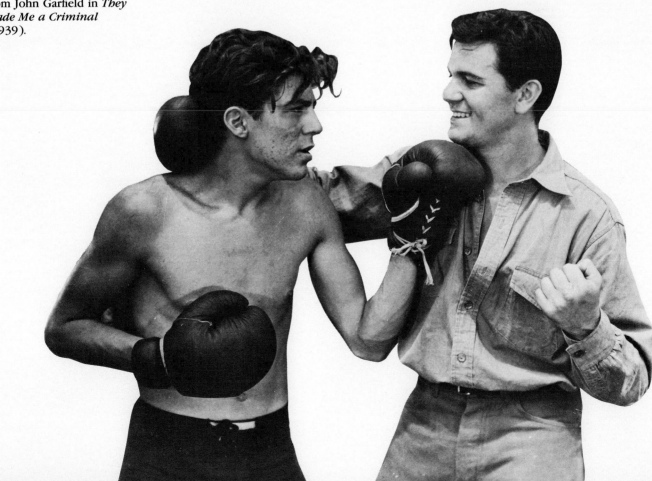

James Cagney with the Dead Enders in *Angels With Dirty Faces* (1938).

as Pasty, and another member of the original gang, Bernard Punsley, as Hunky. The movie starred James Cagney as Rocky Sullivan, a criminal who finds that he has become a hero in his old slum neighborhood, as far as the Dead End Kids are concerned. Pat O'Brien was the local parish priest, who is disturbed about the boys' admiration for a criminal. Cagney and O'Brien both came from the same East Side gutter and they are still friends, but friends at war, and one of them must be destroyed. Father Connolly admits to Sullivan that crime appears to pay. He concedes that recklessness and a distorted kind of heroism tend to glorify the gangster—to make him a juvenile idol. At the end, when Cagney is to go to the electric chair, O'Brien prevails on him to show his courage by acting the coward in order to destroy the boys' hero-worship.

Then came *Little Tough Guys* (1939), in which the Dead End Kids were renamed (for that one picture) the Little Tough Guys. Halop played Johnny Boylan, Hall was Pig, Dell was String, and Punsley was Ape. Leo Gorcey sat this one out, but his brother David was in the cast, playing Sniper. Also appearing was Halley Chester as Dopey. In the picture, Halop's father was accused of a crime he had not committed and the boy took to the streets, becoming the leader of a gang. They commit crimes and Halop ends up in a reform school. Several other juvenile stars were in the film, too—Helen Parrish and Jackie Searl.

The gang was back, billed as the Dead End Kids, in *Angels Wash Their Faces* (1939), which also starred Bonita Granville, with the love interest provided by Ann Sheridan and Ronald Reagan. One of the boys' young friends is thrown into jail for an insurance fire he did not set, and the kids have to find the arsonist. During the filming, the Dead End Kids had terrorized the rest of the cast by throwing firecrackers under people's chairs and putting mice in women's dressing rooms. Off-screen it was Ronald Reagan who took command and made them stop.

In *Hell's Kitchen* (1939) the Dead End Kids leave reform school and become the victims of the brutal superintendent of the Hell's Kitchen Shelter (Grant Mitchell), but are rescued by an ex-racketeer (Ronald

Reagan again) who is on parole and working at the shelter. In *You Can't Get Away with Murder* (1939), Billy Halop was a good kid who was led astray and into prison by Humphrey Bogart. Bobby Jordan was sent to reform school in *Off the Record* (1939), after a newspaper reporter (Joan Blondell) conducts an exposé of the slot-machine rackets. She feels responsible, and she and Pat O'Brien take Jordan under their wings. Finally, in *The Dead End Kids on Dress Parade* (1939), they were in a military school, being rebellious, but heroism during a fire won them the respect of the other cadets.

Obviously, the Dead End Kids were scraping the bottom of the barrel. By then, the pattern was set. The Dead End Kids were rough and tough on the surface, but good at heart, always willing to be taught the honest way of doing things, and ready to help a pal in need. It was a pattern that lasted for many years.

The group broke up briefly in the late 1930s. Huntz Hall was at Universal Studios, and Leo Gorcey was at Monogram Pictures making "East Side Kids" features. Of the original Dead End Kids, one splinter group became known as the Little Tough Guys (whose mainstays were Frankie Thomas, Leo's brother David Gorcey, and Billy Benedict), another as the East Side Kids, and yet another (later) as the Bowery Boys—but there was overlapping, and it was hard to remember who belonged to which group.

Gorcey and Hall were reunited when Hall moved over to Monogram in 1946 to launch the Bowery Boys series. Gorcey enlisted not only his brother David, but his father, Bernard, who played Louie, the owner of the ice-cream shop where the gang hung out. Following Gorcey and Hall's zany commands were David Gorcey, Billy Benedict, Gabriel Dell, and Bobby Jordan.

The Bowery Boys films, which ran for about an hour each, were made to a rigid formula. The leader of the group was Slip Mahoney, played by Leo Gorcey. Most of Slip's efforts were devoted to fixing problems caused by his devoted but incredibly dense sidekick Satch Jones, played by Huntz Hall. A plot twist that never failed to appear was the bestowal of some unusual talent on Satch: mind-reading powers, a great singing voice, remarkable strength.

The boys were always having run-ins with gangsters, or being sent off to some exotic locale like Africa or Paris, or running into ghosts or monsters. None of these details seemed to matter; neither did the Poverty-Row sets provided by Monogram, decidedly a budget-minded studio. And neither did the age of the "boys." Leo Gorcey retired in 1955, when he was 40, but Huntz Hall kept going a few years after that. Indeed, between 1946 and 1948, when Gorcey was 33 and Hall was 28, they made 48 low-budget features, at first using fairly realistic themes but later straying into fantasy. Their appeal was based on puns and slapstick, and although the films were basically quite awful, they have retained a certain nostalgia value. What killed the series was not the sight of potential grandparents playing teenagers, but the decline of the double feature. Otherwise, the Bowery Boys might have gone on forever.

Left: Bonita Granville with the Dead End Kids in *Angels Wash Their Faces* (1939).

Below: Many of the Dead End Kids showed up with the East Side Kids—*Let's Get Tough* (1940), with Tom Brown.

In addition to regular features such as *The Ghost Creeps* (1940), *Pride of the Bowery* (1940), *Spooks Run Wild* (1941), and *Docks of New York* (1945), the gang was in serials. There was *Junior G-Men* (1940), followed by *Sea Raiders* (1941). Hall, Dell, and Punsley were in *Junior G-Men of the Air* (1943), in which they foiled the attempts of Lionel Atwill, made up as a Japanese, to wreck America's defenses. What is perhaps most impressive about the films today is their innocence. One would certainly expect that movies about such upright, well-to-do youths as Henry Aldrich and Andy Hardy would avoid the seamy side of life. After all,

the 1930s and '40s expected innocence from its teenagers. They were allowed a touch of puppy love, but no more than that, and they always hung out at the local soda fountain— nothing as strong as beer would ever pass the lips of Andy Hardy. But the Bowery Boys were supposed to be tough slum kids who lived on the Lower East Side of New York, surrounded by tenements and gangland types. Nevertheless, the plot had them invariably hanging out in an ice-cream shop run by a character named Louie Dumbrowski (Bernard Gorcey). No language stronger than "golly" was ever heard. The air of total unreality that surrounded the whole enterprise didn't seem to matter. As long as the audience would watch Huntz Hall make faces at the camera and Leo Gorcey swat him over the head with his folded-up hat, they were satisfied. When Monogram gave up the series, it was continued by Allied Artists. The last Bowery Boys film, *In the Money*, was made in 1958. Considering the quality of the material and the obvious aging of the cast, it was about time.

A double phenomenon appeared in movie theaters in 1937. Errol Flynn starred in a screen adaptation of Mark Twain's *The Prince and the Pauper*, and appearing in the title roles were 12-year-old twins, Billy and Bobby Mauch (1925–). They were extremely appealing, and Warner Bros. tried desperately to do something with them after

this film triumph. Unfortunately, the studio cast them in a series of butcheries of the Booth Tarkington *Penrod* books. First was *Penrod and Sam* (1937). Never mind that in the book the two boys were not related. Never mind that Warners turned them into miniature G-Men. The film would have sunk no matter what. Then came *Penrod and His Twin Brother* (1938), another Mauch disaster in which the twin brother materializes from Chicago and they both become detectives once again. Perhaps the best, although that isn't saying much, was *Penrod's Double Trouble* (1938), in which Penrod is kidnapped, then rescued by his dog, which leads his friends into the deserted old house in which he is imprisoned. Tarkington must have been turning in his grave.

Opposite: The Mauch twins, Billy and Bobby, in *The Prince and the Pauper* (1937), with the reclining Errol Flynn.

Below: Flynn protects the Mauch twins in a publicity still from *The Prince and the Pauper*.

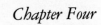

Above: Donald O'Connor (left) with Buck Jones and Helen Twelvetress in *Unmarried* (1939).

Opposite: Bing Crosby, producer-director Wesley Ruggles, and Donald O'Connor discuss *Sing You Sinners* (1938).

Donald O'Connor (1925–   ) is probably the most underestimated child star in history. A fine actor and singer, and a great dancer, he never learned choreographic shorthand and always danced by observation. His father had been a circus acrobat and strong man, and his mother was a bareback rider. They went into vaudeville, and Donald joined the act when he was an infant. His father dropped dead on stage, and his mother had to care for the family of four kids—three others had died soon after their births. The breezy, sprightly, eternally youthful song-and-dance comedian made his film debut at the age of 11, performing a specialty routine with his two brothers in *Melody For Two* (1937). In 1938 he was signed by Paramount to play adolescent roles in such films as *Tom Sawyer—Detective* (1938, in which he was Huckleberry Finn) and *Beau Geste* (1939, in which he was the young Beau, who grew up to be Gary Cooper). After some more years in vaudeville, he was back in Hollywood, making a string of low-budget Universal musicals in which he played the juvenile lead, often opposite Peggy Ryan, Gloria Jean, Ann Blyth, or Susanna Foster.

But O'Connor's career was sagging, even though he was busy: the studio used him in many films that didn't take full advantage of his talent. The year before he went into the Army, he and Peggy Ryan had made 12 musicals together for Universal. In *This is the Life* (1944) he was dropped by Susanna Foster for an older man—an army officer played by Patric Knowles (why he was in the United States Army with a British accent was not explained). Between song-and-dance numbers, many of them with Peggy Ryan, O'Connor won back Foster. He was with Ryan in *Chip Off the Old Block* (1944), playing a naval cadet on leave who is chased by Ryan. Their dance numbers together, some of them quite athletic, were superb.

When O'Connor returned from military service, the studio continued to underestimate his ability, and he was put into a series of horrible comedies that featured Francis,

Left: A poster for *Tom Sawyer—Detective* (1938), in which O'Connor (left) played Huckleberry Finn, opposite Bill Cook's Tom.

Opposite top: O'Connor, Peggy Ryan, and George Raft in *Follow the Boys* (1944).

Opposite below: Peggy Ryan, Donald O'Connor, Arthur Treacher, and Ann Blyth in *Chip off the Old Block* (1944), one of the many musicals made by the team of O'Connor and Ryan.

the Talking Mule. O'Connor suddenly realized that he was 25 years old and his career wasn't going anywhere. Fed up with Francis, he asked to be released from his contract, and the studio let him go. He had also acquired a drinking problem, but he was able to overcome it.

During the 1950s O'Connor co-starred in several major musical films, most notably *Singin' In the Rain* (1952), in which he almost stole the show. He scored other triumphs in *Call Me Madam* (1953) and *There's No Business Like Show Business* (1954). In television, he won an Emmy as the star of the "Colgate Comedy Hour." Then he played comedian Buster Keaton in *The Buster Keaton Story* (1957)—another triumph.

In a complete turnabout in his career, O'Connor began composing classical music, conducting the Los Angeles Philharmonic in the premiere performance of his first symphony, *Reflections d'un Comique*. An album of his music was recorded in Europe by the Brussels Symphony Orchestra.

One of O'Connor's most durable, likable, and effervescent co-stars was Peggy Ryan

(1924–   ). She began as a child performer in vaudeville and made her film debut in 1937, when she was 13 years old. That was in *Top of the Town*. After a small role in *The Grapes of Wrath* (1940), she went on to make countless "B" musicals for Universal, and ended her film career with *All Ashore* (1953). Ryan then moved to Hawaii, opened a dancing school, and returned to show business, playing Jack Lord's secretary in the television series "Hawaii Five-O."

Joan Leslie (1925–) was born Agnes Theresa Sadie Brodel, and she made her stage debut before she was three years old. She became a professional performer when she was nine, in a song-and-dance act with her two sisters, billed as "The Three Brodels." When she was ten, she was a New York model, and when she was 11, she made her screen debut as Robert Taylor's little sister in *Camille* (1937). Still under the name Joan Brodel, she appeared in such films as *Men with Wings* (1938), *Nancy Drew—Reporter* (1939), and *Laddie* (1940).

In 1941 Brodel signed with Warner Bros. as Joan Leslie and played typical girl-next-door types in such movies as *High Sierra*

Above: At the far right is Joan Brodel (later Joan Leslie) in *Nancy Drew–Reporter*. Nancy Drew was played by Bonita Granville (center).

Opposite top: Leslie (second row, left) played Gary Cooper's wife in *Sergeant York* (1942).

Opposite below: Leslie (second from right) appeared in *High Sierra* (1941) with Humphrey Bogart (left).

(1941), *Sergeant York* (1942), *Yankee Doodle Dandy* (1942), *This Is the Army* (1943), and *Rhapsody in Blue* (1945). Leslie's career seemed to decline after she left Warners in 1946, and she retired from the screen after *The Revolt of Mamie Stover* (1956). She then became a very successful dress designer.

Marjorie Lord (1922–) made her screen debut at the age of 15 in *Border Cafe* (1937) and went on to make three other films that year—*Forty Naughty Girls*, *Hideaway*, and *On Again—Off Again*. During the late 1930s, the 1940s, and the early '50s, she was in routine films except for her role opposite James Cagney in *Johnny Come Lately* (1943). Her chief fame came from her role as Danny Thomas' wife in the television series "Make Room for Daddy."

The story of the child star Sabu (1924–63) is one of the strangest in the history of films. He was born in Karapur, Mysore, India, and became a stable boy at the court of an Indian maharajah. While he was so employed, he was discovered by the legendary documentary movie-maker Robert Flaherty, and was immediately cast in the title role of the film *Elephant Boy* (1937), a British picture. He went on to play Indian boys in *Drums* (1938) and *The Thief of Baghdad* (1940). Sabu then went to Hollywood, where he was typecast in such exotic epics as *The Jungle Book* (1942) and *Tangier* (1946). Perhaps his finest role was that of a maharajah in a remote part of India in *The Black Narcissus* (1947), with Deborah Kerr. But the Arabian Nights fantasies craze died in the late 1940s, and Sabu tried to resurrect his career in Europe, where he died of a heart attack at the age of 39.

Peggy Ann Garner (1931–) was the daughter of a British-born attorney and an extremely ambitious stage mother. Before she was six years old, her mother had her working in summer stock and as a model. She made her movie debut when she was seven, in a bit part in *Little Miss Thoroughbred* (1938). She then won the role of Carole Lombard's daughter in *In Name Only* (1939), but reverted to small roles in *Blondie Brings Up Baby* (1939) and *Abe Lincoln in Illinois* (1940). She was enormously effective in a 1942 film, *The Pied Piper*, in which bearded Monty Woolley played an Englishman who managed to get a gaggle of children out of France as the Germans marched in. And she was excellent playing the title character as a child in *Jane Eyre* (1944). However, Garner had her biggest break in *A Tree Grows in Brooklyn* (1945), in which, as Francie Nolan, she dominated the movie, which

Opposite: Sabu was most appealing in his first
picture—*Elephant Boy* (1937).

Above: Little Peggy Ann Garner with Carole Lombard:
In Name Only (1939).

featured veteran stars: Dorothy McGuire, James Dunn, Joan Blondell, and Lloyd Nolan. Dunn played her alcoholic father, winning the Academy Award for Best Supporting Actor, and Garner won a Special Academy Award as "the outstanding child actress of 1945."

Garner made a few good films after that, but only a few, appearing in *Junior Miss* (1945), *Home, Sweet Homicide* (1946), and *Daisy Kenyon* (1947). After that it was downhill all the way, although her performances were always good. In the late 1940s she was playing in such films as the Monogram Studios cheapie *Bomba, the Jungle Boy* (1949), opposite Johnny Sheffield, the former "Boy" of the Tarzan films—proving that outstanding child actresses can go out of date as fast as yesterday's newspaper.

Garner had loved her movie work as an escape from her problem-filled relationship with her mother. When she made *A Tree Grows in Brooklyn*, she was glad to live on the lot in Shirley Temple's former bungalow, as she said, "to keep me safe so I didn't come to work with bags under my eyes from crying all night, wondering 'Is Mother coming home?'" From 1950 to 1960, Garner lived in New York with the newspaper columnist and television host Ed Sullivan and his family (she was a close friend of his daughter), partly to escape the bad times at home and partly to learn her craft. Those were, she said, the happiest years of her life.

Garner made her stage debut on Broadway in *The Man* (1950) with Dorothy Gish, followed by *A Royal Family* (1951) and *Home Is the Hero* (1954). She also worked extensively in summer stock and on television. Her biggest disappointment was the loss of the lead role in *Bus Stop* (1955) to Kim Stanley; she had been the first choice of the playwright, William Inge. Later, Garner would tour with the play with her second husband, actor Albert Salmi (she had been married to actor Richard Hayes from 1951 to 1953). She and Salmi stayed together from 1956 to 1963. After their divorce Garner married a real-estate broker and got into the real-estate business, although the marriage did not last. In the 1970s she became sales manager for a Pontiac dealer in Santa Monica, California.

Opposite: Dorothy Mc-Guire, James Dunn, and Peggy Ann Garner in *A Tree Grows in Brooklyn* (1945). Dunn won the Oscar for Best Supporting Actor for his performance as the alcoholic father, and Garner won a Special Academy Award for her work in the picture.

Right: George Raft and Peggy Ann Garner in *Nob Hill* (1945).

Another child star with an ambitious stage mother was Darryl Hickman (1931–). Indeed, she had named him for movie czar Darryl F. Zanuck although it is not known whether or not that helped his career. Hickman was put into dancing class at the age of three and was soon a child extra in films. When he was five, he was a member of a kiddie troupe, and he made his real film debut at the age of seven in *If I Were King* (1938). Hickman was Henry Fonda's little brother in *The Grapes of Wrath* (1940), and he went on to play many child roles, then juvenile leads, in more than 50 movies.

In 1945 Hickman grew up to be Herbert Rudley (who played Ira Gershwin) in *Rhapsody in Blue* and Fred MacMurray (who played Eddie Rickenbacker) in *Captain Eddie*. He was also Cornel Wilde's crippled brother in *Leave Her to Heaven* (1945). In that film, the evil Gene Tierney character let him drown, which was Hickman's most traumatic experience in years of movie-making. The water was so cold that his double wouldn't work in it, and Hickman was immersed for days while the scene was being shot. He caught pneumonia.

When Hickman's film career began to decline in the late 1950s, he switched to television, appearing in dramas and becoming involved in the production end of the business. Eventually, he became executive producer of daytime programming at CBS and of the soap opera "Love of Life." Hickman did go back to films later, in a supporting role in *Network* (1976)—his first movie in 17 years.

Hickman's brother, Dwayne Hickman (1934–), began his movie career with his

Above: Shirley Temple and Darryl Hickman played teenagers in *A Kiss for Corliss* (1949).

Opposite: Darryl Hickman had a brief fling as a member of Our Gang. Here he is seated at the desk.

Above: Darryl Hickman played the crippled brother of Cornel Wilde in *Leave Her to Heaven* (1945).

Below: Dwayne Hickman and Kathy Grant in *Rally 'Round the Flag Boys!* (1958).

brother in *Captain Eddie* (1945) at the age of 11. He played supporting child roles in such films as *The Return of Rusty* (1946) and *The Boy With Green Hair* (1948), then switched to television in the 1950s. He was a regular on the situation comedy "The Bob Cummings Show" and had the lead in the series "The Many Loves of Dobie Gillis," becoming typecast as a bumbling, slightly moronic teenager. In the late 1960s he tried Hollywood again, but got stuck in mindless teen-oriented beach-blanket films like *How to Stuff a Wild Bikini* (1965) and *Dr. Goldfoot and the Bikini Machine* (1965). *Dr. Goldfoot* was a simple-minded disaster. It was an energetic farce whose trendy tastelessness was as appealing as a day-old fast-food hamburger. It told the story of a mad scientist (Vincent Price) who built an army of well-stacked robots to control the world's power brokers. Not surprisingly, Hickman retired from the screen, and turned to running a Las Vegas public relations firm.

Child star Terry Kilburn, born in London (1926–   ), came to America at an early age and broke into show business by appearing for a time on Eddie Cantor's radio show. By the time he was 12, he was appearing in Hollywood films, such as *Lord Jeff* (1938), with Freddie Bartholomew, and *Sweethearts* (1938), with Jeanette MacDonald and Nelson Eddy. His most memorable early role, however, was as Tiny Tim in *A Christmas Carol* (1938), in which Reginald Owen played Scrooge and Gene Lockhart, Bob Cratchit. He was also outstanding in the classic *Goodbye, Mr. Chips* (1939), with Robert Donat in the title role. In this moving story of a beloved English classics master, he played four roles—four generations of boys from the same family.

The Swiss Family Robinson (1940) featured Kilburn with Freddie Bartholomew and Tim Holt in an adaptation of the Johann David Wyss novel about a shipwrecked family building a new life on a deserted island. The film was made for financial reasons, as the

Above: Terry Kilburn in *The Swiss Family Robinson* (1940).

Below, left and right: Kilburn in two of his four roles as members of different generations of the same family—with a young and old Robert Donat—in *Goodbye, Mr. Chips* (1939).

novel was in the public domain, having run out of copyright, so the author's heirs didn't have to be paid. Thomas Mitchell played the father in this movie that was remade by Walt Disney in 1960.

Kilburn appeared in occasional films as a young adult, but many of them were pretty bad—*Bulldog Drummond at Bay* (1947), *Slaves of Babylon* (1953), and *Fiend Without a Face* (1957), for example. His drama studies at UCLA led him to reevaluate his career, and he became a stage actor and later a director. Eventually, he moved to Rochester, Michigan, to become artistic director of the Meadowbrook Theatre.

London-born Roddy McDowall (1928–) began making British films when he was eight years old, the most notable being *Scruffy, Murder in the Family, Hey! Hey! USA* (all 1938) and *This England* (1941). He had appeared in more than 30 movies, usually in minor roles, when he and his mother were evacuated to the United States during the London blitz in 1940. He was an enormous hit in *How Green Was My Valley* (1941), Darryl F. Zanuck's production about a Welsh mining town, in which he played a sensitive boy who was destined to become a coal miner. McDowall did his share of growing up to be someone else over the following years: he grew up to be Tyrone Power in *Son of Fury* (1942), a swashbuckler; Gregory Peck in *The Keys of the Kingdom* (1945), a film about a priest in China; and Peter Lawford in *The White Cliffs of Dover* (1945).

McDowall did some of his finest early film work in movies as a young friend of animals. *My Friend Flicka* (1943) cast him as an American boy who loved a rebellious horse. Audiences accepted Roddy in the role of the son of a Western family despite his accent, and the film led to a sequel, *Thunderhead— Son of Flicka* (1945). Meanwhile, moviegoers were also seeing him as a British boy in love with a dog who managed to find its way home even though it had been sold and taken far away; *Lassie Come Home* (1943)—which was child star Elizabeth Taylor's second film—started a long series that went on well into the television years.

In 1945, when McDowall was moving into what looked like his awkward teenage years, his contract with MGM came to an end. He left Hollywood for a time to concentrate on stage work and television drama, moving into adult roles. Then he returned to film work in a broad range of parts. In the 1960s he had good roles in a couple of epics—*Cleopatra* (1962) and *The Greatest Story Ever Told* (1965). He also became part of the Walt Dis-

Opposite: Roland Young, Terry Kilburn, and Billie Burke in *Topper Takes a Trip* (1939). Alan Mowbray is in the background.

Above right: A young and sad Roddy McDowall being comforted by man's best friend in *Lassie Come Home* (1943).

Right: Roddy McDowall with another of his animal friends in *My Friend Flicka* (1943).

McDowall's first acting triumph—in *How Green Was My Valley* (1941) with Sara Allgood and Walter Pidgeon.

ney stock company, appearing in several of Disney's family-oriented comedies—*That Darn Cat* (1965) with Haley Mills and *Bedknobs and Broomsticks* (1971) with Angela Lansbury, among others. Then came the ape movies. The first of the series was *Planet of the Apes* (1968), which starred Charlton Heston as an American astronaut marooned on a planet where chimpanzees, orangutans, and gorillas rule and humans are hunted and despised creatures fit only for slavery. The picture went over so well at the box office that four sequels followed, and McDowall was in four of these five films, speaking his lines through an ape's face mask and playing Cornelius, the gentle, intelligent chimpanzee who eventually became the hero of the series. The makeup was wonderful, but it took as long as five hours to apply. At mealtimes, the ape actors had to use mirrors at first just to find their mouths; drinking was done through straws.

Left: Dame May Whitty played McDowall's nurse in *The White Cliffs of Dover* (1945).

Below: McDowall (left) appeared with Jane Darwell (standing) in *On the Sunny Side* (1942).

Overleaf: Roddy McDowall and Jane Powell in *Holiday in Mexico* (1946).

Left: Aunt Polly (May Robson) confronts Tom Sawyer (Tommy Kelly) when he shows up at his own funeral in *The Adventures of Tom Sawyer* (1938).

Below: Tommy Kelly (left) as Tom Sawyer in a confrontation with his cousin Sid (David Holt, the brother of Tim Holt); May Robson and Margaret Hamilton (right) look on: *The Adventures of Tom Sawyer* (1938).

Opposite top: Edward G. Robinson, Ruth Hussey, and Bobs Watson in *Blackmail* (1939).

Opposite below: Bobs Watson (front row, right) in *Men of Boys Town* (1941). With him are Spencer Tracy (center) as Father Flanagan, Sidney Miller (to Tracy's left), and Charles Smith (between Tracy and Miller).

For a while it appeared that McDowall would never get the mask off. Television started a "Planet of the Apes" series, and he got the leading role. Then, for better or worse, the series flopped, and he went back to playing human beings, which he did well. Many of his later films were of less than Academy-Award caliber—*Embryo* (1976), *Scavenger Hunt* (1979), *Fright Night* (1985) and *Dead of Winter* (1987)—but he always turned in intelligent, debonair performances.

In addition to his acting talents, McDowall is a superb photographer who has published books of his still photographs. He also did a good directing job on *The Devil's Widow*, a film starring Ava Gardner, which started production in 1968 but was not released until 1971. His hobby is collecting old motion pictures, and he has one of the best private collections in the world. Still, McDowall has never forgotten his roots as a child star. Recently he owned a red Alfa Romeo automobile to which he had affixed the license plate *X MOPPET.*

The child actor with perhaps the shortest career was the freckle-faced all-American boy Tommy Kelly (1928–   ). He was magnificent in the title role in *The Adventures of Tom Sawyer* (1938), the best-ever version of the Mark Twain classic, produced by David O. Selznick. Kelly was 10 at the time, and

Ann Gillis (Becky Thatcher) was 11, but May Robson, who played Aunt Polly, had to lie about her age. She was 80, and she thought that might sound too old for the part, so she told them that she was 74 and won the assignment. Kelly went on to star with Spanky McFarland in *Peck's Bad Boy with the Circus* (1938), in which he was full of pranks, fell in love with a child bareback rider, and discovered chicanery behind the big top. But for all practical purposes, Kelly's acting career was over.

Hands down, the champion crier among the child stars was Bobs Watson (1930–). One of the nine Watson children of Hollywood, Bobs appeared in 125 movies during his short career. Even today, he laughingly recalls that they called him "the crybaby of Hollywood." He had appeared in short subjects while he was still in diapers, but his first big year was 1938, when he was eight years old and appeared in *Kentucky, In Old Chicago,* and *Boys' Town.*

It was in *Boys' Town,* in which he played little Pee Wee, that Watson made his first big impression. The star was Spencer Tracy, who played Father Flanagan and won the Academy Award for best actor for his performance. After he got his Oscar, Tracy sent Watson a telegram which read, "Dear Bobs, part of this Oscar belongs to you. Uncle Spence."

Watson went on to appear in *On Borrowed Time* (1939), another tear-jerker. He played Pud, a youngster whose grandfather (Lionel Barrymore) isn't ready to die, so he chases Death (Sir Cedric Hardwicke) up a tree and won't let him down. Eventually, of course, the grandfather learns that no one on earth is dying and many are in great pain, so he lets Death descend, knowing that he, too, will die. Watson flooded the screen with his tears.

Watson retired from the screen in the early 1940s and returned only occasionally for character roles, as in *What Ever Happened to Baby Jane?* (1962) and *First to Fight* (1967). In 1968 he was ordained a minister of the United Methodist Church.

Baby Sandy (1938–) was born Sandra Lee Henville and debuted in films when she was less than a year old. The first picture in which this cute tot appeared was *East Side of Heaven,* in which Bing Crosby played a cab driver who finds Baby Sandy in his cab and has to become a surrogate father. Sandy was ten months old at the time, which made it possible for the film baby to be a boy. In *Unexpected Father* (1939), Dennis O'Keefe finds himself with a cute gurgling talent named Baby Sandy, but he can't keep her, according to a judge, until he and his girl friend (Shirley Ross) patch up their differences and get married.

Baby Sandy became so popular that she made the cover of *Life* magazine and was voted "Baby of the Year" by *Parents* magazine in 1940 when she was two years old. In *Sandy Is a Lady* (1940), the studio hired a stand-in because some of the scenes involved her trying to cross a traffic-filled street and walking on a steel girder high above it. By the time she made *Bachelor Daddy* (1941), Sandy was aging. This time she was deserted by her parents, and her three bachelor brothers had to care for her. The brothers were played by Edward Everett Horton, Donald Woods, and Raymond Walburn, who were, respectively, 55, 37, and 54 years old—pretty rickety to have a three-year-old sister. Sandy's meteoric career faded out before she turned five. She retired, and much later became a legal secretary.

Born Suzanne DeLee Flander Larson, Susanna Foster (1924–   ) was an operatic singer from her childhood. When she was 11 years old, some friends sent a recording of her voice to MGM. This was at the time when Deanna Durbin had just left that studio for Universal, and MGM wanted a talented replacement. Foster was signed by MGM when she was 12 and given a singing coach, who, according to Foster, almost ruined her voice. The studio finally dropped her option —she had been there almost three years and had yet to make a movie.

Paramount signed her for a walk-on in *The Great Victor Herbert* (1939), and her singing so impressed director Le Roy Prinz that he gave her a big part in the movie. A Paramount contract followed, and she did three more pictures there—*Glamour Boy* (1941, with Jackie Cooper), *There's Magic in Music* (1941), and *Star Spangled Rhythm* (1942). But when her option came up for renewal, Paramount refused to include a raise, and Foster went to Universal, where she made her best picture: *The Phantom of the Opera* (1943), opposite Claude Rains and Nelson Eddy.

As it turned out, however, Universal had signed Foster as a threat to Durbin, and it worked. Deanna kept getting the best singing

Above: Susanna Foster and Darryl Hickman in *Glamour Boy* (1941).

Below left: Baby Sandy, Joan Blondell, and Bing Crosby in *East Side of Heaven* (1939).

roles after she toed the studio line in the face of competition. Foster appeared only in such low-budget movies as *Follow the Boys* (1944), *Bowery to Broadway* (1944), *Frisco Sal* (1945), and *That Night With You* (1945). When her option was up in 1945, she told Universal that she was retiring because she was not getting decent parts. The best that they offered was the lead in a dreadful vehicle—*The Countess of Monte Cristo*— which was eventually made by Sonja Henie in 1948.

Foster considered going into opera, but later said, "I knew enough about opera to know that the politics were even worse than in the studio. I was never really ambitious. At least not in the cutthroat way that's required to succeed. The truth is that I hated a career and everything that went with it."

In 1948 Foster married Wilbur Evans, the Broadway musical-comedy star. The marriage lasted 12 years, during which period she appeared in operettas with him. The divorce was a bitter one, involving litigation about the support of their two sons, Michael and Philip. Foster then went to work as a clerk with a Wall Street brokerage firm, and steadfastly refused offers to do plays, television, and night-club work, saying, "I want to do what I want to do, and that does not include anything in show business."

Above: Bing Crosby and Gloria Jean in *If I Had My Way* (1940)—her second picture.

Opposite: Gloria Jean and W. C. Fields (right) in *Never Give a Sucker an Even Break* (1941).

Deanna Durbin's success meant that every studio had to have a wholesome teenage singing star. A hundred flowers bloomed, most of them briefly. It was no coincidence that Joe Pasternak, the Universal producer who had picked Durbin out of a crowd, came up with another winner, Gloria Jean (1928–   ), who was born Gloria Jean Schoonover. It was also no coincidence that both teenagers' careers tailed off badly after Pasternak left Universal—it was Gloria Jean's bad luck that he left after working with her for only a couple of years. She had been a professional vaudeville and radio vocalist from the age of three, and she was signed by Universal in 1939, when she was 11, being groomed as a replacement for Durbin, who was switching to ingenue roles. She dropped her last name and made her screen debut in *Under Pup* (1939), in which she played a poor girl who sang her way to popularity in a snooty summer camp for the rich. It made her a star.

In her next film, *If I Had My Way* (1940), Gloria Jean sang alongside no less a personality than Bing Crosby. She played an orphan whom Crosby takes to New York City to search for her rich uncle. The rich uncle is not interested in taking her in, but another uncle, a vaudevillian played by Charles Winninger, is.

Jean made only a few more films before Pasternak left Universal, but one of them was the indescribable *Never Give a Sucker an Even Break* (1941), in which she played the niece of W. C. Fields. The script was written by Fields himself, and it made as little sense as anything that has ever been put on film. What with the great comic jumping out of airplanes, meeting gorillas face to face, and being lowered in a basket from a mountain-top retreat, Gloria Jean more or less got lost in the shuffle. But while they were making the movie, Fields taught her how to shoot pool, which may have been some consolation.

Get Hep to Love (1942) was obviously an attempt to position Jean as a reincarnation of Durbin. She was a budding concert soprano who runs away from her nasty aunt and ends up being adopted by a childless couple. Her high-school classmates are Donald O'Connor, Cora Sue Collins, and Peggy Ryan, So naturally, they put on a show.

Things were beginning to go downhill when Jean made *Destiny* (1944), in which she was a blind farm girl who shelters an unjustly accused prison escapee, Alan Curtis, in her father's home. In *Easy to Look At* (1945), she tried a more adult role as a costume designer who is unjustly accused of being a design thief—naturally, everything turned out all right. Jean never achieved Durbin's popularity with adult moviegoers, although she was a favorite with the younger set, and her attempt at adult roles was a disaster. Eventually, she retired and became a receptionist and switchboard operator with a California cosmetics company.

Diana Lynn (1926–71), born Dolores Loehr, was a musical prodigy. At the age of 10, she was playing the piano professionally, and she made her movie debut when she was 13 as one of a group of students performing classical pieces in the background of *They Shall Have Music* (1939), a picture that featured violinist Jascha Heifetz. Her first speaking role came in *There's Magic in Music* (1941)—she didn't have many lines, but she did play part of the Grieg *Piano Concerto*. At the time she was billed as Dolly Loehr.

In 1941 Loehr signed a long-term contract with Paramount and changed her name to Diana Lynn. After a great deal of drama coaching, she made her real acting debut as the precocious little roommate of Ginger Rogers in Billy Wilder's *The Major and the Minor* (1942). She became known for her irrepressibility, intelligence, and humor in such films as *The Miracle of Morgan's Creek* (1944) and *Our Hearts Were Young and Gay* (1944). After that she had to try adult roles, as she was nearing 20, and her career declined. In the 1950s she shifted to television and became a star again in that new medium, but she died of a stroke at 45 while trying to make a movie comeback.

It has often been said that in show business, you have to have a gimmick. In the case of Johnny Sheffield (1931–   ), that gimmick appeared to be a loincloth, but actually it was his physical ability. Sheffield was the son of actor Reginald Sheffield, and he made his stage debut on Broadway in the original cast of *On Borrowed Time* when he was seven years old (in the film version, Bobs Watson had the role). MGM liked his performance, and he was signed to play Tarzan's foundling son, "Boy," in *Tarzan Finds a Son* (1939), with Johnny Weissmuller and Maureen O'Sullivan. In this picture he followed his new dad through every vine and jungle pool. Actually, when he got the part, Sheffield didn't know how to swim. But since Weissmuller had chosen him to play Boy, he felt close to the former Olympic swimming champion and confided his problem. After he had signed the contract, Weissmuller secretly taught him to swim.

Sheffield soon learned that playing Boy wasn't an easy way to earn money. Although the actors never left Hollywood, even the back-lot jungle required a good deal of physical effort. Swinging from trees and dodging jungle animals, however tame they are, is hard work. But there were long breaks from the jungle routine. Sheffield appeared with Mickey Rooney and Judy Garland in *Babes in Arms* (1939), played with Pat O'Brien in *Knute Rockne—All-American* (1940), and acted with Priscilla Lane in *Million Dollar Baby* (1941) before stripping down to his loincloth again for *Tarzan's Secret Treasure* (1941), *Tarzan's New York Adventure* (1942), *Tarzan Triumphs* (1943), and *Tarzan and the Huntress* (1947).

A funny thing happened to this Tarzan series: everyone outgrew it. Maureen O'Sulli-

van was the first to go, dropping out for more serious roles in 1943. While the Tarzan films continued through and past the war years, both Weissmuller and Sheffield were growing—Sheffield up and Weissmuller sideways. At just about the time that Weissmuller got a bit too bulky to be Tarzan, Sheffield got too big to be playing a character called Boy.

Johnny Weissmuller put on the uniform of an African big-game hunter and became Jungle Jim in a series of standard, low-budget features that lasted until 1955. Johnny Sheffield, now a strapping six feet tall and 190 pounds, stayed in his loincloth, but became *Bomba, the Jungle Boy* (1949). That first picture had Peggy Ann Garner as the female lead. The series went on for 11 more films, until 1955, and featured such gems as *Bomba and the Jungle Girl* (1952) and *Safari Drums* (1953). It was killed by television, which also did away with Weissmuller's Jungle Jim series. Both series were intended for the bottom half of double features, in an era when Americans went to the movies for a whole evening's entertainment. When television came in, they got used to staying at home. Double features died, and with them died Bomba, the Jungle Boy. Sheffield turned in his loincloth and enrolled at UCLA. □

Opposite left: Diana Lynn (left) and Gail Russell in *Our Hearts Were Young and Gay* (1944).

Opposite right: A publicity shot of Sheffield and Weissmuller in their Tarzan and Boy loincloths.

Right: The young Johnny Sheffield with Johnny Weissmuller in *Tarzan Finds a Son* (1939).

Overleaf: Johnny Weissmuller (Tarzan), Brenda Joyce (Jane), Tommy Cook, and Johnny Sheffield (Boy) in *Tarzan and the Leopard Woman* (1946).

Above left: Joan Carol in *Walking Down Broadway* (1938).

Above right: June Lockhart (right) in *All This and Heaven Too* (1940).

Below: Gene Reynolds, El Brendel, Bonita Granville in *Gallant Sons* (1940).

Above: Janet Chapman and John Litel in *Little Miss Thoroughbred* (1938).

Opposite: John Payne, Billy Burrud, Betty Furness in *Fair Warning* (1937). Burrud grew up to be the host of a television wild-animal show and Furness became a television consumer advocate.

Right: Sybil Jason (with crown) starred with Pat O'Brien and Ann Sheridan in *The Great O'Malley* (1937).

1940~1949

The War Years and Beyond

One of the first child stars to make it big in the 1940s was Terry Moore (1929–), who started out as a child model and made her screen debut when she was 11. Her first two pictures were *Maryland* (1940) and *The Howards of Virginia* (1940), in which she had bit parts under her real name, Helen Koford. Later she would be known as Judy Ford, then Jan Ford, before settling on Terry Moore.

Moore went on to other juvenile roles in such films as *My Gal Sal* (1942), *Since You Went Away* (1944), *Gaslight* (1944), and *Son of Lassie* (1945), but got her first attention playing an adolescent opposite a giant gorilla in *Mighty Joe Young* (1949). She was the best friend of the huge simian, and he would occasionally hold Moore and her piano over his head while she played "Beautiful Dreamer." Moore went on to become known mainly as a busty Hollywood sexpot, but she received an Academy Award nomination for Best Supporting Actress for her fine work in *Come Back, Little Sheba* (1952). However, Moore generally got less press coverage for her roles than she did for her off-screen escapades, which belied the girl-next-door look that put her on more than 30 magazine covers. She had grown up in a strict Mormon household, and omnipotent studio heads took over during her adolescence, with decrees about whom she could date and what she could wear. But a powerful inventor, aviator, and moviemaker over at RKO became interested in her when she was only 18 and he was 42: she and Howard Hughes were secretly married in 1947. By 1951 Moore, tired of Hughes' womanizing and jealousy, married someone else, committing bigamy. Then she divorced her second husband and went back to Hughes for another four years. They broke up in 1955, but felt that there was no reason to get a divorce, since no one knew about their marriage. According to Moore, Hughes paid her off handsomely.

Moore then married another millionaire, Eugene McGrath, and divorced him to make a 12-year-long marriage to Stuart Cramer. She went on to write a book about her relationship with Hughes called *The Beauty and the Billionaire*. Moore had many publicized dates—among them, Henry Kissinger —and in 1984, at the age of 55, posed nude for *Playboy* magazine. Little Terry had certainly grown up.

Born Angela Maxine O'Brien, Margaret O'Brien (1937–) became arguably the best little actress ever seen in the movies. This

Opposite: Margaret O'Brien says her prayers in *Journey for Margaret* (1942).

charming, natural child star symbolized the new child of the wartime early 1940s—helpless and vulnerable in a world threatened by wholesale devastation. She began modeling at the age of three and went before the Hollywood cameras at the age of four in a small role with Mickey Rooney and Judy Garland in *Babes on Broadway* (1941).

O'Brien became a star in her second picture, *Journey for Margaret* (1942), in which she played a little English girl, orphaned in the London blitz, who is adopted by an American reporter and his wife (Robert Young and Larraine Day). She changed her screen name from Maxine O'Brien to Margaret O'Brien because of that role as little Margaret. In the film she showed that she had an emotional range beyond that of most adult actresses, and she immediately captured the hearts of moviegoers.

MGM knew they had a good thing when they saw it, and Margaret was hard at work in no time. She made three films in 1943 (*Dr. Gillespie's Criminal Case, Thousands Cheer,* and *Madame Curie*) and another five in 1944. In one of those, *Lost Angel,* she played a child prodigy who was being raised by a group of psychology professors and was introduced to the real world and shown the joys of childhood by a newspaper reporter (James Craig). "The tiny tot firmly establishes herself as a marvel of the current cinema," reported one reviewer.

In *Music For Millions* (1944), O'Brien was a waif adopted by a symphony orchestra. And in *The Canterville Ghost* (1944), she played opposite Charles Laughton, who was a seventeenth-century spirit. O'Brien later recalled that film rather flippantly. "All they had to do to make me cry," she said, "was to tell me that Charles Laughton was going to steal the scene." That year O'Brien won a Special Academy Award for being "the out-

Above: George Murphy, Margaret O'Brien, and Rhys Williams in *Tenth Avenue Angel* (1948).

Left: Joan Carroll, Lucile Bremer, Judy Garland, Hank Daniels, and Margaret in *Meet Me in St. Louis* (1944).

Opposite: The young Margaret O'Brien.

Below: Margaret (left) in *Little Women* (1948).

standing child actress of 1944." One fanmagazine writer gushed, "Before we've completely forgotten about the natural charms and talents of Shirley Temple as the wonderchild of the movies, her place is being filled on the screen by another infant prodigy." Margaret was seven years old at the time.

Margaret's talent was undeniable. She could be funny with Red Skelton in *Thousands Cheer* and with Laughton in *The Canterville Ghost*. She could be serious with Greer Garson in *Madame Curie* and even hold her own alongside that masterful actor Orson Welles in *Jane Eyre* (1944, in which she played a ballet-dancing French moppet). Many critics felt that she did her best work as Judy Garland's kid sister in the classic film musical *Meet Me in St. Louis* (1944). Dancing a cakewalk with Judy to the tune of "Under the Bamboo Tree," giving a convincing portrayal of a child's fear at the possibility of having to leave her beloved home because her father had been offered a new job, Margaret gave a memorable performance. Partly because of her contribution, *Meet Me in St. Louis* is regarded as one of the best film musicals ever made.

The Margaret O'Brien boom continued all through the 1940s, although the pace slowed down. She made only one film in 1945, playing alongside Edward G. Robinson and Jackie "Butch" Jenkins in *Our Vines Have Tender Grapes*, about a Norwegian farmer in Wisconsin. One of two films in 1946 was a typical Wallace Beery Western called *Bad Bascomb*, in which he played a bandit who was tamed by the influence of a child.

O'Brien's big film in 1947 was *Tenth Avenue Angel*, in which she spread sweetness and light in the tenements of New York City. Her only picture in 1948 was *Big City*, in which she played a waif befriended by a Jewish cantor (Danny Thomas), a Protestant minister (Robert Preston), and a Roman Catholic policeman (George Murphy). She was great as Beth in the remake of *Little Women* (1948), more than holding her own in an all-star cast that included Elizabeth Taylor, June Allyson, Peter Lawford, Janet Leigh, and Mary Astor. After she made *The Secret Garden* (1949) at the age of 12, she retired for a time.

When O'Brien came back to the screen, she had become an adolescent, which was painfully evident in *Her First Romance* (1951). It was a plodding film whose only highlights were O'Brien in her first grownup role and O'Brien getting her first real screen kiss. The once-irresistible moppet was resistible as a teenager. She retired again, but returned to appear in an occasional forgettable picture. *Glory* (1956) and *Heller in Pink Tights* (1960) were not all that bad, but who today remembers *Diabolic Wedding* (1971) and *Annabelle Lee* (1972), both of them Peruvian movies?

O'Brien enjoyed moderate success on television and on the dinner-theater circuit, but she began to gain weight, married twice, and settled down to being a mother who made occasional acting appearances. Fortunately, her earnings had been put away in a trust fund, and she had no financial problems.

Stanley Clements (1926–81) won an amateur singing contest at the age of 11, and made his screen debut in *Tall, Dark and Handsome* (1941) at the age of 15. He was usually cast as a tough teenager or a jockey. Some of his better pictures were *Sweet Rosie O'Grady* (1943), *Going My Way* (1944), and *Salty O'Rourke* (1945). After military service from 1946 to 1947, he returned to Hollywood, but could get work only in low-budget films. He ended up with the Bowery Boys in the late 1950s.

Elizabeth Taylor (1932–) was one of the few child stars who never went through an awkward age on the screen, but remained a superstar through adolescence into maturity. Indeed, many of her present-day fans have no memory of her childhood career. This highly publicized sex goddess made her first appearance on the screen as a little slip of a girl with a shy, winning manner, a captivating British accent, and the most unbelievably beautiful face in Hollywood.

Henry Daniell gives Elizabeth Taylor a haircut as Peggy Ann Garner looks on—*Jane Eyre* (1944).

Opposite: Carl "Alfalfa" Switzer and Elizabeth Taylor in *There's One Born Every Minute* (1942).

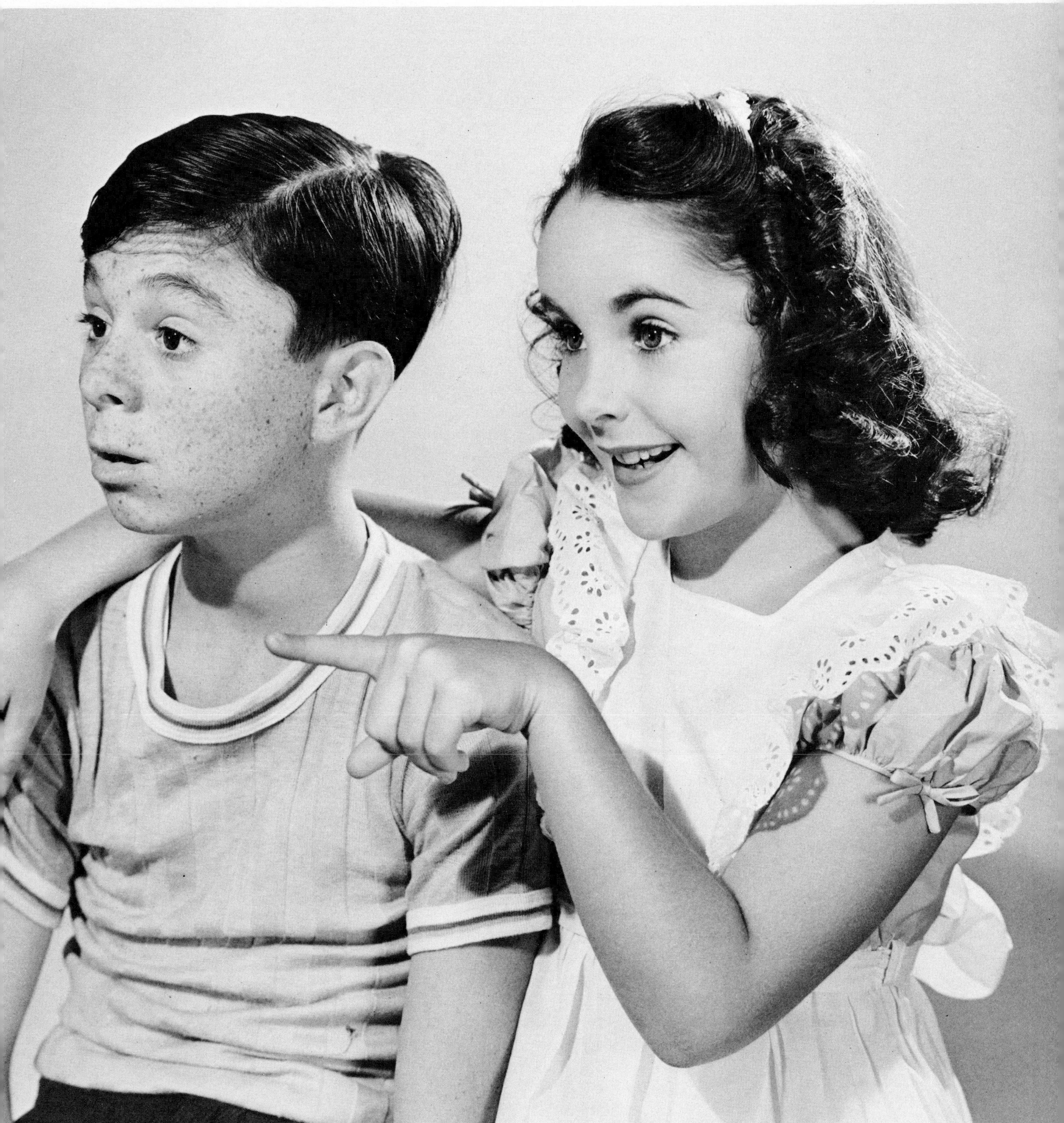

Taylor was born in London to American parents who had long been British residents. She began studying ballet as soon as she could walk, and at the age of three she danced with her class before the British Royal Family. Just before the outbreak of World War II in 1939, the Taylors returned to America and settled in Los Angeles, where Elizabeth's father opened an art gallery at the Beverly Hills Hotel. At the age of ten she was a striking beauty, and the talent scouts soon discovered her. In 1942 she made her screen debut, first in a short subject, *Man or Mouse*, and then with Carl "Alfalfa" Switzer in a low-budget, low-brow comedy, *There's One Born Every Minute*.

Taylor had served her brief apprenticeship, and the following year she signed a contract with MGM and appeared in the movie that got the Lassie series started, *Lassie Come Home* (1943), co-starring Roddy McDowall; this was the start of their lifelong friendship. Her talent and beauty won the hearts of theatergoers all over the country. The next year, she died a plaintive death as Helen, the friend of the heroine, in *Jane Eyre* (1944). That same year, she played the June Lockhart character as a child in a romance about England in World War I, *The White Cliffs of Dover*. But her biggest childhood hit was in the role of a horse-loving British girl who rode her steed to victory in the Grand National race in *National Velvet* (1944), a movie that also starred Mickey Rooney, Jackie "Butch" Jenkins, and Terry Kilburn. The picture was based on an Enid Bagnold best-seller and had a strange history. As early as 1935, producer Pandro S. Berman had wanted to do it at RKO, starring Katharine Hepburn. However, Paramount bought the rights, but couldn't find the proper cast and sold it to MGM in 1937. When the MGM film came out, a critic said that Taylor played the horse-loving title character with "burning eagerness tempered with sweet, fragile charm." Elizabeth was a star.

Adolescence was approaching rapidly, but Taylor made two transitions without much effort at all. The first was from child to teenager in *Courage of Lassie* (1946), *Life with Father* (1947), *A Date with Judy* (1948), and *Little Women* (1949). Almost immediately, she became a starlet as the young bride

in two family comedies, *Father of the Bride* (1950) and its sequel, *Father's Little Dividend* (1951), both with Spencer Tracy and Joan Bennett.

Taylor began her adult career with *A Place in the Sun* (1951), the screen version of Theodore Dreiser's monumental novel, *An American Tragedy*. Montgomery Clift committed murder (doing away with Shelley Winters) for love of her. For the love scenes between Taylor and Clift, director George Stevens used huge close-ups, which impressed youthful intellectuals who did not remember the passionate love scenes between Vilma Banky and Rudolph Valentino in *The Son of the Sheik* (1926). Taylor and Clift would be paired again in *Raintree County*, (1958), the film version of Ross Lockridge's Pulitzer Prize-winning novel about Indiana during the Civil War period.

Taylor was dating Howard Hughes at the age of 17, and at 18 she married Nick Hilton, the son of hotelier Conrad Hilton. This marriage lasted only a few months, but MGM

Above left: Taylor and McDowall in *The White Cliffs of Dover* (1944).

Left: Taylor in *National Velvet* (1944).

Opposite below: With Selena Royle in *Courage of Lassie* (1946).

Below: Taylor in the big race in *National Velvet* (1944).

Liz began her adult career in *A Place in the Sun* (1951) with Montgomery Clift.

Taylor with Jimmy Lydon in *Cynthia* (1947).

was able to use it to promote *Father of the Bride*. Taylor and Hilton divorced in 1957, and she married the flamboyant impresario Mike Todd, after converting to Judaism. The marriage matured her both as a woman and as an actress, but when Todd died the following year in the plane he had named "the Lucky Liz," she was heartbroken.

Then Eddie Fisher, who had been the best man at the wedding of Taylor and Todd, became a suitor despite the fact that he was married to Debbie Reynolds. When Taylor married Fisher in 1959, she became the center of a heated controversy, accused of breaking up the marriage between Fisher and the appealing Reynolds—one of America's favorite film stars. But Taylor's near-fatal bout with pneumonia in the early 1960s, while filming in London, won back her fans. Hollywood, too, relented. She had been nominated for the Academy Award for Best Actress for *Raintree County* and *Cat on a Hot Tin Roof* (both 1958), and for *Suddenly Last Summer* (1959), but had never won. She finally captured the Oscar after her recovery, for *Butterfield 8* (1960), which was certainly not her best screen performance to that date.

Then Taylor's off-screen romance with the British actor Richard Burton hit the headlines. They were working on *Cleopatra* (1963), one of Hollywood's most extravagant flops, when the relationship began. Both got divorces from their current spouses, and they were married in 1964. Taylor and Burton appeared together in several more movies,

From left, Myrna Loy, Elizabeth Taylor, and Spencer Tracy in *Father of the Bride* (1950).

including *The V.I.P.s* (1963), *Who's Afraid of Virginia Woolf?* (1966), and *The Taming of the Shrew* (1967). Taylor won her second Academy Award as Best Actress for *Who's Afraid of Virginia Woolf?* The often stormy Taylor-Burton marriage faltered in the early 1970s, when the couple separated and reconciled several times. They were divorced, then remarried, and redivorced in 1976. Two years later Taylor married John Warner, a former Secretary of the Navy who later became a Senator from Virginia. This marriage, too, ended in divorce. At this writing, Taylor, now well into her 50s, is still a celebrity and a byword for glamor. In 1987 Parfums International, Ltd., unveiled a new product, the fragrance called Elizabeth Taylor's Passion, which Taylor was to promote in an extensive multimedia campaign.

Robert Blake (1934–   ) was born Michael Gubitosi in Nutley, New Jersey, and was thrust into a stage career by his parents before he was two years old. When the family moved to California, "Mickey" caught on as a member of the "Our Gang" crew during the series' last years at MGM. When that assignment ended, he moved on to playing the improbable role of Little Beaver (improbable because he was recognizably an Italian-

Bobby Blake sells Humphrey Bogart a lottery ticket in *The Treasure of the Sierra Madre* (1948).

Bobby Blake, as Little Beaver, steals the villain's six-shooter in one of the Red Ryder "B" movies.

American kid with a New Jersey accent pretending to be an American Indian). Little Beaver was the young sidekick of Red Ryder in a "B"-movie Western series that got its start as a comic strip. It was highly forgettable work—the cheap Westerns that were turned out by the gross in double-feature days vanished without a trace when the double bill went out of style. Blake appeared first with Donald "Red" Barry, whose hair was not red—the nickname came from his character, Red Ryder. Then the title role was assumed by "Wild Bill" Elliott, a taciturn cowboy star who favored the use of kids in his films. He felt that his obvious liking for children would offset the severity of his usual screen characterizations, so he was delighted to get Mickey as Little Beaver.

Mickey Gubitosi then became Bobby Blake, and he picked up a few good roles as he toiled on through the childhood years. Those who love trivia remember him as the little Mexican boy who sold Humphrey Bogart a winning lottery ticket in the 1948 classic of greed and gold, *The Treasure of the Sierra Madre.*

Then came adolescence, and troubles for Bobby Blake. Expelled from several schools, he became heavily involved with drugs. A new age of frankness had begun, and Blake was soon telling interviewers that he had never been happy as a child and that he had indulged in both crime and narcotics during his teen years. In days gone by, that confession would have been enough to end an acting career. But the new climate in Hollywood helped Blake, especially because his talent was obvious. After military service, he returned to Hollywood as Robert Blake and began picking up roles in minor films and on television. His natural toughness held him back, because he refused to compromise—he was literally willing to fight anyone who didn't want to do things his way.

Then came Blake's adult breakthrough, as the merciless killer Perry Smith in the movie version of Truman Capote's novel *In Cold Blood* (1967), which was based upon a real mass murder case in Garden City, Kansas. He was magnificent, but even this role boomeranged on him. Blake became so emotionally involved in the task of portraying the killer he played that his career suffered for

several years from the resultant stress. As a footnote, the drawing of Humphrey Bogart in Perry Smith's jail cell in the film was done by Blake himself.

When Blake got back on the track, he had some good parts, such as the title role in the Western about an independent-minded American Indian, *Tell Them Willie Boy Is Here* (1969). This film was set in California in 1909, and Blake played a renegade who killed the father of the Indian girl (Katharine Ross) he hoped to marry. In the movie, he is tracked down by a deputy sheriff (Robert Redford). Another noteworthy role was that of a tough policeman in *Electric Glide in Blue* (1973). The trouble was that none of his films were big box-office successes. As a result, he missed out on some major roles, like the lead in *Lenny* (1974)—Dustin Hoffman got the part—and the role of Billy Rose in *Funny Lady* (1975), which was played by James Caan. (In the latter case it was alleged that he had insulted the star of the picture, Barbra Streisand, when she asked him to audition for the part.) Even so, Blake, who was at his best in off-beat roles, made it big on television in several series. The most notable of these was "Baretta," which starred him as a streetwise, cockatoo-carrying detective.

Juliet Mills (1941–), born in London, certainly came from an acting family. The older sister of Hayley Mills, and the daughter of the great screen actor Sir John Mills and novelist-playwright Mary Hayley Bell, she made her screen debut as an 11-week-old baby in *In Which We Serve* (1942). The star and co-director of the movie was her godfather, Noël Coward. Although she became famous for her work on the stage, she did appear in several movies, including *So Well Remembered* (1947), *The October Man* (1947), and *The History of Mr. Polly* (1949), before she reached adolescence. She went on to play romantic leads as an adult, and is best remembered as the nanny in the American television series "Nanny and the Professor" in the early 1970s.

Natalie Wood (1938–81) was born Natasha Gurdin, the daughter of an architect of Russian descent and a ballet dancer of French extraction. Like Elizabeth Taylor, she never went through an awkward age in films, progressing easily from child parts to teenage

Above: John Payne, Natalie Wood, and Edmund Gwenn in *Miracle on 34th Street* (1947).

Below: Maureen O'Hara, Natalie Wood, and Fred MacMurray in *Father Was a Fullback* (1949).

Below: Irving Bacon (left) meets Natalie Wood in *The Green Promise* (1949). Also in the movie were, left to right, Ted Donaldson, Connie Marshall, and Walter Brennan.

Natalie Wood and Viveca Lindfors in *No Sad Songs for Me* (1950).

roles and emerging as an accomplished adult actress. Many people have trouble remembering that the woman who played the burlesque stripteaser Gypsy Rose Lee in the musical *Gypsy* (1962) got her start in movies as a little girl. Wood began taking dancing lessons before she could walk very well, and when she was five years old, she debuted in films in a bit part in *Happy Land* (1943), a picture that starred Don Ameche and Frances Dee and used many of the residents of her home town, Santa Rosa, California, as extras. But the director of the movie, Irving Pichel, remembered her performance, and three years later he signed her to appear in a featured role with Orson Welles and Claudette Colbert in a three-handkerchief movie called *Tomorrow Is Forever*.

In 1947 Natalie made a big hit in a picture that still shows up on television every Christmas, and has even been colorized in the highly debated new computerized technique—*Miracle on 34th Street*. She played a cynical little girl who started off being very skeptical about the existence of Santa Claus but ended up as a sentimental believer. In that movie she was Maureen O'Hara's daughter, and Santa Claus (Kris Kringle) was played by Edmund Gwenn. That same year, she was Gene Tierney's daughter in a charming tale of the supernatural, *The Ghost and Mrs. Muir*, with Rex Harrison playing the ghost.

Wood's pattern in her early films was to play the daughter role rather than the childhood portion of an older character's life. She was Walter Brennan's daughter in *The Green Promise* (1949); Fred MacMurray's daughter in *Father Was a Fullback* (1949); Joan Blondell's daughter in *The Blue Veil* (1951); and Bette Davis' daughter in *The Star* (1953). After a brief pause in her career, she was back in films in a big way opposite James Dean and Sal Mineo in *Rebel Without a Cause* (1955). The film showed that she had that elusive something called star quality and brought her an Academy Award nomination. Later she would get nominations for *Splendor in the Grass* (1961) and *Love With the Proper Stranger* (1963).

Wood starred opposite Tab Hunter in *The Burning Hills* (1956), a movie about a young rancher (Hunter) who clashes with the son (Skip Homeier) of a cattle baron who had killed his brother. Wood, playing a half-Mexican, half-Yankee girl, befriends Hunter. The two appeared again in *The Girl He Left Behind* (1956).

Wood had her share of good parts after that—with Gene Kelly in *Marjorie Morningstar* (1958), with Warren Beatty in *Splendor in the Grass* (1961), and especially in two big musicals, *West Side Story* (1961) and *Gypsy* (1962). But in the late 1960s, after some less than impressive roles, her career began to fade. Wood made a big comeback in a 1969 comedy, *Bob & Carol & Ted & Alice*, and earned a lot of money because she had a share in the profits.

Natalie Wood was married to actor Robert Wagner in 1957. They divorced in 1963 and remarried in 1972. It was in 1981 that she accidentally drowned at the age of 43. Despite her magnificent talent, many critics were unmoved by her acting. The *Harvard Lampoon*, for example, initiated the annual "Natalie Wood Award for the worst performance by an actress." Wood took it in stride, however: she felt that her youthful acting career had been like playing house. And she once remarked that the psychiatric bills she had accumulated during her Hollywood career were "at least the equal of the annual defense budget of most Central American nations."

Bobby Driscoll (1937–68) appeared in his first movie, *Lost Angel* (1943), when he was six years old. He was the first "live" actor to sign a long-term contract with the Walt Disney animation studios, and he starred in many of their most endearing features, such as *Song of the South* (1946), *So Dear to My Heart* (1948), and *Treasure Island* (1950), in which he played the young Jim Hawkins opposite Robert Newton's magnificent Long John Silver. Perhaps his best picture, however, was *The Window* (1949), in which he played a child who is in the habit of telling tall tales. In this *film noir*, he sees a murder from his fire escape one evening, but because of his record, no one will believe him. The killers, however, realize that they have been seen and plot to kill the boy. Driscoll won a

Bobby Driscoll (right) in *Song of the South* (1946).

Special Academy Award that year for being "the outstanding juvenile actor of 1949."

Driscoll's career began to falter when he hit his teenage years. He found it almost impossible to find screen or television work. In the depths of depression, he turned to drugs and was arrested several times on various charges. He moved to New York City in 1965, and in 1968, when he was 31, his body was found in an abandoned tenement building. He had had a heart attack. Driscoll was buried in a pauper's grave, and it wasn't until a year later that his body was identified through fingerprints.

Gigi Perreau (1941–   ) was born Ghislaine Elizabeth Marie Thérèse Perreau-Saussine (really). She was the daughter of French fugitives from Nazi-occupied Paris who had emigrated to Los Angeles. Her parents had met while living in Japan and then gone back to France. When World War II broke out, they were fortunate enough to escape the country, and Gigi was born just three months after they arrived in America.

The way Perreau broke into films is a Hollywood story of the kind they don't seem to

make any more. Mrs. Perreau had motion-picture ambitions for her son, Gerald, and she took him to MGM for a screen test one day, but she had to take his younger sister along because she could not find a baby sitter. Naturally, it happened that MGM was in desperate need of a cute little girl that day, because the moppet who was scheduled for the part had thrown a temper tantrum. Gigi was quickly thrust before the camera, looked good, and so made her movie debut at the age of two in *Madame Curie* (1943), playing the famous scientist, Marie Curie, as a baby.

Gigi had several minor roles in the next few years, as in *Mr. Skeffington* (1944), *Yolanda and the Thief* (1945), and *Green Dolphin Street* (1947), but she didn't start rolling in high gear until she was seven years old. Samuel Goldwyn was looking for a boy and a girl to play the David Niven and Teresa Wright characters as children for a movie called *Enchantment* (1949). Once again, Gerald went to try out for one of the parts, and Gigi tagged along. This time they both were hired. (Audiences didn't know that they were brother and sister because Gerald used

Opposite: Bobby Driscoll, as young Jim Hawkins, discovers pirate treasure in *Treasure Island* (1950).

Right: Gigi Perreau (on the sofa with Charles Coburn) in *Has Anybody Seen My Gal?* (1952). Rock Hudson and Piper Laurie (standing left) played the love interest.

Peter Miles, Jimmy Hunt, Fred MacMurray, Gigi Perreau, and Claudette Colbert in *Family Honeymoon* (1949).

the stage name of Peter Miles.) Goldwyn liked Perreau enough to sign her to a seven-year contract—he was looking for a child star to match Margaret O'Brien at MGM—and before long she was not only making movies and stage appearances, but also earning an estimated $180,000 a year on commercial endorsements.

Like other child stars of that time, Perreau worked hard. She made three films in 1949, four in 1950, and three more in 1951. Along the way, she appeared in *Shadow on the Wall* (1949) with Zachary Scott and Nancy Davis (who would become Mrs. Ronald Reagan); *Family Honeymoon* (1949) with Fred Mac-Murray and Claudette Colbert; *My Foolish Heart* (1959) with Dana Andrews and Susan Hayward; and *Reunion in Reno* (1951) with Frances Dee and Leif Erickson. In the latter picture, she played a nine-year-old who goes to Reno to get a divorce from her parents, thereby predating the plot of *Irreconcilable Differences* (1985), in which little Drew Barrymore pulled the same trick on her parents, Ryan O'Neal and Shelley Long.

In 1951 came *Weekend With Father*, in which Perreau and her sister, Janine, appeared with other child actors, Tommy Rettig and Jimmy Hunt. In the movie, Van Heflin and Patricia Neal played a widower and a widow, each with two children, who meet at a train station as they are sending the kids off to camp.

Then things began to go downhill for Perreau. In 1952 there was *Bonzo Goes to College*, a sequel to *Bedtime for Bonzo* (1951), in which Ronald Reagan had been upstaged by a chimpanzee. This time the chimp ends up leading the college football team to victory. It was a bomb, and even the fine cast of Perreau, Maureen O'Sullivan, Edmund Gwenn, David Janssen, Irene Ryan, and Gene Lockhart couldn't save it. In 1952 there was nothing. Despite her personal charm and proven acting ability, Perreau's stardom was over. Despite all the awards she had won, despite all the big money, she could not retain her screen appeal after early childhood. Perreau didn't appear in a movie again until 1956, and then the parts were few and rather small. She and her brother Gerald did make a television appearance or two (they had appeared together in a half dozen or more

Right: Edward Arnold, Jackie "Butch" Jenkins, Peter Lawford, and Beverly Tyler in an exciting race-track scene from *My Brother Talks to Horses* (1946).

Opposite: Jackie Jenkins in a tender scene with Elizabeth Taylor in *National Velvet* (1944).

films), but the good old days were over. Gigi's last film appearance was in 1967, when she made a cheapie movie called *Hell on Wheels*, and she quietly drifted away from acting after that.

Jackie "Butch" Jenkins (1937–) was a freckled little charmer who looked just enough like the ideal average American boy to make it in films. His buck teeth stuck out a mile, his freckles sprawled all over his face, and every mother and father in the country could identify with him. He was also lucky on two counts. He was born in Los Angeles, and if a Hollywood producer was looking for a child actor, why not look in the neighbor-

hood of Hollywood? Secondly, his mother was Doris Dudley, the daughter of New York drama critic Bide Dudley, and an actress who had appeared on Broadway and in a few Hollywood movies.

By the time he was six years old, Jackie had earned a reputation among the lifeguards in Santa Monica as "the Holy Terror." In spite of all the trouble he got into, he was never thought of as a brat. (Jackie had once started a fire at home, but his mother felt that she should keep an eye on him rather than stifle his exuberance.) While she was making *The Moon and Sixpence* (1942), playing a minor role, someone noticed young Jackie.

MGM was looking for just such a boy to play Ulysses Macauley in the film version of William Saroyan's novel *The Human Comedy* (1943), a warm story about Armenian life in California, which was to star Mickey Rooney and Edward G. Robinson. Jackie, it turned out, had a total lack of the theatrical mannerisms so typical in child actors, and he almost stole the show from Rooney and Robinson.

Everyone loved Butch, as he was now known, and the good roles came thick and fast. He appeared with Rooney and Elizabeth Taylor in *National Velvet* (1944) and with Margaret O'Brien and Robinson in *Our Vines Have Tender Grapes* (1945). He was with Peter Lawford in *My Brother Talks to Horses* (1946), in which he made money on bets by conversing with race horses. He was in *Boys' Ranch* (1946) with two other young actors, Skip Homeier and Darryl Hickman; *Little Mr. Jim* (1946) with James Craig and Laura La Plante; *The Bride Goes Wild* (1948) with Van Johnson and June Allyson; *Summer Holiday* (1948, a musical version of Eugene O'Neill's *Ah! Wilderness*, in which he played the part originated by Mickey Rooney in the first film version); and *Big City* (1948) with Margaret O'Brien, Danny Thomas, Robert Preston, and George Murphy.

And that was it. The pressures were too much, and Butch began to stutter. Nothing could stop it, and his mother took him out of the movies. They moved to Texas, where Butch settled down to a normal life at last—at the age of 11. He went on to attend Iowa State University, marry twice, and end up owning a chain of car washes and the firm that supplies water to four Texas counties. Much later he said, "I have never regretted leaving the picture business and am very grateful to my mother for taking me away from it. I enjoyed the first few years of acting in movies but I certainly don't miss it. In fact, when I've had offers to return a few times I wasn't even tempted. There may be a better way to live than on a lake with a couple of cows, a wife, and children, but being a movie star is not one." Still, he has never lost his stutter.

Born George Vincent Homeier, Skippy (later Skip) Homeier (1930–) began his show business career on radio at the age of six. His first film was *Tomorrow the World* (1944), and it was probably his best. He repeated his Broadway role as a Nazi brat named Emil Brückner—a vicious Hitler Youth member who brings his totalitarian tactics to the United States when his father dies and he is adopted by an American couple—Fredric March and Betty Field. At the end, he is deprogrammed and rehabilitated, but it is hard going. First of all, he is appalled to find out that Field is Jewish. This leads him to observe that "America is a cesspool. The only true American is a Navajo Indian." When he sees a young boy helping his mother by hanging out her wash, he berates him for doing " women's work"—apparently thinking that the boy should be out planting land mines. The adults suggest that he might want an Erector set for his birthday, and Emil growls, "I do not vant an Erector set. I vant a gold watch with an illuminated dial. One that can be useful for night marches." In short, he is thoroughly obnoxious; even his adoptive sister observes, "Gee whiz, Emil, you're such a drip."

After *Tomorrow the World*, Homeir was often typecast as a juvenile delinquent. When he reached maturity, he usually appeared in war films and Westerns, and he had some success doing television commercials.

Jane Powell (1929–   ) was born Suzanne Burce; after becoming a teenage singing star, she made her film debut in *Song of the Open Road* (1944), which was a showcase for her vocal talents. She became the young leading lady of MGM musicals and light romances, gaining immense popularity for her engaging personality and wide-ranging coloratura voice. This vivacious, blue-eyed blonde often played sweet young maidens going through their first romances. Some of Powell's early successful films were *Delightfully Dangerous* (1945), *Holiday in Mexico* (1946), and *A Date With Judy* (1948). But by the time she was 19 years old, she was suffering from an ulcer because of the pressures of stardom.

Perhaps Powell's biggest musical up to this time was *Royal Wedding* (1951), opposite Fred Astaire. Judy Garland was supposed to have had the lead in this film, but she

Above: Skippy Homeier with Betty Field and Fredric March in *Tomorrow the World* (1944).

Left: Homeier and Gregory Peck in *The Gunfighter* (1950).

missed or delayed so many rehearsals that she was replaced by Powell. MGM was trying to cash in on the Princess Elizabeth-Prince Philip wedding season, and went so far as to hire Sir Winston Churchill's actress daughter, Sarah, for her only Hollywood movie. The film was set in London and concerned the attempts of Astaire and Powell, a brother-and-sister dance team, to perform at the time of the wedding. Among the songs was a ballad for Powell, "Too Late Now," and Astaire sang the song with perhaps the longest title in musical history: "How Could You Believe Me When I Said I Love You When You Know I've Been a Liar All My Life?"

When the picture was going into production, Powell asked Astaire, "Tell me, Mr. Astaire, when did you stop dancing with your sister?" (Adele Astaire). He told her that it had been in 1929. Said Jane, "That's the year I was born." They didn't talk much after that.

217

Above: Jane Powell in *Luxury Liner* (1948).

Left: Powell (top center) with Ann E. Todd, Jose Iturbi, Jeanette MacDonald, and Elinor Donahue in *Three Daring Daughters* (1948).

Powell's screen career reached its peak in the musical *Seven Brides for Seven Brothers* (1954). It was based on Stephen Vincent Benét's *Sobbin' Women* which, in turn, was based on the story of the rape of the Sabine women. *Seven Brides* was the saga of six fur-trapping brothers who come to town to find wives after their eldest brother (Howard Keel) has married Jane Powell. It included kidnapping and many delightful musical numbers before the happy conclusion. Among the songs were "When You're In Love," "Wonderful Day," "Bless Yore Beautiful Hide," "Spring," and "Lonesome Polecat." The movie worked in every department, and actually created a new style of film musicals.

After *Seven Brides*, Powell's career began to decline. Even though she was approaching 30, she was unable to shake her eternal-adolescent image. After a few more pictures, she retired from the screen in 1958, and began to work on television, in stock companies, and in night clubs. In 1973 she replaced Debbie Reynolds as the star of the Broadway revival of *Irene*.

Jean Simmons (right) in *Great Expectations* (1946).

Jean Simmons and Dennis Price in *Hungry Hill* (1947), which was based on a novel by Daphne DuMaurier.

Jean Simmons (1929–   ), the beautiful and talented star of British and American films, made her screen debut as Margaret Lockwood's sister in *Give Us the Moon* (1944) when she was 15. She was chosen for the role after being discovered in a group of dance students. The strange thing about her early career was that she was not permitted to play younger roles. One exception was the film version of George Bernard Shaw's *Caesar and Cleopatra* (1945), but even there she played a Cleopatra who was old beyond her years. Another possible exception was the excellent film version of the Dickens novel *Great Expectations* (1946), in which Simmons did play a young girl—the spoiled Estella.

Simmons became an established screen personality after she was selected by Laurence Olivier to star with him, as Ophelia, in his screen production of *Hamlet* (1948)—a role that won her the Best Actress prize at the Venice Festival and a nomination for an Oscar. In 1950 she married the British actor Stewart Granger, and when he was called to Hollywood, she went along, making her American film debut in another George Bernard Shaw adaptation—*Androcles and the Lion* (1953)—playing Lavinia. She went on to star in *Young Bess* (1953), as Queen Elizabeth I; in *The Robe* (1953) and *The Egyptian* (1954); and as *Desirée* (1954), opposite Marlon Brando as Napoleon. In 1955 she was

Dean Stockwell starred with Randolph Scott in *Home, Sweet Homicide* (1946).

back with Brando again in the musical *Guys and Dolls*—a complete departure for her—in which she played the demure Sarah Brown and exhibited a fine singing voice. She divorced Granger in 1960 and married director Richard Brooks, who had worked with her in *Elmer Gantry* (1960), that wonderful adaptation of the Sinclair Lewis novel that also starred Burt Lancaster.

Simmons' career continued through the 1960s, when she made such memorable pictures as *All the Way Home* (1963), *Life at the Top* (1965), and *Mister Buddwing* (1966). She was once again nominated for an Oscar for her work in *The Happy Ending* (1969), and she largely retired from films in the early 1970s. But she could be seen occasionally on television, and she toured for two years in the musical play *A Little Night Music*.

Dean Stockwell (1936–) made his stage debut at the age of seven in the Theatre Guild production of *The Innocent Voyage*, alongside his brother, Guy Stockwell. Two years later he charmed movie audiences in the sparkling musical *Anchors Aweigh* (1945), with Gene Kelly, Frank Sinatra, and Kathryn Grayson (he played her younger brother) and in *The Valley of Decision* (1945), with Greer Garson and Gregory Peck.

For several years Stockwell had a string of good roles as a juvenile. In *The Green Years* (1946) he played the younger Tom Drake in

Above: Richard Widmark and Dean Stockwell in *Down to the Sea in Ships* (1949).

Right: Errol Flynn (left) with Dean Stockwell, who played the title role in *Kim* (1950).

Opposite: Stockwell with Wallace Beery in *The Mighty McGurk* (1946). In the film, Stockwell was adopted by a punchy prizefighter (Beery).

the film adaptation of the A. J. Cronin novel about a boy growing into manhood. He was an orphan befriended by a tough but gentle prizefighter, Wallace Beery, in *The Mighty McGurk* (1946). He was a country boy in *The Romance of Rosy Ridge* (1947), and a suburban boy in *Gentleman's Agreement* (1947), one of the first films to speak out against anti-Semitism. Stockwell won a Golden Globe Award for his work in this picture, after which he played Nick Charles, Jr., in the last of the Thin Man series—*Song of the Thin Man* (1947).

In 1948 Stockwell played the title role in an impressive flop, *The Boy with Green Hair*. It was a misbegotten sermon about discrimination that aimed high, but missed with theater audiences. "Would you want your sister to marry someone with green hair?" one character asks indignantly. The movie also featured as its theme song a weird number entitled "Nature Boy" (later parodied on records by Jo Stafford as "Serutan Yob"), composed by a mystic named eden ahbez, who held that no name should be capitalized except that of God.

Stockwell was a cabin boy in *Down to the Sea in Ships* (1949), with Lionel Barrymore. Then came his most memorable performance—in the title role of *Kim* (1950), adapted from the Rudyard Kipling novel. Starring with him was Errol Flynn as Redbeard. Stockwell then played an invalid who was nursed back to health by Margaret O'Brien in *The Secret Garden* (1951). His last childhood role was in *Cattle Drive* (1951), when he was 15.

Dean Stockwell has played adult film roles, but none as good as those he had as a child. He remained in the theatrical world, appearing in television features and movies, acting on the stage, and directing some plays. He was married for a time to actress Millie Perkins. But those who want to recapture the old Dean Stockwell will have to go into the film archives to see those movies of the 1940s.

Claude Jarman, Jr. (1934–), made his film debut in *The Yearling* (1946), adapted from the novel by Marjorie Kinnan Rawlings about the farm boy whose best friend is a deer. Gregory Peck and Jane Wyman played his parents. After a single appearance in movies, Jarman won a Special Academy Award as "the outstanding child actor of 1946." In *The Sun Comes Up* (1948), Jeanette MacDonald's last movie, she played a singing widow who adjusts to her loss with the help of a country boy, Jarman, and his dog, Lassie. Jarman gave a memorable performance in *Intruder in the Dust* (1949), a film based upon the novel by William Faulkner, in which he played opposite Juano Hernandez. He was also in *Rio Grande* (1950), in a teenage role as John Wayne's son, who fails math at West Point and enlists in the cavalry. He ends up serving under his father. Maureen O'Hara, playing Wayne's estranged wife, goes West to try to bring him home. She isn't successful, and Jarman proves his courage in a battle against marauding Apache Indians.

Jarman didn't make the adjustment to adult roles, and his movie career faded into obscurity. He attended Vanderbilt University and later went into show-business management. He became the executive director of the San Francisco Film Festival and was the executive producer of the rock-concert feature film, *Fillmore* (1972). He also became the manager of the San Francisco Opera House.

Born in London, John Howard Davies (1939–) had a very short but distinguished career as an actor. He made his film debut in the title role of *Oliver Twist* (1948), with an all-star cast including Alec Guinness, Robert Newton, Kay Walsh, Francis L. Sullivan, and Anthony Newley. Davies went on to play the little boy in the eerie film *The Rocking Horse Winner* (1949), which was based on a D. H. Lawrence story about a tot who had the knack for picking race-track winners while furiously riding his rocking horse. Finally, he played the title role in the 1951 version of *Tom Brown's Schooldays*, And that was about it. Davies became a director for the BBC, specializing in the "Monty Python's Flying Circus" comedy series.

Below: John Howard Davies in the title role of the 1948 version of *Oliver Twist*.

Opposite: In *Oliver Twist* Davies gets a thrashing at the hands of his employer. Francis L. Sullivan, as the beadle, center, malevolently looks on.

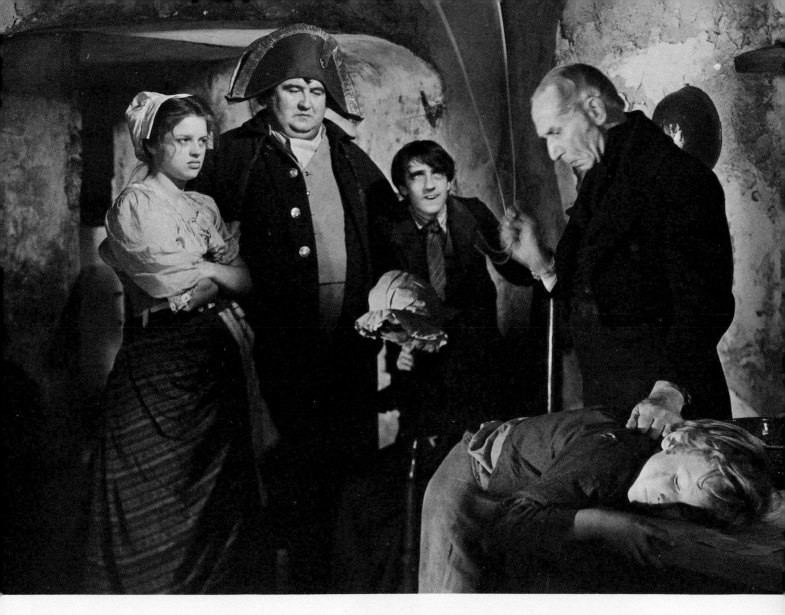

Russ Tamblyn (1934–   ), billed as Rusty Tamblyn, began in show business at an early age on radio and on the stage. His first film work was a small part in *The Boy with Green Hair* (1948), and he was noticed favorably as one of Elizabeth Taylor's brothers in *Father of the Bride*. But his dazzling ability as an acrobatic dancer was not discovered until he played one of the younger brothers in the musical *Seven Brides for Seven Brothers* (1954). Tamblyn, now billed as Russ, had been in pictures for ten years before he got his first starring role in *tom thumb* (1958), in which he played the title role. It was a smash. He came back to demonstrate his magnificent dancing in *West Side Story* (1961), and his acting ability in *The Haunting* (1963), a chiller based on the Shirley Jackson novel. Tamblyn was nominated for an Academy Award as Best Supporting Actor for his work in *Peyton Place* (1957). □

Russ Tamblyn

Opposite top: Richard Lyon, Irene Dunne, Lee J. Cobb, and Rex Harrison in *Anna and the King of Siam* (1946).

Opposite left center: Jack Carson, Robert Arthur, and Rosalind Russell in *Roughly Speaking* (1945).

Opposite bottom: John Payne, Douglas Croft, and Claudette Colbert in *Remember the Day* (1941).

Opposite right below: Jimmy Hunt confronts a Martian in *Invaders from Mars* (1953).

I DONT WANT TO BE ALONE
The Squeezeroo Kids

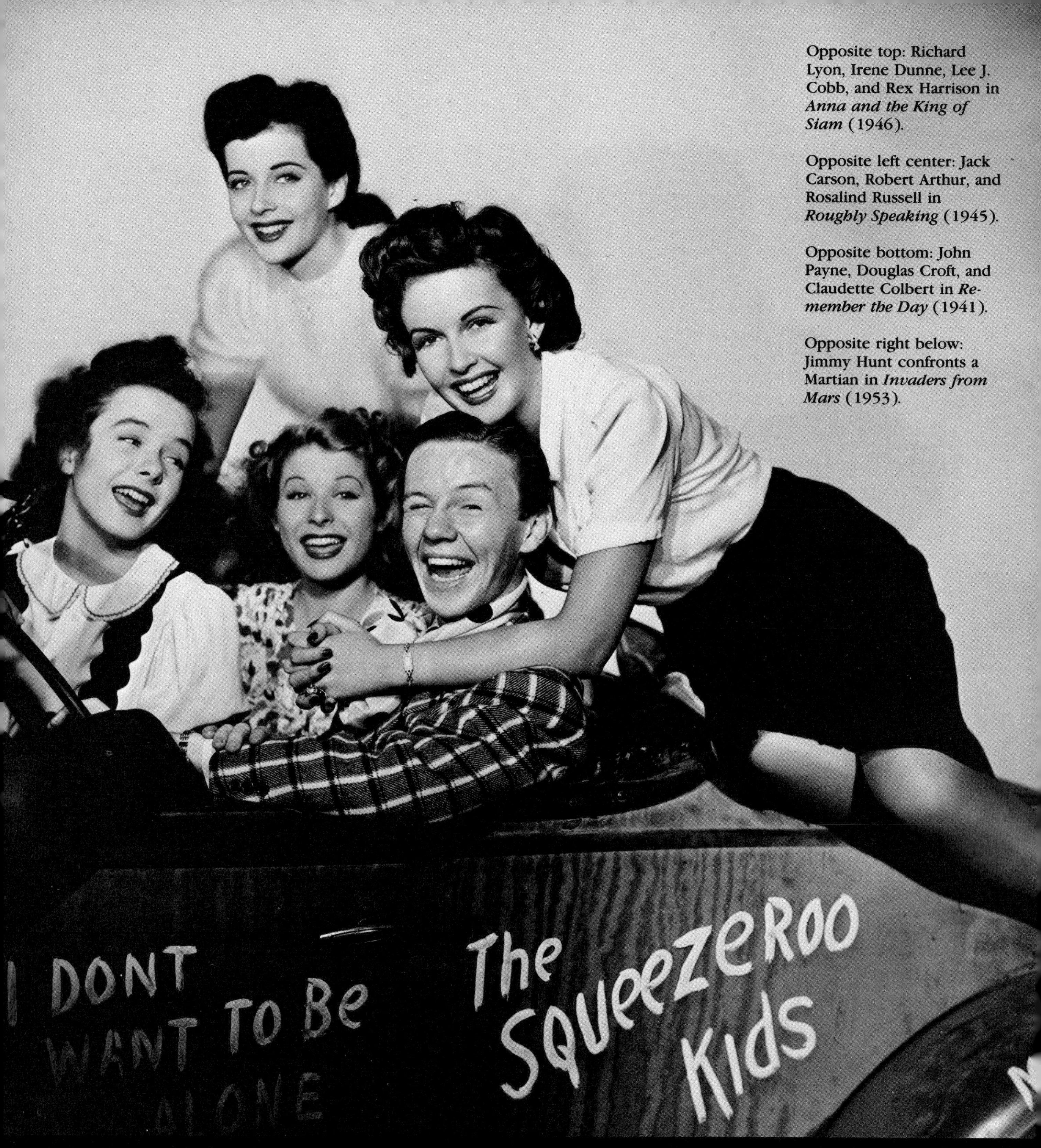

Above: Diana Lynn, Anne Rooney, and Jimmy Lydon (seated) with Gail Russell and Frances Gifford in *Henry*

1950~1959
The Retreat of the Juveniles

O ne of the first young stars to emerge on the scene in the 1950s was a small girl with an incredible voice. Anna Maria Alberghetti (1936–) was born in Pesaro, Italy, to musical parents. By the time she was 12, she was on a European concert tour, and at 14 had made her American debut at New York's Carnegie Hall. That same year she appeared in her first film, the movie version of Gian-Carlo Menotti's chilling two-act opera *The Medium* (1950), playing Monica, the ingenuous daughter of the scheming occultist, Madame Flora. She was sensational, but this success had no sequel. In fact, it seemed that each of her subsequent films was worse than the one before. They included such forgotten movies as *Here Comes the Groom* (1951), *The Stars Are Singing* (1953), *The Last Command* (1955), *10,000 Bedrooms* (1957), *Duel at Apache Wells* (1957), and, with Jerry Lewis, *Cinderfella* (1960). Anna Maria retired from the screen, but gained back some of her celebrity by playing the lead in the Broadway musical *Carnival* (1961), which was based on the great film *Lili* (1953). Alberghetti went on to appear as a young matron in television commercials.

Tommy Rettig (1941–) started his show-business career at the age of six, touring with Mary Martin in the Irving Berlin musical comedy *Annie Get Your Gun*. Before he was nine he had made his screen debut, appearing, in 1950 alone, in *Panic in the Streets*, *The Jackpot*, *Two Weeks With Love*, and *For Heaven's Sake*. Eventually, he made 17 pictures, of which the most notable was *The 5,000 Fingers of Dr. T.* (1953). However, Rettig was best known for playing Jeff Miller, Lassie's master from 1954 to 1958, in the "Lassie" television series. He was the first to play the part in the long-running series, which he began when he was 13 years old. Four years later, he was no longer acceptable as a kid star. It was a bitter blow for a boy who had shared an Emmy won by the show. Rettig tried to keep his career going, but didn't succeed. He retired with his wife to a California farm, where he was arrested in 1972 for growing marijuana. In one of the unhappier endings to a show-business story, he was arrested on charges of smuggling cocaine in 1975 and sentenced to five years in a federal penitentiary.

Patty McCormack (1945–) was a 1950s throwback to the days of Bonita Granville and Skip Homeier—the nasty kid—in contrast to the typical child star, who said things like "jeepers," and guzzled malted

Opposite: Patty Duke (right) and Anne Bancroft in a violent scene from *The Miracle Worker* (1959).

231

classmate who beat her out in a writing contest—and almost everyone who suspects her of the deed. Finally, her mother Christine (Nancy Kelly) realizes that the child has inherited "the bad seed" from her grandmother, a convicted murderess, and must be destroyed. Heckert and Jones also repeated their Broadway roles in the movie. Of course, the Johnson Office (Eric Johnson had succeeded censor Will Hays in 1945) insisted that the girl die as punishment for her sins, although in the play, she is saved when neighbors hear the shot that Christine has used to end her own life after giving Rhoda an overdose of sleeping pills. But Mervyn LeRoy, the director, softened Rhoda's fate in the film by having his cast take a sort of curtain call at the end of the movie, in which Kelly takes McCormack over her knee and spanks her.

In real life McCormack was anything but bad. The daughter of a Brooklyn fireman named Frank Russo (her stage name came from her grandmother), she managed the difficult job of being a star and a good kid simultaneously. She had an ordinary parochial-school education and cheerfully played good-kid parts as well as monsters (she was one of the family in "Mama," a warm-hearted television series about a Scandinavian family in San Francisco). McCormack continued her split personality on screen, playing such roles as *Kathy O'* (1958)—a famous child star "loved by millions, yet loved by no one," who was really a rat—then shifting to the sweet role of Joanna in *The Adventures of Huckleberry Finn* (1960).

Along the way, McCormack played the young Helen Keller in the television version of the drama *The Miracle Worker*. The play was a vigorous rendition of the story of Helen Keller, the deaf and blind child who was educated by the efforts of her devoted teacher, Annie Sullivan. The powerful play depicted a series of violent physical bouts—throwing chairs, banging tables, pushing and shoving—as Sullivan tried to get through to her frustrated young ward. McCormack also starred in the short-lived television series "Peck's Bad Girl."

Donna Corcoran (1943–) was another child star who had a short but memorable career. The daughter of a maintenance super-

milks. She was discovered at the age of four in a New York restaurant—her mother had taken her on a shopping tour because no baby sitter was available. The restaurant where they were having lunch staged a modeling contest, and Patty won. That started her on a modeling career, which led to a small part in the film *Two Gals and a Guy* (1951), with Janice Paige and Robert Alda. Then Broadway offered a starring role in the frightening play *The Bad Seed*, with Nancy Kelly, Eileen Heckart, and Henry Jones. McCormack played a little girl who was born vicious and who murdered three people in the course of the action. It went over so big that she got the role in the film. (Audiences who had once wanted sweetness and light were now ready to applaud a child star who was rotten to the core.) When McCormack played little Rhoda again in the film version of *The Bad Seed* (1956), she was 11 years old. In the film she murders the

Above: Patty McCormack was still nasty in *The Young Runaways* (1968), with Lynn Bari.

Right: Marilyn Monroe, Elisha Cook, Jr., Gloria Blondell, Jim Backus, and Donna Corcoran in *Don't Bother to Knock* (1952).

Opposite: Patty Mc-Cormack in *The Bad Seed* (1956).

intendent at MGM, she began her film work at the age of seven, in *Angels in the Outfield* (1951)—an engaging fantasy in which heavenly forces help the Pittsburgh Pirates start winning games. She was the little orphan who contacts the angels on behalf of the team manager, played by Paul Douglas. It was a captivating performance, and Corcoran seemed to have some of the old Margaret O'Brien magic. She made several more films in the early 1950s, such as *Gypsy Colt* (1953), based on an Eric Knight novel, and *Moon-fleet* (1955), but retired from the screen at the age of 11.

Brandon de Wilde (1942–72) proved the truth of the adage about being in the right place at the right time. His father was a stage manager in New York and his mother was an actress, but his parents had not planned an acting career for their son. However, his father was engaged as the stage manager for the Broadway play *The Member of the Wedding*, which had a role for a young boy. Someone suggested that Brandon might be good for the role, which was hard to cast, and he did get the part. The play opened in 1950 and ran for more than 500 performances. The seven-year-old Brandon won cri-

George Stevens and starring Alan Ladd in the title role. De Wilde played Joey Starrett, the son of a pioneering family in the West (Van Heflin and Jean Arthur were his parents), and Ladd played the gunman whose past was shrouded in mystery and who finally shot it out with Jack Palance, the gunman imported by the villain to drive the farmers off the range. The last scene, in which Ladd rides numbly into the distance, bleeding from wounds suffered in the gunfight, while Brandon shouts over and over, "Shane, come back!," is memorable. De Wilde was nominated for an Academy Award for his role and the film earned more than $8 million—and that was in 1953.

Brandon de Wilde never topped his role in *Shane*, although he appeared in other good movies during his brief career. In 1953–54 he appeared in his own television series, "Jamie," and went on to play youthful roles in a variety of films, most notably *Blue Denim* (1959), *All Fall Down* (1962), and *Hud* (1963). After he grew up, de Wilde remained in the theater. He was touring with the play *Butterflies Are Free*, in which he was a blind young man trying to adjust to living on his own, when he was killed in an automobile accident near Denver. He was 30 years old.

Born George Wentzlaff, George "Foghorn" Winslow (1946–   ) was a young star who had a gimmick. As his nickname indicates, he achieved his fame on the strength of his deep bass voice. From the time he appeared on the popular television show "People Are Funny," with Art Linkletter, his booming voice made him a public favorite. His television appearances led to his first movie role, in *Room for One More* (1952), in which Cary Grant and Betsy Drake, then Grant's wife, played a soft-hearted couple who just couldn't resist adopting unwanted kids.

Winslow played opposite Grant in another 1952 film, *Monkey Business*, which also starred Marilyn Monroe. In between he acted with Richard Widmark in a weepy movie about parental love called *My Pal Gus* (1952). Winslow appeared opposite Monroe again in *Gentlemen Prefer Blondes* (1953), a musical comedy in which he played a very young millionaire. The plot centered on the efforts of Monroe and Jane Russell to marry money,

tical acclaim and became the first child to win the Donaldson Award for an outstanding stage performance. This led to the same part in the 1952 movie version.

The next year, de Wilde appeared in a film that provided his most unforgettable role— the classic Western *Shane* (1953), directed by

Right: George "Foghorn" Winslow gets a word of advice from Cary Grant in *Room for One More* (1952).

Below: George "Foghorn" Winslow played a young millionaire opposite Marilyn Monroe in *Gentlemen Prefer Blondes* (1953).

Opposite top: Jodie Starrett, played by Brandon De Wilde, listens to a bedtime story as told by his mother (Jean Arthur) in *Shane* (1953).

Opposite below: De Wilde was a teenager in *Blue Denim* (1959). With him are Macdonald Carey and Marsha Hunt, (seated) and Warren Berlinger.

and it was an amusing twist to have the little rich boy making suggestive remarks to Marilyn in his surprisingly grown-up voice.

However, as little George got older, his charm began to dim. He was a success with Clifton Webb in *Mister Scoutmaster* (1953), and got some work in television, but he could not stop the relentless march of time. By 1958, when he was 12 years old, the little-boy-with-the-big-voice gimmick had outlived its effectiveness, and Winslow's career in movies was over. He enlisted in the Navy and disappeared in the crowd.

Richard Beymer (1939–) was performing on a Los Angeles kiddie show at the age of 12, and at 14 made his movie debut in *Indiscretion of an American Wife* (1953), directed by Vittorio De Sica, with Jennifer Jones and Montgomery Clift. Then came *So Big* (1953), one of several film versions of the Edna Ferber novel. Beymer had juvenile leads and got great reviews in such films as *The Diary of Anne Frank* (1959) and *West Side Story* (1961, in which he played the lead, Tony), but he never clicked with audiences and retired from the screen in 1963. Then he went to New York to study at the Actors Studio. The following year he traveled to Mississippi for the civil-rights drive to register black voters, making a documentary film of the activities that won a prize at the Mannheim, West Germany, Film Festival. In the 1970s he turned his hand to directing.

One of the brothers of Donna Corcoran, Kevin "Moochie" Corcoran (1949–), began his show-business career at the age of two, and later became one of the Mouseketeers gang on television's "The Mickey Mouse Club." He got his nickname from a character he played in one of the Disney kid series on the show, *Adventures in Dairyland*. Corcoran went on to appear, and sometimes star, in several films, including such Disney features as *Old Yeller* (1957), *The Shaggy Dog* (1959), *Toby Tyler* (1960), *Pollyanna* (1960), *The Swiss Family Robinson* (1960), and *Babes in Toyland* (1961).

At the age of three, Tuesday Weld, born in 1943, became the sole support of her widowed mother and two siblings. She worked as a child model and then appeared as an actress on television as well; she had her first nervous breakdown at the age of nine. A year later she was drinking heavily, and she tried suicide at the age of 12. Weld made her film debut when she was 13, in *Rock, Rock, Rock* (1956), a rock 'n' roll exploitation film in which her voice was dubbed by Connie Francis. She went on to play unpredictable, cherubic-faced, often predatory, nymphets.

Because she was generally cast in low-grade exploitation movies and soap-opera films, Weld was largely ignored by the critics. Most of her press coverage came from gossip columnists who deplored her freewheeling style of life, calling it a menace to

Left: Sandra Dee (left) has a chat with her father (played by Rex Harrison) in *The Reluctant Debutante* (1958). In the background, left to right, are Kay Kendall, Diane Clair, and Angela Lansbury.

Opposite left: Richard Beymer and Montgomery Clift in a tense moment in a Rome railway station—*Indiscretion of an American Wife* (1953).

Opposite right: Tommy Kirk and Kevin "Moochie" Corcoran in *Old Yeller* (1957)

Below: David Ladd, Anne Seymour, Arthur O'Connell, and Pam Smith in *Misty* (1961).

the reputation of the industry. Then came a period of depression and seclusion. She married, had a child, divorced, and saw her house burn down. Her film career was all but over. Finally, audiences began to notice that she was a good actress who had been cast in bad films. In the mid-1960s she began coming into her own in such top-drawer pictures as *Soldier in the Rain* (1963), with Steve McQueen and Jackie Gleason, and *The Cincinnati Kid* (1965), also with McQueen. She went on to distinguish herself in films like *Pretty Poison* (1968), *Play It As It Lays* (1972), *Looking for Mr. Goodbar* (1977), and *The Serial* (1979).

Sandra Dee (1942–   ) was born Alexandra Zuck, but obviously that had to change. Dee began modeling while she was in elementary school, broke into television, and made her first movie when she was 14—*Until They Sail* (1957). It was a soapy courtroom drama in which she played the sister of Joan Fontaine, Jean Simmons, and Piper Laurie. Paul Newman was the star. She was excellent in the title role of *The Reluctant Debutante* (1958), in which her parents were Rex Harrison and Kay Kendall, and *The Restless Years* (1958),

in which she played an illegitimate girl in a small town. But generally she was the star of teenage-oriented movies playing cute, glamorous postpubescents. From 1960 to 1967 she was married to teen idol Bobby Darin, which set her young fans' hearts aflutter.

David Ladd (1947–   ) was the son of actor Alan Ladd and actress Sue Carol and the half-brother of producer Alan Ladd, Jr. He had some success as a child actor, beginning with *The Big Land* (1957), when he was ten years old. He later made occasional films as a young adult, usually playing supporting roles in movies that included *A Dog of Flanders* (1960), *Misty* (1961), *The Klansmen* (1973), *The Day of the Locust* (1975), and *Evil in the Deep* (1976).

Patty Duke (1946–) became a professional actress at the age of seven. By the time she zoomed to stardom on Broadway at the age of 12, as the young Helen Keller in *The Miracle Worker* (1959), she had appeared in two films, *The Goddess* (1958) and *Happy Anniversary* (1959); some 50 television programs; and many stage plays. In the film version of *The Miracle Worker* (1962) she re-created her stage role as the blind and deaf child who was guided by her teacher into making contact with the world. The teacher, Annie Sullivan, was played by Anne Bancroft, who had also had the role on Broadway. At 16 Duke won the Academy Award for Best Supporting Actress for her work in the film; she was the first child star to get a real Oscar, rather than a Special Oscar. The violence in the film was so realistic that both the stars had to wear pounds of padding under their clothes. Duke even wore a baseball catcher's chest guard. Later in the 1960s, Duke gained additional popularity with her television series "The Patty Duke Show," in which she played a dual role as an American girl and her visiting British cousin.

Patty Duke's personal life has not been free of difficulties. She grew up in a family adversely affected, and finally broken, by her father's alcoholism. She once said that "If I hadn't become an child star ... I might have turned into a prostitute." On the screen she was lovable; off screen, she was a terror. She gained a reputation for throwing tantrums, and it was impossible to predict what she would say in public.

At the age of 17 Duke dropped out of films "to grow up, to function for myself." During the next few years, she went through unsuccessful marriages to director Harry Falk, Jr., and rock promoter Michael Tell; a miscarriage; psychoanalysis; and a much-publicized affair with Desi Arnaz, Jr., whose child she bore. But her acting was as good as ever (she won an Emmy for her television

The Kids' Private Lives

Quite possibly it began with Patty Duke. All the details of her private life were not only disclosed, but given wide publicity. That was quite a change for Hollywood.

Where audiences had once been shielded from even a hint, for example, that Judy Garland might be having trouble with pills, moviegoers were increasingly supplied with every bit of information about their child stars' private lives, no matter how young those stars might be. More than that, child stars began playing roles that Hollywood had once thought unsuitable even for seasoned professionals. Under the new regime of candor, Patty Duke's temper tantrums were discussed in print all over the country. Brooke Shields stated publically that she intended to remain a virgin until marriage. Tatum O'Neal had a baby out of wedlock and no one seemed to notice. It's a sign of the times that began in the late 1950s.

Kids began appearing in movies that they might not legally have been permitted to see. Some were appearing nude, others were playing child pimps and prostitutes. A young black actor named Larry B. Scott played a 13-year-old heroin addict in *A Hero Ain't Nothin' But a Sandwich* (1978), and audiences watched him inject the drug into his arm.

All the old stardust had been knocked off the child actors, leaving, it seemed, little innocence behind. In the old Hollywood, a movie about kids and baseball was pure idealism, which always ended with the hero getting a big hit that knocked in the winning run. In *The Bad News Bears* (1976), a comedy about kid baseball players, the one outstanding feature was the foul language—the kind of language that was once forbidden in any Hollywood movie. Audiences, it seemed, would accept almost anything from kids.

role in the drama *My Sweet Charlie*), despite her problems.

When Duke returned to the screen, she was ridiculed for her role in the film version of the ghastly *Valley of the Dolls* (1967). But the story has a happy ending. In 1972 she married the actor John Astin, best known for his portrayal of the ghoulish character Gomez Addams in the television comedy series "The Addams Family." They made a number of television appearances together, became domestic, and at last report were raising a fine family. Duke now bills herself as Patty Duke Astin.

Hayley Mills (1946–   ) is the daughter of actor Sir John Mills and novelist-playwright Mary Hayley Bell, and the younger sister of actress Juliet Mills. She made an auspicious screen debut at the age of 13 in *Tiger Bay* (1959), playing the part of a frightened little witness in the film, which starred her father as a detective pursuing a fugitive. The movie was supposed to have a young boy as the witness—the script change was made after the producer saw Hayley. For the role, she won an acting award at the Berlin Film Festival.

Above: Hayley Mills won a Special Academy Award for her work in *Pollyanna* (1960). Here she is with Kevin "Moochie" Corcoran.

Left: Mills played a dual role as a pair of twins in *The Parent Trap* (1961), when Elvis was the rage.

Walt Disney saw *Tiger Bay* and signed Hayley to a long-term contract. Sweetness and light were the words at the Disney studio, where Mills played the lead role in a new version of *Pollyanna* (1960), in which she emerged as a captivating child star and won a Special Academy Award "for the most outstanding juvenile performance in 1960." She went on to play innocent children and adolescents in such films as *In Search of the Castaways* (1962), a Jules Verne swashbuckler; *The Chalk Garden* (1963), a remake; *The Moonspinners* (1964), a thriller; and *That Darn Cat* (1965), a comedy. She was also

offered the role of a sexy young teenager in *Lolita* (1962), a part she turned down.

When she was 21, Mills shattered her Pollyanna screen image with a nude scene in the sex-centered British comedy *The Family Way* (1967), in which she played a young married woman. At the time, she was also having a well-publicized affair with producer-director Roy Boulting, who was 33 years older than she. They were married in 1971 and later divorced. Hayley Mills continues to make good films.

Ron Howard (1954–) started his career at the age of two, appearing with his parents,

Ron Howard was nine when he made *The Courtship of Eddie's Father* (1963) with Dina Merrill and Glenn Ford.

Hayley Mills at age 14—1960.

Above: Ronny Howard in *The Music Man* (1962)

Below: The Howard boys—Clint (left) and Ron—with Steve Forrest in *The Wild Country* (1971).

Rance and Jean Howard, in a Baltimore stage production of *The Seven Year Itch*. He made his first television appearance in the black-and-white days of 1956, on an episode of "Kraft Television Theatre." Howard made his screen debut in *The Journey* (1959) with Deborah Kerr and Yul Brynner.

It isn't often that an audience can watch a child grow up over many years, but that's what happened to Ron Howard fans. Then billed as Ronny Howard, he began playing Opie Taylor, the son of Sheriff Andy Taylor, on "The Andy Griffith Show" on television in 1960. He was to remain on the show for eight years, appearing in most of the weekly episodes.

Howard took time off to make films, too. He appeared in *Five Minutes To Live* (1961) and was captivating as the lisping young brother of librarian Marian Paroo in the film version of the smash Broadway musical *The Music Man* (1962), starring Robert Preston and Shirley Jones. He was also in *The Courtship of Eddie's Father* (1963) and *Village of the Giants* (1965).

As a young leading man, Howard returned to the screen in the early 1970s, and was outstanding playing Steve Bolander, opposite Cindy Williams as Laurie Henderson, in George Lucas' *American Graffiti* (1973). It was hailed as the most authentic retrospective film about the 1950s. It had no narrative line, but was a kind of collage covering the adventures of four high-school friends in a small town over a period of 12 hours. Steve was about to leave for college. He breaks up, then makes up, with his girl friend, Laurie. This was only Lucas' second feature film, and it was shot mostly at night over a period of 28 days in Modesto, California. It cost a mere $750,000 and made a profit of $10,300,000. For the next ten years, Howard was the star of the television spinoff from the picture, "Happy Days," in which he played Richie Cunningham.

Howard continued to act in films until it was clear that he might become permanently typecast as a teenager; he then turned to directing. His first directorial job was *Grand Theft, Auto* (1977), but that was just the beginning. By the mid-1980s he was turning out such excellent films as *Splash!* (1984) and *Cocoon* (1986). He had become a director to be reckoned with. □

Still More Also Rans . . . . .

Above: Inger Stevens, Malcolm Broderick, and Bing Crosby in *Man on Fire* (1957).

Right: Fred MacMurray and Kurt Russell in *Follow Me, Boys!* (1966).

Below: Gary Cooper, Richard Eyer, and Anthony Perkins in *Friendly Persuasion* (1975).

Chapter Seven

1960~The Present

The End of Innocence

*I*n the 1960s, children were playing parts that, in general, demanded a wider range of acting abilities than had been called for previously. One of the first young stars to meet this demand was Martin Stephens (1949–   ), a British boy. He began his screen career at the age of 12 in *The Hellfire Club* (1961), but is best remembered for his role in *Village of the Damned* (1962)—one of the all-time great science-fiction thrillers. It was based on the novel *The Midwich Cuckoos*, by John Wyndham, and it starred a group of child movie monsters. The expectant mothers in a small English village bear children from another realm who have strange futuristic powers and are prepared to take over the world. The film, which was modestly made but absorbing and logical, starred George Saunders and Barbara Shelley. Stephens played the leader of the young changelings, who masquerade as human beings—Saunders' son, David Zellaby. Cold, emotionless, articulate, and self-assured, he was chilling. At the end of the movie, as he prepares to kill Saunders, he says dispassionately, "Father, I want to talk to you." It was a terrifying, perfectly delivered line.

Stephens co-starred in *The Innocents* (1962), again as a sinister child. In *The Battle of the Villa Fiorito* (1965), he played one of three children who try to break up the romance of their parents—Maureen O'Hara, who has left her husband, and Rossano Brazzi, a widower. It was a three-handerchief film with beautiful scenery around Lake Garda in Northern Italy. Stephens, for all practical purposes, ended his screen career in *The Witches* (1966), when he was 17.

Pamela Franklin (1950–   ) was another fine child actor of the era. She was born in Tokyo to British parents and trained as a ballet dancer. Her first film was made when she was 11 years old: *The Innocents* (1961)—one of the landmark movies about ghosts, adapted from the Henry James novel *The Turn of the Screw*. The book's theme was the idea that children may be incapable of handling "adult" carnal knowledge without falling prey to evil. The picture told the tale of a spinster in Victorian times (Deborah Kerr) who becomes the governess of two children (Franklin, and Martin Stephens), a beautiful brother and sister who suggest the ambience of an incestuous relationship. As the film

Opposite: Tatum O'Neal on the set of *Paper Moon* (1973).

The Present

Pamela Franklin (right) was one of the students of Maggie Smith in *The Prime of Miss Jean Brodie* (1969).

continues, an indefinable sense of evil permeates the lovely country-house setting. People about whom the neurotic young governess knows nothing seem to appear and disappear. The children behave oddly. From the housekeeper, the governess hears about two former servants—a man called Peter Quint and her predecessor as governess, Miss Jessel—who were vile people involved in an illicit relationship that precipitated their deaths. Kerr is convinced that they are haunting the place and are using the two children for their own evil purposes. The governess vows to save the children, and interposes herself between them and the evil spirits, upon which the girl collapses into hysterics and the boy dies in her arms. In the book, the reader is left with the feeling that the ghosts might have been figments of the governess' imagination, but in the movie, the audience is led to believe that they are sharing a real experience.

Franklin was magnificent in *The Innocents*, and she went on to play other roles, gradually maturing into juvenile and ingenue parts.

The Present

Above: Jenny Agutter in *Sweet William* (1980).

Below: Richard Harris and Jenny Agutter in *The Snow Goose,* a television special.

She was outstanding in such movies as *The Nanny* (1965), *The Prime of Miss Jean Brodie* (1969), and as Dora in *David Copperfield* (1970). Then came *The Legend of Hell House* (1973), in which she starred with Roddy McDowall. It was a story of occult phenomena, in which four researchers agree to spend a week in a house haunted by malevolent spirits who have killed previous psychic investigators. It was one of the most absorbing ghost-breaker yarns on film.

Like Pamela Franklin, Jenny Agutter (1952–) progressed from child to adult roles almost without a hitch. She trained as a ballet dancer and made her screen debut at the age of 12 in *East of Sudan* (1964), a British movie. Her first American film was *Star!* (1968), in which Julie Andrews played the title role in the biopic of British comedienne and musical-comedy star Gertrude Lawrence. Agutter starred in the Australian film *Walkabout* (1971), in which she was lost in the Australian outback. She was also noteworthy in the American science-fiction picture *Logan's Run* (1976) and in the psychological drama *Equus* (1977). She is still active in films.

The Present

Above: Mark Lester starred with Dirk Bogarde in *Our Mother's House* (1967). Bogarde played a worthless father who shows up after his children have adjusted to the death of their mother.

Above right: "Please, sir, I want some more"—Mark Lester in the title role of *Oliver!* (1968).

Right: After their triumph in *Oliver!,* Mark Lester and Oliver Reed were together again in *Crossed Swords* (1977), a remake of *The Prince and the Pauper* in which Lester played a dual role.

Born in London, Mark Lester (1958–) was a cherubic blond star of motion pictures at the age of six. This son of an actor and an actress had appeared on British television before he debuted in *The Counterfeit Constable* (1964). He had small parts in, among other things, *Fahrenheit 451* (1966) and *Our Mother's House* (1967), which also starred Dirk Bogarde and Pamela Franklin, before making his mark in the title role of the musical-comedy film *Oliver!* (1968). He was magnificent in the part of Oliver Twist and proved to be a fine singer into the bargain. Lester also turned in fine performances as a young boy in such films as *Black Beauty* (1971) and *Crossed Swords* (1977), the latter in a dual role.

Olivia Hussey (1951–) was born in Buenos Aires, Argentina, to British parents. She debuted in *The Battle of the Villa Fiorito* (1965) with Martin Stephens, Maureen O'Hara, and Rossano Brazzi. Then came her most magnificent performance, when, at the age of 15, she was cast as Juliet in Franco Zeffirelli's production of *Romeo and Juliet* (released in 1968), with Leonard Whiting, Milo O'Shea, and Michael York. Hussey went on to make such pictures as *Lost Horizon* (1973) and *Death on the Nile* (1978).

Linda Blair (1959–) was making mustard commercials for television before she ever broke into pictures. She made her screen debut in 1970, when she was 11, in *The Way We Live Now*. Then came *The Sporting Club* (1971), a bomb about promiscuity in Northern Michigan—it had enough violence and gore to last a lifetime. Her big break came in *The Exorcist* (1973), in which she played Regan MacNeil, the 12-year-old daughter of a movie actress, who is possessed by an evil spirit. The California Welfare Authorities had forbidden the appearance of a young child in this shocking film, so *The Exorcist* was shot in the Georgetown section of Washington, D.C. Blair was nominated as Best Supporting Actress by the Academy Awards Committee.

The Exorcist was based on the novel by William Peter Blatty, and told the story of the young girl, Regan, who is forced into grotesque and terrifying acts by the demon who possesses her. Her head turns completely around; she levitates, curses, and vomits in people's faces; she produces poltergeist phenomena and develops self-inflicted wounds. Her mother (Ellen Burstyn) finally enlists the help of an experienced exorcist—a priest played by Max Von Sydow—who struggles to free the girl from the devil and succeeds at the cost of his life and a fellow priest's.

The film quickly became the biggest box-office grosser of any horror movie in history. But in fact, *The Exorcist* had a lot more going for it than a number of shocking scenes. It was a well-acted, tightly directed picture that held up, and can now be considered a genuine horror classic.

Blair went on to make a few forgettable films such as *Airport 1975* (1974), *Exorcist II: The Heretic* (1977), and *Hard Ride to Rantan* (1979). After a drug arrest in her native Westport, Connecticut, she seemed to drift into sexploitation pictures, appearing as a young girl being victimized in a women's prison, for example. She later said about her career, "You have to grow up early. I've been working and supporting myself since I was six years old. I missed going to Daddy and saying, 'Give me money, I want to go off and do this or that.' I competed with kids whose parents supported them. It was very hard. I paid my dues. I was never carefree."

Linda Blair in her grotesque makeup as Regan MacNeil, the girl possessed by the devil in *The Exorcist* (1973).

Overleaf: Olivia Hussey was Juliet opposite Leonard Whiting in *Romeo and Juliet* (1968).

The Present

Jodie Foster in *Foxes* (1980).

Above: Jodie Foster (right) appeared with Helen Hayes in the suspense drama *Candleshoe* (1977).

Below: Foster (center) in *The Hotel New Hampshire* (1984).

Jodie Foster (1963–) began to perform professionally at the age of three, and appeared in many Disney television productions before she made her screen feature debut in 1972, when she was nine. That year she appeared in *Napoleon and Samantha* and *Kansas City Bomber.* She also played Becky Thatcher in *Tom Sawyer* (1973).

Foster took off the year of 1974 to play the role of Addie (which Tatum O'Neal had originated in the 1973 film), in the short-lived television series *Paper Moon.* She turned in an expert performance in *Alice Doesn't Live Here Anymore* in 1975. While continuing to play conventional roles in family pictures for Disney and other studios, this amazingly mature child star electrified the film community and shocked many moviegoers with her characterizations in roles that far exceeded her chronological age in maturity and sophistication.

Foster was not quite 13 when she played Iris, the drug-addicted precocious prostitute in *Taxi Driver*, and Miss Tallulah, the bawdy

speakeasy queen in *Bugsy Malone* (both 1976). She was going on 14 when she portrayed a child murderess in *The Little Girl Who Lived Down the Lane* (1977), in which she was replaced by her older sister in the nude scenes.

Foster was a brilliant young woman, who recalled that in childood, "The only doll I played with was a G. I. Joe." She had attended the bi-lingual Lycée Française in Hollywood, and so was able to star in a French film, *Moi, Fleur Bleu*, in 1977. After making *Ladies of the Valley* (1979), she turned her back on Hollywood and began her studies at Yale University.

The daughter of actor Ryan O'Neal and actress Joanna Moore, Tatum O'Neal (1963–) showed audiences how much the movies had changed since the 1960s. By the time she made her first film, *Paper Moon* (1973), innocence was out of style, both on and off screen. Nine-year-old Tatum made her movie debut as a cigarette-smoking, prematurely wise assistant to a traveling, Bible-selling con man (played by her father). Shirley Temple had sung and danced her way into the hearts of America, but Tatum O'Neal became the biggest child star in the New Hollywood by lying and cheating her way through life on film, faithful only to the swindler who had picked her up. She had been expelled from a private school just before the *Paper Moon* part of Addie came up and was discovered while visiting her father on the set of one of his films, *The Thief Who Came to Dinner*, where she was noticed by the wife of a rising young director named Peter Bogdanovich. A few months later, Bogdanovich went over to the O'Neal house to see Tatum, who supposedly knew nothing about a possible movie role. As soon as he walked into the house, Tatum asked, "Is this the guy who's going to direct the movie?" She got the part anyway. Not only that, but she won the Academy Award for Best Supporting Actress for her performance—the youngest person ever to win the Oscar—and accepted it wearing a boy's tuxedo.

Once upon a time, it was standard for everyone who worked with a child star to have nothing but praise for the kid's hard work and intelligence. Any indication that the child needed help in acting, or that the

Tatum O'Neal and her father Ryan were the stars of *Paper Moon* (1973), for which she won an Oscar.

The Present

Above: Brooke Shields and
Keith Carradine in *Pretty
Baby* (1978).

Right: Shields and Christopher Atkins in *The Blue
Lagoon* (1980).

Opposite: Henry Fonda,
Peter Fonda, and Brooke
Shields in *Wanda Nevada*
(1979).

moppet's behavior was less than perfect, was avoided. But Bogdanovich, in the new atmosphere of the 1970s, admitted freely that he had spent long hours coaching Tatum (she had never had an acting lesson) and that he had helped her to get her lines right by offering her bribes that started out at 50 cents and ended at 50 dollars. It all paid off. *Paper Moon* made more than $45 million at the box office, and Tatum O'Neal became an overnight celebrity. Her parents had separated when she was two years old, and she spent some years with her mother on a San Fernando Valley ranch, where Joanna Moore became addicted to methadrine and Tatum grew flowers in a wrecked car in the front yard. "She really hated me," her mother said later. "She spit in my face." When she was eight years old, Tatum went to live with her father, and then started her career. The secret of her success, according to Bogdanovich, was that "It's always amusing if a child behaves older than she is by about 30 years."

Tatum O'Neal left the screen for three years after *Paper Moon*. Then one day she told her father that she wanted to use her movie earnings to buy a horse ranch. "You only made $16,000," said O'Neal. "That won't buy it." So she went back to work, getting a contract for *The Bad News Bears* (1976) that paid her $350,000 and nine percent of the film's net profits. She played the part of a fearless Little League pitcher and was the highest-paid child star in the history of Hollywood. Tatum had learned what money could buy, and was getting more than her share of publicity. It wasn't the old style of Hollywood publicity, which was heavy on gingham dresses and ice cream cones. Tatum O'Neal was part of the jet set. She was seen in fancy discothéques, interviewed by Andy Warhol, went shopping in London, was photographed for *Vogue* magazine, drove around in a Mercedes, and made the nightclub scene. She fought with co-star Walter Matthau on the set of *The Bad News Bears*, although they ended as friends. She acknowledged that she had been smoking cigarettes for three years before her role in *Paper Moon*. In short, she was the very model of a 1970s child star, a million light years away from the old innocent stereotype.

In 1978 Tatum was in England to film *International Velvet*, a sequel to Elizabeth Taylor's big 1944 hit, *National Velvet*. She was 15 years old and on top of the world. She couldn't take a fall from a horse in the film, because the insurance company wouldn't allow it—an ex-jockey doubled for her. She was making just one film a year, going to high school between roles, and was rapidly approaching the time of life when most child stars face their greatest challenge—growing up. In a way, she ducked the challenge. She went to live with tennis star John McEnroe, and after a time bore his son, Kevin. They were married in 1986.

Probably the most stunningly beautiful child star since Elizabeth Taylor is Brooke Shields (1965–). She started as a baby model and made her film debut in a bit part in a film called *Holy Terror* (1977). It was a piece

The Future of the Child Star

Ricky Schroder and Jon Voight repeated the roles that Jackie Cooper and Wallace Beery had performed so ably in the remake of *The Champ* (1979).

The era of the child star may never return. Certainly, there will always be a need for children in movies, but the current trend toward sex and violence in films militates against their becoming stars—at least until the pendulum swings the other way and the public demands motion pictures about homey, simple people again. As it stands now, however, Hollywood could never get away with another Andy Hardy film, a *Boys' Town*, a *Little Miss Marker*.

There are young actors who are established stars, such as Gary Coleman and Tatum O'Neal, but there is no studio system to support them anymore—no flack department to give them a buildup. Besides, it takes so long to conceive a movie, to shoot it, and to release it that these child stars may reach puberty after just a few pictures. In the old days, a Roddy McDowall would make five pictures in the same year in which he appeared in *How Green Was My Valley* (1941), and a Dickie Moore could make 40 pictures (not counting his "Our Gang" comedies) between 1931 and 1935.

For a time it looked as though young Ricky Schroder might assume the mantle of the genuine old-fashioned Hollywood kid. He is a fine actor, and audiences empathize with him. Besides, like all the great former kid stars, he could cry on cue. The veteran child actor turned director and producer, Gene Reynolds, said of Schroder's performance in the remake of *The Champ* (1979): "I kept counting how many times they were cranking up that kid to cry, because in the master shot he'd be crying. Then I'd see the over-the-shoulder shot and he'd be crying. Then I'd see a close-up and he'd be crying. And I know how long it takes to go from setup to setup. So this kid had to stop crying, dry up, and then start again. The poor kid never stopped crying." Unfortunately for movie audiences, Schroder is out of the running. He opted for television and the "Silver Spoons" situation comedy, and now he is past puberty. Perhaps the only remaining old-time child star type is Peter Billingley, who was so good in *Memories Never Die* (1982) and absolutely magnificent in the comedy *A Christmas Story* (1983). But he'll have to get many more roles in a hurry.

Albert Finney, as Daddy Warbucks, and Aileen Quinn in the title role of *Annie* (1982).

The Present

Five-year-old Heather O'Rourke is kidnapped in *Poltergeist* (1982).

of nothing that asked the question, "Did 12-year-old Alice [Paula Sheppard] kill her sister, parents, aunt, etc.?" Shields got knocked off in the first reel of this movie that had the distinction of being filmed in Paterson, New Jersey. So unsure (and rightly so) were the producers about the merits of the film that they also released it as *Communion* and *Alice, Sweet Alice.*

Shields did, however, become a legitimate child star in her next film, *Pretty Baby* (1978), when she was 13. This was director Louis Maille's American film about a marriage between a 12-year-old New Orleans prostitute (Shields) and an older photographer, set around the time of World War I. Shields was striking in the role. After a few more movies came *The Blue Lagoon* (1980), a pale remake of the great Jean Simmons classic.

Shields' next film was *Endless Love* (1981), a teenage drama that, unfortunately, left critics rolling in the aisles. Shields was the girl friend of a Chicago boy who breaks into her

Henry Thomas played Elliott in *E. T. The Extraterrestrial* (1982). Here he is with his alien friend.

Danny Lloyd was the terrified child in *The Shining* (1980), here clutching his mother as she tries to protect him from her crazed homicidal husband.

bedroom (there were a number of embarrassing sex scenes); when her father forbids him the house, he sets fire to it in order to "rescue" the family from the blaze. Things went wrong and the house burned down. The film was absolute tripe, even though the acting wasn't half bad, and Brooke Shields left Hollywood to attend Princeton University.

But where are the child stars of tomorrow going to come from? And who will they be? Even though a baby is eligible for a State of California work permit at the age of 15 days, there seem to be pretty slim pickings for the movies at the moment.

For a time it looked as if Ricky Schroder would be the new tot king of Hollywood, after he made such an impressive job of his role in the tear-jerking remake of *The Champ* (1979). But he opted for television in the sitcom "Silver Spoons," and even his wonderful work as *Little Lord Fauntleroy* with Alec Guinness was in a made-for-television film. Then came Aileen Quinn, who was great in the movie version of the Broadway musical *Annie* (1982), but one movie does not make a child star of enduring fame. The same might be said of Henry Thomas, who was so winning as the younger brother in *E.T. The Extraterrestrial* (1982). A similar case is that of Danny Lloyd, the gifted child who rode his tricycle around the haunted hotel in *The Shining* (1980).

For the time being, we'll have to bank on Drew Barrymore, who is piling up some effective credits, including *E.T.* (she was Thomas' sister), *Firestarter* (1984), and *Irreconcilable Differences* (1985). But even she has begun to dabble in the made-for-television movie, most notably in *Babes in Toyland* (1986).

Still, children are always trying to break into the movies. In 1982 alone, there were between 750 and 900 work permits issued by the city of Los Angeles to potential child actors. Who knows—perhaps the next big child star will flash before our eyes this very evening on television. Maybe it will be that baby who is having its diapers changed. Or maybe it will be a kid who is already out in Hollywood, trying out for that big chance on the silver screen, dreaming of being discovered in a drug store and becoming the world-famous star who drives around in a Rolls Royce and gives autographs. For all we know, another crop of great child stars may be just around the corner, and we can take our handkerchiefs to the theater and watch the little darling sing and dance his way into our hearts, or hear, once again, "I know, kids, let's put on a show!"   □

262

Final Takes

Kristy McNichol in *Little Darlings* (1980).

Shirley Temple

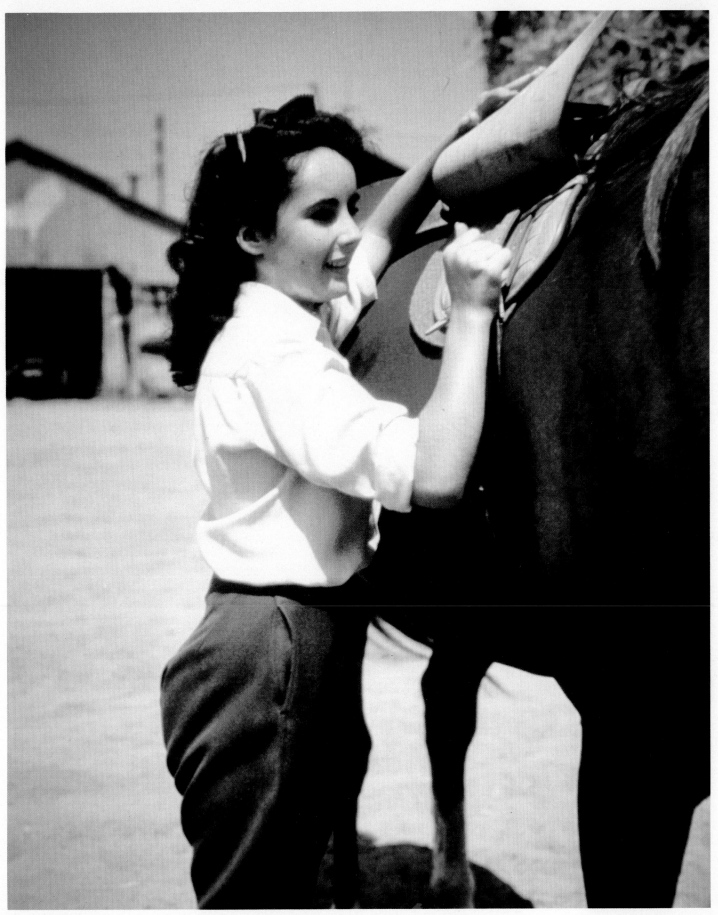

Elizabeth Taylor

Freddie Bartholomew

Gloria Jean

Judy Garland and Margaret O'Brien in *Meet Me in St. Louis.*

Dean Stockwell

River Phoenix, left, and Wil Wheaton in *Stand By Me*.

Anthony Michael Hall and Molly Ringwald in *The Breakfast Club*.

Kelly Reno and Mickey Rooney in *The Black Stallion*.

Selected Filmography

Agutter, Jenny: *East of Sudan* (64), *Star!* (68), *The Railway Children* (70), *Logan's Run* (76), *Equus* (77), *The Riddle of the Sands* (79), *An American Werewolf in London* (81), *China 9, Liberty 37* (84).

Alberghetti, Anna Maria: *The Medium* (51), *Here Comes the Groom* (51), *The Stars Are Singing* (53), *The Last Command* (55), *Cinderfella* (60).

Alexander, Ben: *Each Pearl a Tear* (16), *Hearts of the World* (18), *Flaming Love* (25), *All Quiet on the Western Front* (30), *Stage Mother* (33), *Western Gold* (37), *Criminals Within* (41), *Dragnet* (54), *Pay the Devil* (57).

Astor, Mary: *The Beggar Maid* (21), *Beau Brummel* (24), *Don Q, Son of Zorro* (25), *Don Juan* (25), *Holiday* (30), *The Lost Squadron* (32), *Red Dust* (32), *Dodsworth* (36), *The Prisoner of Zenda* (37), *Midnight* (39), *Turnabout* (40), *The Great Lie* (41), *The Maltese Falcon* (41), *The Palm Beach Story* (42), *Meet Me in St. Louis* (44), *Act of Violence* (49), *Little Women* (49), *Return to Peyton Place* (61), *Hush . . . Hush Sweet Charlotte* (64).

Bartholomew, Freddie: *Fascination* (30), *Lily Christine* (32), *David Copperfield* (35), *Anna Karenina* (35), *Little Lord Fauntleroy* (36), *The Devil Is a Sissy* (36), *Lloyds of London* (36), *Captains Courageous* (37), *Kidnapped* (38), *Lord Jeff* (38), *The Swiss Family Robinson* (40), *Tom Brown's School Days* (40), *The Town Went Wild* (44), *St. Benny the Dip* (51).

Beckett, Scotty: *Gallant Lady* (33), *Anthony Adverse* (36), *Conquest* (38), *The Bluebird* (40), *King's Row* (42), *Ali Baba and the Forty Thieves* (43), *Corky of Gasoline Alley* (51), *Three for Jamie Dawn* (56).

Beery, Noah, Jr.: *The Mark of Zorro* (20), *Heroes of the West* (26), *The Road Back* (37), *Only Angels Have Wings* (39), *Of Mice and Men* (40), *Riders of Death Valley* (41), *Gung Ho!* (44), *Red River* (48), *Destination Moon* (50), *Inherit the Wind* (60), *The Seven Faces of Dr. Lao* (64), *Little Fauss and Big Halsy* (70), *Walking Tall* (73), *The Best Little Whorehouse in Texas* (82).

Beymer, Richard: *So Big* (52), *Johnny Tremain* (57), *The Diary of Anne Frank* (59), *High Time* (60), *West Side Story* (61), *Hemingway's Adventures of a Young Man* (62), *The Stripper* (62), *Cross Country* (83).

Blair, Linda: *The Exorcist* (74), *Airport 75* (75), *The Exorcist II: The Heretic* (77), *Hell Night* (81), *Night Patrol* (84).

Blake, Robert: *Andy Hardy's Double Life* (43), *The Horn Blows at Midnight* (45), *The Treasure of the Sierra Madre* (48), *Pork Chop Hill* (60), *In Cold Blood* (67), *Tell Them Willie Boy Is Here* (69), *Electric Glide in Blue* (73), *Second Hand Hearts* (80).

Brown, Tom: *The Hoosier Schoolmaster* (24), *Tom Brown of Culver* (32), *Freckles* (35), *Maytime* (37), *The Quiet Gun* (57), *The Choppers* (61).

Coogan, Jackie: *Skinner's Baby* (16), *The Kid* (21), *Peck's Bad Boy* (21), *Oliver Twist* (22), *A Boy of Flanders* (24), *Tom Sawyer* (30), *Huckleberry Finn* (31), *College Swing* (38), *High School Confidential* (58), *Marlowe* (69), *Cahill—U.S. Marshal* (73), *The Escape Artist* (81).

Cooper, Jackie: *Sunny Side Up* (29), *The Champ* (31), *Skippy* (31), *When a Feller Needs a Friend* (32), *Divorce in the Family* (32), *The Bowery* (33), *Broadway to Hollywood* (33), *Treasure Island* (34), *Peck's Bad Boy* (34), *Dinky* (35), *Tough Guy* (36), *Gangster's Boy* (38), *Seventeen* (40), *French Leave* (48), *Chosen Survivors* (74), *Superman* (78), *Superman III* (83).

Crawford, Michael: *Soap Box Derby* (50), *Blow Your Own Trumpet* (54), *The War Lover* (56), *The Knack, and How to Get It* (65), *A Funny Thing Happened on the Way to the Forum* (66), *The Jokers* (66), *How I Won the War* (67), *Hello, Dolly!* (69), *Alice's Adventures in Wonderland* (72), *Condorman* (81).

Darro, Frankie: *So Big* (24), *The Circus Kid* (28), *Wild Boys of the Road* (33), *Broadway Bill* (34), *No Greater Glory* (34), *Racing Blood* (37), *Laughing at Danger* (40), *Trouble Makers* (48), *Across the Wide Missouri* (51), *Operation Petticoat* (59), *Hook, Line and Sinker* (69).

Dee, Sandra: *Until They Sail* (57), *Gidget* (59), *Imitation of Life* (59), *A Summer Place* (59), *Tammy Tell Me True* (61), *Tammy and the Doctor* (63), *You've Got to Be Kidding* (67), *Rosie* (68), *The Dunwich Horror* (70), *Ad Est di Marsa Matruh* (71).

De Haven, Gloria: *Modern Times* (36), *The Great Dictator* (40), *Susan and God* (40), *Best Foot Forward* (43), *Two Girls and a Sailor* (44), *Yes Sir, That's My Baby* (49), *The Girl Rush* (55), *Evening in Byzantium* (78).

Dern, Laura: *Alice Doesn't Live Here Anymore* (75), *Mask* (85), *Smooth Talk* (86), *Blue Velvet* (86).

De Wilde, Brandon: *Member of the Wedding* (52), *Shane* (53), *Goodbye, My Lady* (56), *Night Passage* (57), *Blue Denim* (59), *Hud* (63), *In Harm's Way* (65), *The Calloways* (65), *The Deserter* (70), *Wild in the Sky* (72).

Dillon, Matt: *Over the Edge* (79), *Little Darlings* (80), *My Bodyguard* (80), *Tex* (82), *The Outsiders* (83), *Rumble Fish* (83), *The Flamingo Kid* (84), *Target* (85), *Rebel* (86), *Native Son* (86).

Donaldson, Ted: *Once Upon a Time* (44), *A Tree Grows in Brooklyn* (45), *The Decision of Christopher Blake* (48), *Phone Call from a Stranger* (52).

Dors, Diana: *The Shop at Sly Corner* (46), *Oliver Twist* (78), *It's a Grand Life* (53), *A Kid for Two Farthings* (55), *Yield to the Night* (56), *Hannie Caulder* (71), *Theatre of Blood* (73), *Steaming* (released in 86).

Downs, Johnny: *Valley of the Giants* (27), *The Crowd* (28), *College Scandal* (35), *College Holiday* (38), *Hold That Co-Ed* (38), *All-American Co-Ed* (41), *Harvest Melody* (43), *The Right to Love* (45), *Cruising Down the River* (53).

Driscoll, Bobby: *Lost Angel* (43), *Song of the South* (46), *The Window* (49), *Treasure Island* (50), *The Happy Time* (52), *The Scarlet Coat* (55), *The Party Crashers* (58).

Duke, Patty: *I'll Cry Tomorrow* (55), *Somebody Up There Likes Me* (56), *Country Music Holiday* (57), *My Goddess* (58), *Happy Anniversary* (59), *4-D Man* (59), *The Miracle Worker* (62), *Billie* (65), *Valley of the Dolls* (67), *Me, Natalie* (69), *You'll Like My Mother* (72), *The Swarm* (78), *Hard Feelings* (82).

Durbin, Deanna: *Every Sunday* (36), *Three Smart Girls* (36), *One Hundred Men and a Girl* (37), *Mad About Music* (38), *That Certain Age* (38), *It Started with Eve* (41), *Can't Help Singing* (44), *Up in Central Park* (47), *For the Love of Mary* (48).

Fabares, Shelley: *Never Say Goodbye* (56), *Summer Love* (58), *Ride the Wild Surf* (64), *Happy Girl* (65), *Hold On* (66), *Spinout* (66), *Clambake* (67).

Fairbanks, Douglas, Jr.: *Party Girl* (20), *Stella Dallas* (25), *The Jazz Age* (29), *The Dawn Patrol* (30), *Outward Bound* (30), *Little Caesar* (30), *Morning Glory* (33), *Catherine the Great* (34), *The Prisoner of Zenda* (37), *The Young in Heart* (38), *Gunga Din* (39), *The Corsican Brothers* (41), *Sinbad the Sailor* (47), *State Secret* (50), *Ghost Story* (81).

Fellows, Edith: *Madame X* (29), *Daddy Long Legs* (31), *Emma* (32), *Riders of Death Valley* (32), *Jane Eyre* (34), *Pennies from Heaven* (36), *The Five Little Peppers* (39), *Nobody's Children* (40), *Girls' Town* (42), *Her First Romance* (47).

Foster, Jodie: *Kansas City Bomber* (72), *Tom Sawyer* (73), *One Little Indian* (73), *Alice Doesn't Live Here Anymore* (74), *Bugsy Malone* (76), *Taxi Driver* (76), *The Little Girl Who Lives Down the Lane* (76), *Candleshoe* (77), *Foxes* (80), *O'Hara's Wife* (82).

Foster, Susanna: *The Great Victor Herbert* (39), *There's Magic in Music* (41), *Glamour Boy* (41), *Top Man* (43), *The Climax* (44), *This Is the Life* (44), *Frisco Sal* (45), *That Night with You* (45).

Franklin, Pamela: *The Innocents* (61), *The Lion* (62), *A Tiger Walks* (64), *The Third Secret* (64), *The Nanny* (65), *Our Mother's House* (67), *The Prime of Miss Jean Brodie* (69), *The Food of the Gods* (76).

Funicello, Annette: *Johnny Tremain* (57), *The Shaggy Dog* (61), *Babes in Toyland* (61), *The Misadventures of Merlin Jones* (63), *Bikini Beach* (64), *The Monkey's Uncle* (65), *Fireball 500* (66).

Garland, Judy: *Pigskin Parade* (36), *Broadway Melody of 1938* (37), *Thoroughbreds Don't Cry* (38), *Everybody Sing* (38), *Love Finds Andy Hardy* (38), *The Wizard of Oz* (39), *Babes in Arms* (39), *Strike Up the Band* (40), *Ziegfeld Girl* (41), *For Me and My Gal* (42), *Girl Crazy* (42), *Meet Me in St. Louis* (44), *The Clock* (45), *The Harvey Girls* (46), *The Pirate* (47), *Easter Parade* (48), *In the Good Old Sum-*

mertime (49), *Summer Stock* (50), *A Star Is Born* (54), *Judgment at Nuremberg* (60), *A Child Is Waiting* (62), *I Could Go on Singing* (63).

Garner, Peggy Ann: *Little Miss Thoroughbred* (38), *In Name Only* (39), *The Pied Piper* (42), *Jane Eyre* (44), *A Tree Grows in Brooklyn* (45), *Bomba, the Jungle Boy* (49), *The Black Forest* (54), *The Cat* (67), *A Wedding* (78).

Gillis, Ann: *The Garden of Allah* (36), *Off to the Races* (37), *The Adventures of Tom Sawyer* (38), *Beau Geste* (39), *Little Men,* (40), *Nice Girl* (41), *In Society* (44), *Big Town After Dark* (47), *2001: A Space Odyssey* (68).

Gish, Dorothy: *An Uneasy Enemy* (12), *The Sisters* (14), *Susan Rocks the Boat* (16), *Hearts of the World* (18), *Battling Jane* (18), *Remodeling Her Husband* (20), *Orphans of the Storm* (22), *Romola* (24), *Nell Gwyn* (26), *Madame Pompadour* (27), *Our Hearts Were Young and Gay* (44), *The Whistle at Eaton Falls* (51), *The Cardinal* (63).

Gish, Lillian: *An Unseen Enemy* (12), *The Madonna of the Storm* (13), *The Birth of a Nation* (14), *The Lily and the Rose* (15), *An Innocent Magdalene* (15), *Intolerance* (16), *Broken Blossoms* (18), *True Heart Susie* (20), *Way Down East* (20), *Orphans of the Storm* (22), *The White Sister* (23), *Romola* (24), *La Boheme* (26), *The Scarlet Letter* (26), *Annie Laurie* (27), *The Wind* (28), *His Double Life* (34), *The Commandos Strike at Dawn* (43), *Miss Susie Slagle's* (46), *Duel in the Sun* (46), *Portrait of Jennie* (48), *The Cobweb* (55), *The Night of the Hunter* (55), *Orders to Kill* (58), *Follow Me, Boys* (66), *The Comedians* (67), *A Wedding* (78), *Sweet Liberty* (86), *The Whales of August* (87).

Gorcey, Leo: *Dead End* (37), *Mannequin* (38), *Crime School* (38), *Angels With Dirty Faces* (38), *Mr. Wise Guy* (42), *Bowery Bombshell* (46), *Bowery to Bagdad* (55), *It's a Mad Mad Mad Mad World* (63), *The Sphynx* (69).

Granville, Bonita: *Westward Passage* (32), *Silver Dollar* (32), *Cavalcade* (33), *Ah Wilderness* (35), *These Three* (36), *Maid of Salem* (37), *Nancy Drew, Detective* (38), *Hitler's Children* (43), *Love Laughs at Andy Hardy* (46), *The Lone Ranger* (56), *The Magic of Lassie* (78).

Green, Mitzi: *The Marriage Playground* (29), *Honey* (30), *Transatlantic Merry-Go-Round* (34), *Walk With Music* (40), *Bloodhounds of Broadway* (52).

Grey, Virginia: *Uncle Tom's Cabin* (27), *The Michigan Kid* (28), *Misbehaving Ladies* (31), *Dames* (34), *Test Pilot* (38), *The Big Store* (41), *Idaho* (43), *Unconquered* (47), *Target Earth* (54), *Back Street* (61), *Rosie* (67), *Airport* (70).

Hall, Huntz: *Dead End* (37), *Angels With Dirty Faces* (38), *Spooks Run Wild* (41), *Bowery Bombshell* (46), *Ghost Chasers* (51), *Dig That Uranium* (56), *Spook Chasers* (57), *The Love Bug Rides Again* (73), *Valentino* (77), *The Escape Artist* (81).

Halop, Billy: *Dead End* (37), *Angels With Dirty Faces* (38), *Hell's Kitchen* (39), *Mob Town* (41), *Gas House Kids* (46), *Air Strike* (55), *Fitzwilly* (56).

Hayes, Helen: *Jean and the Calico Doll* (10), *The Weavers of Life* (17), *The Sin of Madelon Claudet* (31), *Arrowsmith* (31), *A Farewell to Arms* (32), *The White Sister* (33), *What Every Woman Knows* (34), *Stage Door Canteen* (43), *Anastasia* (56), *Airport* (70), *Candleshoe* (77).

Hickman, Darryl: *If I Were King* (38), *The Grapes of Wrath* (40), *Meet Me In St. Louis* (44), *Boys' Ranch* (45), *Rhapsody in Blue* (45, *Submarine Command* (51), *Tea and Sympathy* (56), *The Tingler* (59), *Network* (76).

Hickman, Dwayne: *Captain Eddie* (45), *Rally 'Round the Flag, Boys!* (59), *Cat Ballou* (65), *Dr. Goldfoot and the Bikini Machine* (65), *Doctor, You've Got to Be Kidding* (67).

Homeier, Skip: *Tomorrow the World* (44), *Boys' Ranch* (46), *Fixed Bayonets* (51), *Beachhead* (54), *Comanche Station* (60), *Starbird and Sweet William* (76), *The Greatest* (77).

Howard, Ron: *The Journey* (59), *The Music Man* (62), *American Graffiti* (73), *The Shootist* (76), *More American Graffiti* (79).

Jean, Gloria: *The Under-Pup* (39), *A Little Bit of Heaven* (40), *Never Give a Sucker an Even Break* (41), *Moonlight in Vermont* (43), *Copacabana* (57), *The Ladies' Man* (61), *The Madcaps* (63).

Jenkins, Jackie "Butch": *The Human Comedy* (43), *National Velvet* (44), *Our Vines Have Tender Grapes* (45), *Boys' Ranch* (46), *My Brother Talks to Horses* (46), *Summer Holiday* (48).

Jarman, Claude, Jr.: *The Yearling* (46), *High Barbaree* (47), *The Sun Comes Up* (49), *Intruder in the Dust* (49), *Rio Grande* (50), *The Great Locomotive Chase* (56).

Jones, Marcia Mae: *Mannequin* (26), *King of Jazz* (31), *These Three* (36), *Heidi* (37), *The Adventures of Tom Sawyer* (38), *Secrets of a Co-Ed* (42), *Arson, Inc.* (49), *Chicago Calling* (52), *The Way We Were* (73).

Jordan, Bobby: *Dead End* (37), *Angels With Dirty Faces* (38), *That Gang of Mine* (40), *Bowery Champs* (44), *Hard Boiled Mahoney* (47), *This Man Is Armed* (56).

Kelly, Tommy: *The Adventures of Tom Sawyer* (38), *Peck's Bad Boy With the Circus* (38).

Kilburn, Terry: *A Christmas Carol* (38), *Goodbye, Mr. Chips* (39), *The Swiss Family Robinson* (40), *National Velvet* (45), *Only the Valiant* (51), *Lolita* (62).

Lake, Arthur: *Jack and the Beanstalk* (17), *Indiscreet* (31), *Topper* (37), *Blondie* (38), *Three Is a Family* (44), *Beware of Blondie* (50).

Le Roy, Baby: *A Bedtime Story* (33), *Alice in Wonderland* (33), *The Lemon Drop Kid* (34), *It's a Great Life* (36).

Leslie, Joan: *Camille* (36), *Men With Wings* (38), *High Sierra* (41), *Sergeant York* (46), *The Male Animal* (42), *Yankee Doodle Dandy* (42), *Hollywood Canteen* (44), *Too Young to Know* (45), *Royal Flush* (46), *Northwest Stampede* (49), *Born to Be Bad* (51), *The Woman They Almost Lynched* (53), *Jubilee Trail* (54), *The Revolt of Mamie Stover* (56).

Lester, Mark: *The Counterfeit Constable* (64), *Oliver!* (68), *Run Wild, Run Free* (69), *Black Beauty* (71), *The Prince and the Pauper* (77).

Lockhart, June: *A Christmas Carol* (38), *All This and Heaven, Too* (40), *Meet Me in St. Louis* (44), *The She-Wolf of London* (46), *The Yearling* (47), *Time Limit* (57).

Louise, Anita: *The Sixth Commandment* (24), *What a Man* (30), *A Midsummer Night's Dream* (35), *Anthony Adverse* (36), *Submarine* (41), *Retreat, Hell!* (52).

Lydon, James: *Back Door to Heaven* (39), *Tom Brown's School Days* (40), *Henry Aldrich for President* (41), *Life With Father* (47), *Island in the Sky* (53), *Brainstorm* (65), *Vigilante Force* (76).

Lynn, Diana: *They Shall Have Music* (39), *The Major and the Minor* (43), *The Miracle of Morgan's Creek* (43), *Our Hearts Were Young and Gay* (44), *My Friend Irma* (49), *The Kentuckian* (55).

McCallister, Lon: *Stella Dallas* (37), *Stage Door Canteen* (43), *Home in Indiana* (44), *The Big Cat* (50), *Combat Squad* (54).

McCormack, Patty: *Two Gals and a Guy* (51), *The Bad Seed* (56), *Kathy O'* (58), *The Mini-Skirt Mob* (68), *Bug* (75).

McDowall, Roddy: *Murder in the Family* (36), *This England* (40), *How Green Was My Valley* (41), *My Friend Flicka* (43), *Lassie Come Home* (43), *The White Cliffs of Dover* (44), *Thunderhead, Son of Flicka* (45), *Macbeth* (50), *The Longest Day* (62), *Cleopatra* (63), *The Loved One* (65), *That Darned Cat* (65), *Planet of the Apes* (67), *Escape from the Planet of the Apes* (71), *Bedknobs and Broomsticks* (71), *Conquest of the Planet of the Apes* (72), *The Poseidon Adventure* (72), *The Legend of Hell House* (73), *Battle for the Planet of the Apes* (73), *Funny Lady* (75), *The Cat from Outer Space* (78), *Fright Night* (85), *Dead of Winter* (87).

McFarland, Spanky: *Day of Reckoning* (33), *O'Shaughnessy's Boy* (35), *Trail of the Lonesome Pine* (36), *General Spanky* (36), *Peck's Bad Boy With the Circus* (39), *The Woman in the Window* (44).

Mauch, Billy and Bobby: *The Prince and the Pauper* (37), *Penrod and Sam* (37), *Penrod and His Twin Brother* (38), *Penrod's Double Trouble* (38).

Mills, Hayley: *Tiger Bay* (59), *Pollyanna* (60), *The Parent Trap* (61), *Whistle Down the Wind* (61), *The Chalk Garden* (64), *The Moonspinners* (65), *The Family Way* (66), *Endless Night* (72), *The Kingfisher Caper* (75).

Mills, Juliet: *In Which We Serve* (42), *The History of Mr. Polly* (49), *No, My Darling Daughter!* (61), *Carry On, Jack* (64), *Oh! What a Lovely War* (69), *Avanti!* (72), *Barnaby and Me* (77).

Minter, Mary Miles: *The Nurse* (12), *Melissa of the Hills* (17), *Anne of Green Gables* (19), *The Trail of the Lonesome Pine* (23).

Moore, Dickie: *The Beloved Rogue* (27), *No Greater Love* (32), *Oliver Twist* (33), *Little Men* (35), *Sergeant York* (41), *Miss Annie Rooney* (42), *The Dangerous Years* (47), *Member of the Wedding* (52).

Moore, Terry: *Maryland* (40), *Son of Lassie* (45), *Mighty Joe Young* (50), *Come Back, Little Sheba* (52), *King of the Khyber Rifles* (54), *Peyton Place* (57), *Platinum High School* (60), *Waco* (66), *Death Dimension* (77).

Nelson, Rick: *Here Come the Nelsons* (52), *Rio Bravo* (59), *The Wackiest Ship in the Army* (60), *Love and Kisses* (65).

O'Brien, Margaret: *Babes on Broadway* (41), *Journey for Margaret* (42), *Thousands Cheer* (43), *Lost Angel* (43), *Madame Curie* (43), *Jane Eyre* (43), *The Canterville Ghost* (44), *Meet Me in St. Louis* (44), *Music for Millions* (45), *Our Vines Have Tender Grapes* (45), *Bad Bascomb* (46), *Three Wise Fools* (46), *The Unfinished Dance* (47), *Big City* (48), *Little Women* (49), *Her First Romance* (51), *Heller in Pink Tights* (60), *Annabelle Lee* (72), *Amy* (81).

O'Connor, Donald: *Sing You Sinners* (38), *On Your Toes* (39), *Beau Geste* (39), *Mister Big* (43), *Patrick the Great* (45), *Francis* (49), *Singin' in the Rain* (52), *Call Me Madam* (53), *There's No Business Like Show Business* (54), *The Buster Keaton Story* (57), *That Funny Feeling* (65), *Ragtime* (81), *Pandemonium* (82).

O'Driscoll, Martha: *Collegiate* (35), *The Secret of Dr. Kildare* (40), *The Lady Eve* (41), *Ghost Catchers* (44), *House of Dracula* (45), *Criminal Court* (47).

O'Neal, Tatum: *Paper Moon* (73), *The Bad News Bears* (76), *Nickelodeon* (76), *International Velvet* (78), *Circle of Two* (80), *Little Darlings* (80), *Split Image* (82), *Certain Fury* (85).

O'Neil, Sally: *Sally, Irene and Mary* (25), *Mike* (25), *Slide, Kelly, Slide* (27), *The Sophomore* (29), *Sixteen Fathoms Deep* (33), *Kathleen* (37).

Parrish, Helen: *Baby Comes Home* (27), *The Big Trail* (31), *A Dog of Flanders* (34), *Three Smart Girls Grow Up* (39), *Too Many Blondes* (41), *They Live in Fear* (44), *The Wolf Hunters* (50).

Peggy, Baby: *Peggy Behave* (22), *The Law Forbids* (24), *Arizona Days* (28), *Eight Girls on a Boat* (34).

Perreau, Gigi: *Madame Curie* (43), *Green Dolphin Street* (47), *My Foolish Heart* (49), *The Man in the Gray Flannel Suit* (56), *Tammy Tell Me True* (61), *Follow the Sun* (69).

Pickford, Jack: *The Kid* (10), *Tom Sawyer* (17), *Just Out of College* (21), *Brown of Harvard* (26), *Gang War* (28).

Pickford, Mary: *Her First Biscuits* (09), *The Violin Maker of Cremona* (10), *The Paris Hat* (13), *Madame Butterfly* (15), *Less Than the Dust* (16), *The Little Princess* (17), *Rebecca of Sunnybrook Farm* (17), *Stella Maris* (18), *Pollyanna* (19), *Suds* (20), *Little Lord Fauntleroy* (21), *The Love Light* (21), *Tess of the Storm Country* (22), *Rosita* (23), *Dorothy Vernon of Haddon Hall* (24), *Little Annie Rooney* (25), *My Best Girl* (27), *The Taming of the Shrew* (29), *Coquette* (29), *Kiki* (31), *Secrets* (33).

Quine, Richard: *The World Changes* (33), *Jane Eyre* (34), *My Sister Eileen* (42), *No Sad Songs for Me* (50).

Rettig, Tommy: *Panic in the Streets* (50), *Elopement* (51), *The Egyptian* (54), *The Cobweb* (55), *At Gunpoint* (57).

Reynolds, Gene: *Thank You, Jeeves* (36), *In Old Chicago* (38), *The Blue Bird* (40), *Eagle Squadron* (44), *The Country Girl* (54), *Diane* (55).

Ringwald, Molly: *Tempest* (82), *Sixteen Candles* (84), *The Breakfast Club* (85), *Pretty in Pink* (86).

Rooney, Mickey: *My Pal the King* (32), *A Midsummer Night's Dream* (35), *Ah! Wilderness* (35), *Captains Courageous* (37), *A Family Affair* (37), *Boys' Town* (38), *Love Finds Andy Hardy* (38), *The Adventures of Huckleberry Finn* (39), *Babes in Arms* (39), *Young Tom Edison* (40), *Strike Up the Band* (40), *Babes on Broadway* (41), *The Human Comedy* (43), *Girl Crazy* (43), *National Velvet* (44), *The Bold and the Brave* (56), *Francis in the Haunted House* (56), *Baby Face Nelson* (58), *Breakfast at Tiffany's* (51), *It's a Mad Mad Mad Mad World* (63), *The Comic* (69), *The Black Stallion* (79), *Find the Lady* (80).

Roth, Lillian: *Pershing's Crusaders* (18), *The Love Parade* (29), *The Vagabond King* (30), *Animal Crackers* (30), *Paramount on Parade* (30), *Madam Satan* (30), *Take a Chance* (33), *Communion* (77).

Russell, Kurt: *The Absent-Minded Professor* (60), *Charley and the Angel* (73), *Superdad* (74), *Escape from New York* (81), *The Thing* (82), *Silkwood* (83), *Swing Shift* (84), *Big Trouble in Little China* (86).

Ryan, Peggy: *Top of the Town* (37), *Top Man* (43), *Bowery to Broadway* (44), *All Ashore* (52).

Sabu: *Elephant Boy* (37), *The Drum* (38), *The Thief of Baghdad* (40), *The Jungle Book* (42), *Arabian Nights* (42), *Cobra Woman* (44), *Black Narcissus* (46), *Song of India* (49), *A Tiger Walks* (63).

Searl, Jackie: *Daughters of Desire* (29), *Tom Sawyer* (30), *Skippy* (31), *Huckleberry Finn* (31), *Alice in Wonderland* (33), *No Greater Glory* (34), *Peck's Bad Boy* (34), *Ginger* (35), *Little Lord Fauntleroy* (36), *Angels Wash Their Faces* (39), *My Little Chickadee* (40), *Glamour Boy* (41), *The Fabulous Dorseys* (47), *The Paleface* (48).

Sheffield, Johnny: *Tarzan Finds a Son* (39), *Babes in Arms* (39), *Lucky Cisco Kid* (40), *Tarzan's Secret Treasure* (41), *Tarzan's New York Adventure* (42), *Tarzan Triumphs* (43), *Tarzan and the Huntress* (47), *Bomba, the Jungle Boy* (49), *The Lost Volcano* (50), *The Lion Hunters* (51), *Bomba and the Jungle Girl* (52), *Safari Drums* (53), *The Golden Idol* (54), *Lord of the Jungle* (55).

Shields, Brooke: *Alice, Sweet Alice* (78), *Pretty Baby* (78), *King of the Gypsies* (78), *Tilt* (79), *Wanda Nevada* (79), *Just You and Me, Kid* (79), *The Blue Lagoon* (80), *Endless Love* (81), *Sahara* (84).

Shirley, Anne: *Moonshine Valley* (22), *Riders of the Purple Sage* (25), *Liliom* (30), *So Big* (32), *Anne of Green Gables* (34), *Steamboat 'Round the Bend* (35), *Stella Dallas* (37), *Mother Carey's Chickens* (38), *Saturday's Children* (40), *All That Money Can Buy* (41), *The Powers Girl* (42), *Government Girl* (43), *Murder My Sweet* (44).

Simmons, Jean: *Give Us the Moon* (44), *Caesar and Cleopatra* (45), *Great Expectations* (46), *Black Narcissus* (47), *Hamlet* (48), *The Blue Lagoon* (49), *Young Bess* (53), *The Robe* (53), *Desiree* (54), *Guys and Dolls* (55), *The Big Country* (58), *Home Before Dark* (58), *Elmer Gantry* (60), *Spartacus* (60), *All the Way Home* (63), *Mister Buddwing* (66), *The Happy Ending* (69), *Mr. Sycamore* (75), *Dominique* (79).

Stephens, Martin: *The Hellfire Club* (61), *Village of the Damned* (62), *The Innocents* (62), *The Battle of the Villa Fiorita* (65), *The Witches* (66).

Stockwell, Dean: *Valley of Decision* (45), *Anchors Aweigh* (45), *The Green Years* (46), *Gentleman's Agreement* (47), *The Boy With Green Hair* (48), *The Secret Garden* (49), *The Careless Years* (57), *Compulsion* (59), *Sons and Lovers* (60), *Long Day's Journey into Night* (62), *Psych-Out* (68), *The Dunwich Horror* (70), *The Loners* (72), *Win, Place or Steal* (75), *Tracks* (77), *She Came to the Valley* (79), *Wrong Is Right* (82), *Blue Velvet* (86).

Sweet, Blanche: *The Man With Three Wives* (09), *Judith of Bethulia* (13), *Anna Christie* (23), *The Silver Horde* (30).

Switzer, Carl "Alfalfa": *General Spanky* (36), *Wild and Woolley* (37), *I Love You Again* (40), *The Human Comedy* (43), *Going My Way* (44), *Courage of Lassie* (46), *State of the Union* (48), *A Letter to Three Wives* (49), *Pat and Mike* (52), *The High and the Mighty* (54), *The Defiant Ones* (58).

Tamblyn, Russ: *The Boy With Green Hair* (48), *Father of the Bride* (50), *Seven Brides for Seven Brothers* (54), *Hit the Deck* (55), *Peyton Place* (57), *tom thumb* (58), *West Side Story* (61), *The Wonderful World of the Brothers Grimm* (63), *The Haunting* (63), *Win, Place or Steal* (75), *Human Highway* (82).

Taylor, Elizabeth: *There's One Born Every Minute* (42), *Lassie Come Home* (43), *Jane Eyre* (43), *The White Cliffs of Dover* (44), *National Velvet* (44), *Cynthia* (47), *Life With Father* (47), *A Date With Judy* (48), *Julia Misbehaves* (48), *Little Women* (49), *Conspirator* (49), *Father of the Bride* (50), *Father's Little Dividend* (51), *Quo Vadis* (51), *A Place in the Sun* (51), *Ivanhoe* (52), *Elephant Walk* (54), *Giant* (56),

Raintree County (57), *Cat on a Hot Tin Roof* (58), *Suddenly Last Summer* (60), *Butterfield 8* (60), *Cleopatra* (62), *The VIPs* (63), *The Sandpiper* (65), *Who's Afraid of Virginia Woolf?* (66), *The Taming of the Shrew* (67), *The Comedians* (67), *Reflections in a Golden Eye* (67), *Secret Ceremony* (68), *Under Milk Wood* (71), *Hammersmith Is Out* (72), *Ash Wednesday* (73), *The Blue Bird* (76), *The Mirror Crack'd* (80).

Temple, Shirley: *The Red-Haired Alibi* (32), *To the Last Man* (33), *Stand Up and Cheer* (34), *Little Miss Marker* (34), *Baby Take a Bow* (34), *Bright Eyes* (34), *The Little Colonel* (35), *Curly Top* (35), *The Littlest Rebel* (35), *Captain January* (36), *Poor Little Rich Girl* (36), *Dimples* (36), *Wee Willie Winkie* (37), *Heidi* (37), *Rebecca of Sunnybrook Farm* (38), *Little Miss Broadway* (38), *The Little Princess* (39), *Susannah of the Mounties* (39), *The Blue Bird* (40), *Miss Annie Rooney* (42), *Since You Went Away* (42), *I'll Be Seeing You* (44), *Kiss and Tell* (45), *The Bachelor and the Bobby-Soxer* (47), *That Hagen Girl* (47), *Fort Apache* (48), *Mr. Belvedere Goes to College* (49), *A Kiss for Corliss* (49).

Watson, Bobs: *In Old Chicago* (38), *Boys' Town* (38), *Kentucky* (38), *The Story of Alexander Graham Bell* (39), *On Borrowed Time* (39), *Dr. Kildare's Crisis* (40), *Men of Boys' Town* (41), *The Bold and the Brave* (56), *What Ever Happened to Baby Jane?* (62), *First to Fight* (67).

Weidler, Virginia: *Surrender* (31), *Mrs. Wiggs of the Cabbage Patch* (34), *Freckles* (35), *Trouble for Two* (36), *Souls at Sea* (37), *Mother Carey's Chickens* (38), *The Women* (39), *Young Tom Edison* (40), *The Philadelphia Story* (40), *Barnacle Bill* (41), *Babes on Broadway* (42), *Best Foot Forward* (43).

Weld, Tuesday: *Rock, Rock, Rock* (56), *Rally Round the Flag, Boys!* (58), *The Five Pennies* (59), *Sex Kittens Go to College* (60), *Wild in the Country* (61), *Bachelor Flat* (61), *Soldier in the Rain* (63), *The Cincinnati Kid* (65), *Pretty Poison* (68), *Play It As It Lays* (72), *Looking for Mr. Goodbar* (77), *Who'll Stop the Rain?* (78), *The Serial* (79), *Author! Author!* (82).

Winslow, George "Foghorn": *Room for One More* (52), *My Pal Gus* (52), *Gentlemen Prefer Blondes* (53), *Mr. Scoutmaster* (53), *The Rocketman* (54), *Artists and Models* (56), *An Affair to Remember* (57), *Wild Heritage* (58).

Withers, Jane: *Handle With Care* (32), *Bright Eyes* (34), *The Farmer Takes a Wife* (35), *Pepper* (36), *The Holy Terror* (37), *Rascals* (38), *Boy Friend* (39), *The Girl from Avenue A* (40), *Her First Beau* (41), *The Mad Martindales* (42), *The North Star* (43), *My Best Gal* (44), *Danger Street* (47), *Giant* (56), *The Right Approach* (61), *Captain Newman, MD* (64).

Wood, Natalie: *Happy Land* (43), *Tomorrow Is Forever* (46), *Miracle on 34th Street* (47), *Rebel Without a Cause* (55), *Marjorie Morningstar* (58), *Splendor in the Grass* (61), *West Side Story* (61), *Love With the Proper Stranger* (64), *Inside Daisy Clover* (66), *Bob & Carol & Ted & Alice* (69), *Meteor* (79), *Brainstorm* (83).

Young, Loretta: *Laugh, Clown, Laugh* (28), *Loose Ankles* (29), *Kismet* (30), *The Devil to Pay* (30), *Life Begins* (32), *Zoo in Budapest* (33), *A Man's Castle* (33), *The House of Rothschild* (34), *The Crusaders* (35), *Clive of India* (35), *Call of the Wild* (35), *Ramona* (36), *Suez* (38), *Kentucky* (38), *The Story of Alexander Graham Bell* (39), *The Doctor Takes a Wife* (39), *A Night to Remember* (42), *Along Came Jones* (46), *The Farmer's Daughter* (47), *The Bishop's Wife* (48), *Rachel and the Stranger* (48), *Come to the Stable* (49), *Half Angel* (51), *It Happens Every Thursday* (53).

Index

Acknowledgments and Credits

The publisher and the author wish to thank Jerry Vermilye for providing many of the photographs.

The Kobal Collection
Pgs. 2, 33, 34, 36, 59, 66–7, 99, 102, 103, 106 above, 108, 111, 162, 199, 227 below, 241, 242 above, 244, 247 above, 252, 256, 257, 262, 264, 269.

Phototeque
37, 60, 77, 80, 81, 83, 84–5, 86, 87, 88, 249, 266, 267, 271.

Jerry Ohlinger's
4, 50, 51, 57, 104 above and below, 105, 110, 124, 125, 132 above, 133, 185, 186 right, 187, 192, 194, 195 below, 199 left, 204, 209, 230, 232, 250–51, 259, 260, 260–61, 263, 265, 270, 272.

Film Copyrights

49: *These Three,* © 1936 Samuel Goldwyn

49: *Heart to Heart,* © 1928 First National Pictures, Inc.

50: *Blonde Venus,* 1932, Copyright © by Universal Pictures, a Division of Universal City Studios, Inc. All Rights Reserved. Courtesy of MCA Publishing Rights, a Division of MCA, Inc.

51: *Little Men,* © 1934 Mascot Pictures Corp.

51: *Oliver Twist,* © 1933 Monogram

51: *So Big,* Copyright © 1932 Warner Brothers Pictures, Inc.

52: *There's Always Tomorrow,* 1934, Copyright © by Universal Pictures, a Division of Universal City Studios, Inc. All Rights Reserved. Courtesy of MCA Publishing Rights, a Division of MCA, Inc.

53: *Little Tough Guys,* 1938, Copyright © by Universal Pictures, a Division of Universal City Studios, Inc. All Rights Reserved. Courtesy of MCA Publishing Rights, a Division of MCA, Inc.

53: *First Love,* 1939, Copyright © by Universal Pictures, a Division of Universal City Studios, Inc. All Rights Reserved. Courtesy of MCA Publishing Rights, a Division of MCA, Inc.

56: *Adventures of Huck Finn,* © 1939 Metro-Goldwyn-Mayer, Inc.

57: *Little Lord Fauntleroy,* Copyright © 1936 United Artists Corporation

59: *Judge Hardy and Son,* © 1939 Metro-Goldwyn-Mayer, Inc.

61: *Love Finds Andy Hardy,* © 1938 Metro-Goldwyn-Mayer, Inc.

61: *Strike Up the Band,* © 1940 Metro-Goldwyn-Mayer, Inc.

62: *Boys Town,* © 1938 Metro-Goldwyn-Mayer, Inc.

64: *Topaze,* © 1933 RKO Radio Pictures, Inc.

65: *Tugboat Princess,* © 1936 Columbia Pictures Corp. of California, Ltd.

65: *She Married Her Boss,* © 1935 Columbia Pictures Corp. of California, Ltd.

65: *Pennies From Heaven,* © 1936 Columbia Pictures Corp. of California, Ltd.

68: *The Bowery,* © 1933 20th Century Pictures, Inc.

68: *Treasure Island,* © 1934 Metro-Goldwyn-Mayer, Inc.

68: *The Champ,* © 1931 Metro-Goldwyn-Mayer, Inc.

69: *Broadway to Hollywood,* © 1933 Metro-Goldwyn-Mayer, Inc.

71: *White Banners,* © 1938 Warner Brothers Pictures, Inc.

71: *What a Life!,* 1939, Copyright © by Universal Pictures, a Division of Universal City Studios, Inc. All Rights Reserved. Courtesy of MCA Publishing Rights, a Division of MCA, Inc.

72: *Anna Karenina,* © 1935 Metro-Goldwyn-Mayer, Inc.

73: *David Copperfield,* © 1935 Metro-Goldwyn-Mayer, Inc.

74-75: *Captains Courageous,* © 1937 Metro-Goldwyn-Mayer, Inc.

76: *Kidnapped,* © 1938 Twentieth Century Fox Film Corp.

77: *Little Lord Fauntleroy,* Copyright © 1936 United Artists Corporation

78: *Three on a Match,* © 1932 Warner Brothers Pictures, Inc.

78: *Too Many Parents,* 1936, Copyright © by Universal Pictures, a Division of Universal City Studios, Inc. All Rights Reserved. Courtesy of MCA Publishing Rights, a Division of MCA, Inc.

89: *The Women,* © 1939 Metro-Goldwyn-Mayer, Inc.

90: *The Philadelphia Story,* © 1940 Metro-Goldwyn-Mayer, Inc.

90: *The Youngest Profession,* © 1943 Metro-Goldwyn-Mayer, Inc.

92 & 93: *Baby Take a Bow,* © 1934 Fox Film Corp.

94-95: *Little Miss Marker,* 1934, Copyright © by Universal Pictures, a Division of Universal City Studios, Inc. All Rights Reserved. Courtesy of MCA Publishing Rights, a Division of MCA, Inc.

100-101: *Bright Eyes,* © 1934 Twentieth Century Fox Film Corp.

102: *Littlest Rebel,* © 1935 Twentieth Century Fox Film Corp.

103: *Rebecca of Sunnybrook Farm,* © 1938 Twentieth Century Fox Film Corp.

103: *Heidi,* © 1937, renewed 1965 Twentieth Century Fox Film Corp.

103: *Captain January,* © 1936 Twentieth Century Fox Film Corp.

104: *Curly Top,* © 1935 Twentieth Century Fox Film Corp.

104: *Susannah of the Mounties,* © 1939 Twentieth Century Fox Film Corp.

104: *The Little Princess,* © 1939 Twentieth Century Fox Film Corp.

105: *Captain January,* © 1936 Twentieth Century Fox Film Corp.

105: *Little Miss Broadway,* © 1938 Twentieth Century Fox Film Corp.

105: *The Little Colonel,* © 1935 Twentieth Century Fox Film Corp.

106: *Miss Annie Rooney,* © 1942 Edward Small Productions, Inc.

107: *The Bachelor and the Bobby Soxer,* © 1947 RKO Radio Pictures, Inc.

110: *Pepper,* © 1936 Twentieth Century Fox Film Corp.

112: *Paddy O'Day,* © 1936 Twentieth Century Fox Film Corp.

113: *Gentle Julia,* © 1936 William Fox

114: *Call It a Day,* Copyright © 1937 Warner Brothers Pictures, Inc.

115: *The Mortal Storm,* © 1940 Metro-Goldwyn-Mayer, Inc.

116: *Nancy Drew and the Hidden Staircase,* Copyright © 1939 Warner Bros. Pictures, Inc.

116: *Nancy Drew—Reporter,* Copyright © 1939 Warner Bros. Pictures, Inc.

117: *Nancy Drew—Detective,* Copyright © 1938 Warner Bros. Pictures, Inc.

117: *Nancy Drew—Trouble Shooter,* Copyright © 1939 Warner Bros. Pictures, Inc.

118-119: *Hitler's Children,* © 1942 RKO Radio Pictures, Inc.

121: *Evelyn Prentice,* © 1934 Metro-Goldwyn-Mayer, Inc.

121: *Tillie and Gus,* © 1933 Paramount Pictures, Inc.

122-123: *A Bedtime Story,* 1933, Copyright © by Universal Pictures, a Division of Universal City Studios, Inc. All Rights Reserved. Courtesy of MCA Publishing Rights, a Division of MCA, Inc.

124: *Charge of the Light Brigade,* Copyright © 1936 Warner Brothers Pictures, Inc.

124-125: *Mama's Little Pirate,* © 1935 Metro-Goldwyn-Mayer, Inc.

126: *King's Row,* Copyright © 1941 Warner Brothers Pictures, Inc.

126: *Conquest,* © 1937 Metro-Goldwyn-Mayer, Inc.

126: *My Reputation,* Copyright © 1946 Warner Brothers Pictures, Inc.

127: *Fifteen Wives,* © 1934 Invincible Pictures Corp.

129: *Pigskin Parade,* © 1936 Twentieth Century Fox Film Corp.

130: *Thoroughbreds Don't Cry,* © 1937 Metro-Goldwyn-Mayer, Inc.

131: *Listen, Darling,* © 1938 Metro-Goldwyn-Mayer, Inc.

131: *Everybody Sing,* © 1938 Metro-Goldwyn-Mayer, Inc.

132: *The Wizard of Oz,* © 1939 Metro-Goldwyn-Mayer, Inc.

133: *The Wizard of Oz,* © 1939 Metro-Goldwyn-Mayer, Inc.

134-135: *Babes on Broadway,* © 1941 Metro-Goldwyn-Mayer, Inc.

136-137: *Girl Crazy,* © 1943 Metro-Goldwyn-Mayer, Inc.

138-139: *Ziegfeld Girl,* © 1941 Metro-Goldwyn-Mayer, Inc.

141: *100 Men and a Girl,* 1937, Copyright © by Universal Pictures, a Division of Universal City Studios, Inc. All Rights Reserved. Courtesy of MCA Publishing Rights, a Division of MCA, Inc.

142: *Every Sunday,* © 1936 Metro-Goldwyn-Mayer, Inc.

143: *That Certain Age,* 1938, Copyright © by Universal Pictures, a Division of Universal City Studios, Inc. All Rights Reserved. Courtesy of MCA Publishing Rights, a Division of MCA, Inc.

144: *Three Smart Girls Grow Up,* 1939, Copyright © by Universal Pictures, a Division of Universal City Studios, Inc. All Rights Reserved. Courtesy of MCA Publishing Rights, a Division of MCA, Inc.

146: *High School,* © 1940 Twentieth Century Fox Film Corp.

148: *Rainbow on the River,* © 1936 RKO Radio Pictures, Inc.

149: *The Great Ziegfeld,* © 1936 Metro-Goldwyn-Mayer, Inc.

152: *Dead End,* © 1937 Metro-Goldwyn-Mayer, Inc.

153: *They Made Me a Criminal,* Copyright © 1939 Warner Brothers Pictures, Inc.

154-155: *Angels With Dirty Faces,* Copyright © 1938 Warner Brothers Pictures, Inc.

156-157: *Angels Wash Their Faces,* Copyright © 1940 Warner Brothers Pictures, Inc.

157: *Let's Get Tough,* © 1942 Monogram Pictures Corp.

158 & 159: *The Prince and the Pauper,* Copyright © 1937 Warner Brothers Pictures, Inc.

160: *Sing You Sinners,* 1938, Copyright © by Universal Pictures, a Division of Universal City Studios, Inc. All Rights Reserved. Courtesy of MCA Publishing Rights, a Division of MCA, Inc.

161: *Unmarried,* 1939, Copyright © by Universal Pictures, a Division of Universal City Studios, Inc. All Rights Reserved. Courtesy of MCA Publishing Rights, a Division of MCA, Inc.

162: *Tom Sawyer, Detective,* 1938, Copyright © by Universal Pictures, a Division of Universal City Studios, Inc. All Rights Reserved. Courtesy of MCA Publishing Rights, a Division of MCA, Inc.

163: *Follow the Boys,* 1944, Copyright © by Universal Pictures, a Division of Universal City Studios, Inc. All Rights Reserved. Courtesy of MCA Publishing Rights, a Division of MCA, Inc.

163: *Chip Off the Old Block,* 1944, Copyright © by Universal Pictures, a Division of Universal City Studios, Inc. All Rights Reserved. Courtesy of MCA Publishing Rights, a Division of MCA, Inc.

164: *Nancy Drew, Reporter,* Copyright © 1939 Warner Brothers Pictures, Inc.

165: *Sergeant York,* Copyright © 1942 Warner Brothers Pictures, Inc.

165: *High Sierra,* Copyright © 1941 Warner Brothers Pictures, Inc.

166: *Elephant Boy,* © 1937 London Film Productions, Ltd.

167: *In Name Only,* © 1939 RKO Radio Pictures, Inc.

168: *A Tree Grows in Brooklyn,* © 1945 Twentieth Century Fox Film Corp.

169: *Nob Hill,* © 1945 Twentieth Century Fox Film Corp.

171: *A Kiss For Corliss,* © 1949 Strand Productions, Inc.

172: *Leave Her to Heaven,* © 1945 Twentieth Century Fox Film Corp.

172: *Rally 'Round the Flag, Boys,* © 1958 Twentieth Century Fox Film Corp.